New Orleans
Neighborhoods

New Orleans
Neighborhoods

A CULTURAL GUIDE

by

MAGGY BACCINELLI

with maps by RAY WHITLOW

THE History PRESS

Published by The History Press
Charleston, SC
www.historypress.net

Back cover images: Photo of French Quarter on top by Bruce Cervini. Photo of home on bottom by Lindsay Arvin.

First published 2015

Manufactured in the United States

ISBN 978.1.62619.871.5

Library of Congress Control Number: 2015947680

For Janice Grimes (Miss Janice), the heart of my neighborhood.

Contents

Preface

New Orleans has hundreds of neighborhoods, not seventy-three like the city's map suggests. The city and an architectural firm drew up and named the neighborhoods I write about here in the 1970s, for practical purposes: to provide services and keep track of people, among other reasons. I used the city's map as a guide for practical purposes, too, but not at first. I first went by this map because, as a relatively new transplant when I received this book contract, it was the only New Orleans neighborhood map I knew. It was the one I saw on T-shirts at Storyville and when I searched "New Orleans neighborhood boundaries" in Google. Surely, I thought, distinct histories and cultures would be packaged within these marketed borders.

It took just one day to learn that the opposite is true. While biking around Hollygrove-Dixon, I found that the neighborhood's centerpiece, its Hollygrove Market, is technically in Gert Town. In the corner of the neighborhood with the big houses, I saw that almost every lawn had a "Northwest Carrollton" sign on it—a post–Hurricane Katrina resident effort to secede from the poorer surrounding area. My main interviewee that morning was less concerned with Hollygrove than telling me about Central City's Calliope project, where he grew up. "The city built it on a dump," he said sternly. "Make sure you put that in the book."

That day, it became clear that the real stories are in the inconsistently perceived boundaries, in the movement of people and in the politics of place, race and resource allocation. The real stories are in the overlap, in the micro-neighborhoods that define themselves by churches, bars and community matriarchs, like my own block's Miss Janice. In fact, New

Orleans' all-star historian, Richard Campanella, has written many articles warning transplants about the fallacy of using city's "seventy-three" as "cultural-geographical gospel."[1] Echoing his philosophy is NOLA.com | the *Times-Picayune*, which launched an incredible ongoing neighborhood series in 2015 that is meant to capture these "real" stories.

And yet with so many inconsistencies, so many micro-neighborhoods and so little authority on the topic as someone who was new to the city, the only way to approach this book was to use what already existed as an outline and then to try to weave as much of the good stuff—the messy stuff—into this structure as possible.

Each neighborhood essay in this book begins with "A Note on Identity." Here I aim to capture some of the boundary discrepancies between the city, residents and the Historic District Landmarks Commission. I sometimes include information about how a neighborhood got its name and the real estate market's or community's efforts, like those in Northwest Carrollton, to rebrand different parts of it. This book does not have seventy-three entries because I combine a few of the city's neighborhoods into longer essays. In those cases, I title the essay with the broader area's colloquial name and put the city's names in parentheses.

In the "At the Heart of It" section of each essay, I focus on what is agreed on. While nearly everyone has a different answer about borders, more often than not people agree on what is at the heart of where they live. Each chapter in this book covers a different City Planning District, except the West Bank and Eastern New Orleans chapters, where I have combined several. The maps at the beginning of each chapter identify most of the still-existing locations that I include in the text. These are very abridged lists of neighborhood landmarks. Likewise, each essay's "Festivals and Events" section describes just a few of the many celebrations that happen throughout the city every year. This entire book, in fact, just skims the surface of these New Orleans neighborhoods, many of which could, and do, have their own books entirely.

Please note that you do not need to read this book linearly. Instead, I hope you will turn to the neighborhood you've always wondered about or are even just a little curious about. Once you get a snapshot of its history and culture, I hope it sparks your curiosity and motivates you to dig deeper. Most of all, I hope this book will inspire transplants like me to step outside and open themselves up to the people around them. I hope you will ask questions and listen. I hope you will share your own cultural traditions while learning about and experiencing the ones that have lured you here. I hope you will appreciate and honor the history that surrounds you. I hope you will celebrate your neighborhood and your neighbors.

Acknowledgements

One of my favorite things about New Orleans' vernacular is that when someone does something nice, the recipient of that good deed says, "Appreciate you" instead of "Appreciate that." It's a subtle change to a simple statement, but it cuts to the core of what this city is all about. New Orleans is overwhelmingly personal, and what matters here more than anything else is one another. To the community leaders who dedicate themselves to their neighbors every day and have collectively spent many hours helping me understand complex neighborhood histories, challenges and triumphs, I appreciate you: Jarvain Bingmon, Todd and Vince Craige, Baakir Tyehimba, Kathryn Hobgood, Nicole Bouie, Tilman Hardy, Ronald Lewis, Robert Green, Laura Paul, Sarah Debacher, Thomas Pepper, Lary Hesdorffer, Liz Lichtman, Emily Wolff, Anthony Bean and Ralph Driscoll.

To the many people who told me stories about growing up, Hurricane Katrina and how their neighborhoods have changed and still are changing, thank you for your trust and hospitality; I appreciate you, Jill and Paul Varisco, Sarah and Alex Smith, Martha Wood, Luke Allen, K.C. and Kathleen King, Roland Le Blanc, Christine Hoffman, Natalie Hooks, Erskine Taylor, Viola Johnson and Milton Scheuermann.

I spent a lot of time at libraries, religious sanctuaries, arts and cultural centers and museums. I appreciate the people who assisted me at all of them, including Tulane's Howard-Tilton Memorial Library, Architecture Library and Amistad Research Center; the New Orleans Public Library Mid-City, Algiers, Rosa F. Keller, Milton H. Latter and Main branches; the

Data Center; Williams Research Center; Ellis Marsalis Center for Music; Backstreet Cultural Museum; Community Commitment Education Center; Ashé Cultural Arts Center; Zeitgeist Multi-Disciplinary Arts Center; New Orleans Healing Center; Touro Synagogue; and Mary Queen of Vietnam Church.

Richard Campanella, I appreciate you for your scholarship, painstaking thoroughness and incredible work. New Orleans needs to throw you a festival.

Likewise, I appreciate the following people for their scholarship and journalistic genius: Eve Abrams, producer of the *Along St. Claude* audio documentary; Orissa Arend, author of *Showdown in Desire*; Kimberly Rivers Roberts, whose story is captured in the documentary *Trouble the Water*; Tram Nguyen, author of the article "Pushed Out and Pushing Back in New Orleans"; NOLA.com's neighborhood-beat reporters and the award-winning staff who covered Hurricane Katrina for the *Times-Picayune*; Billy Sothern, author of the article "Goodbye St. Thomas"; Emily Epstein Landau, author of the book *Spectacular Wickedness*; and Alexander Glustrom, director, editor and producer of the film *Big Charity*. These works have been pivotal to my neighborhood exploration. They've moved and inspired me very much.

To my boss, Linda Peal, and my colleagues at Tulane, I appreciate you and your constant encouragement and support. I am so lucky to call you friends: Makenzie Kozojet, Beth Aguillard, Allison Hjortsberg, Mary-Elizabeth Lough, Amanda Labella, Kirby Messinger, Mary Sparacello and Ben Evans.

I appreciate so much the many friends and family members who've shared this experience and New Orleans with me over the last year, including Shannon Mitch and Drew Handwerk; Laurel Coyle and Brandon McCauley; Todd Trulock; JP Botti; Sarah and Andy Schmitt; Kyle O'Donnell and Gary Griffin; MaryKate Lavin; Ashley Novak and Derek Shae; Rhyz Baluyot; Joey Oakley; Jeremy Hartman; Caroline Sweeney; Meryam Bouadjemi; Beth and Colby Stiles; Serena Mendis and Matt Costa; Farin Mendis; Brent Thomas; Claire Keane; James Goddard; F. Stew Bailey; Dustin Fronczak; Joanna and Johnny Price; Jesse Hartley; Nicole DePietro and David Dunn; Adeline Heymann; Jenna, Jessica and Becca Holke; Devon Cortes; Rachel Malkenhorst; Lindsay and Will Arvin; Eric Bernstein; Giacomo Bagarella; and Roxanne and Matthew Mendis.

I appreciate our Passera Court family: Miss Janice, India and Deshaune, Braylon, Neekie, Taylor, Delano, Tyler, Doonie, Tasha and Robbie, RáHji, RáSaan, Abbie, Sarah and Larry, Aaron and Amanda, Bob, Micah, Thanh and Gay.

Mom and Michael, I appreciate you for your strength, love and radical openness to the people and world around you. You've made me, me. I love you.

Dad and Arlene, I appreciate you for your unwavering encouragement and support. I love you.

To Val, Johnny and Nina: Each one of you inspires me every day in your own way. Stay true to your passions. I love and appreciate you.

To Aunt Sue and Uncle Frank: for the guidance, delicious dinners and support, I love and appreciate you.

Sally Asher, I appreciate you so much. Thank you for believing in me, for opening this door and for setting such an incredible example as an artist, historian and friend. I love you. If readers are interested in the colorful characters for whom we have named our streets and neighborhoods, Sally Asher's *Hope and New Orleans* is a must-read.

I appreciate you, Frank Relle, for the dance parties and *Daring Greatly*, but most of all, for daring greatly.

To my commissioning editor, Chad Rhoad, and my project editor, Ryan Finn: thank you for your guidance and patience, I appreciate you.

Bruce Cervini, you are a saint. Thank you for all of your hard work, beautiful photos, advice and support. Thank you, too, for sharing Gentilly with me. I appreciate you so very much.

To Ray Whitlow, the cartographer of this book: Thank you for beautiful work, patience and advice and for getting excited when you talk about neighborhood borders. I appreciate you.

And finally, I appreciate you, Mitchell Mendis, for taking this adventure with me. You are my best friend, and I could not have finished this project without your selfless outpouring of support, encouragement, talent, advice and love. I love you so much, matey.

Introduction

With a few exceptions, each neighborhood essay in this book focuses on life in that neighborhood after it started being developed residentially. There are some things to know about how New Orleans' topography directed that development, and the city's early cultural geographies, before delving in.

In the thousands of years before man started trying to control the Mississippi River, its heavy flow swept up and then deposited sediment into natural levees along its banks.[2] During times of flood, the Mississippi even broke off into different distributaries, which likewise eroded and pushed soil into ridges along their sides.[3] Until the twentieth century, when New Orleans as we know it was successfully drained, these ridges through the city's backswamp, and the levees along its riverfront, made up most of the elevated, and therefore developed, places in the city.

In 1699, Native Americans guided French brothers Pierre Le Moyne d'Iberville and Jean-Baptiste Le Moyne de Bienville along a shortcut from Lake Pontchartrain to the Mississippi River, likely by way of Bayou St. John and the Esplanade Ridge (approximately along today's Esplanade Avenue).[4] This convenient path significantly reduced the time and risk it took to get from the Gulf of Mexico to the Lower Mississippi Valley.[5] Ultimately, it influenced Bienville's decision to found New Orleans in the present-day French Quarter in 1718. Land grants were given to colonists, and plantations soon lined the river all the way up to today's Carrollton and down to the Lower Ninth Ward, as well as on the West Bank. Long and skinny, they fronted the water and ran back toward the swamp.

In 1788, New Orleans expanded from the French Quarter to today's Central Business District, when the plantation here was subdivided and developed as the city's first "faubourg." Literally translating to "false town," "faubourg" meant "suburb" to the Spanish, who ruled New Orleans during that time.[6] In 1803, the Louisiana Purchase was signed, and New Orleans became an American city. Plantations continued to be subdivided and developed. Downriver faubourgs, like today's Marigny neighborhood, were mostly populated by Creoles—both white and Creoles of color—which then was likely synonymous with *native*, or having ancestry here that dated back to the city's colonial rule.[7] Wealthy Americans settled across Canal Street in today's Garden District and uptown.

The swampy, mosquito-infested land behind these early neighborhoods was sometimes called the "back of town."[8] In the 1800s, as New Orleans' gentry moved to grand avenues like St. Charles and Esplanade, hundreds of thousands of immigrants and African Americans settled here and on the immediate riverfront, which was lined with wharves and industry.[9] Many (especially Irish immigrants) dug canals to New Orleans' lakefront, which itself started to develop as a port and then a resort destination.

This information is a dramatic oversimplification of New Orleans' early history, but it should ground your reading. If it has piqued your interest in New Orleans' founding and cultural and topographical geographies, let Richard Campanella be your guide on those topics going forward.

New Orleans
Neighborhoods

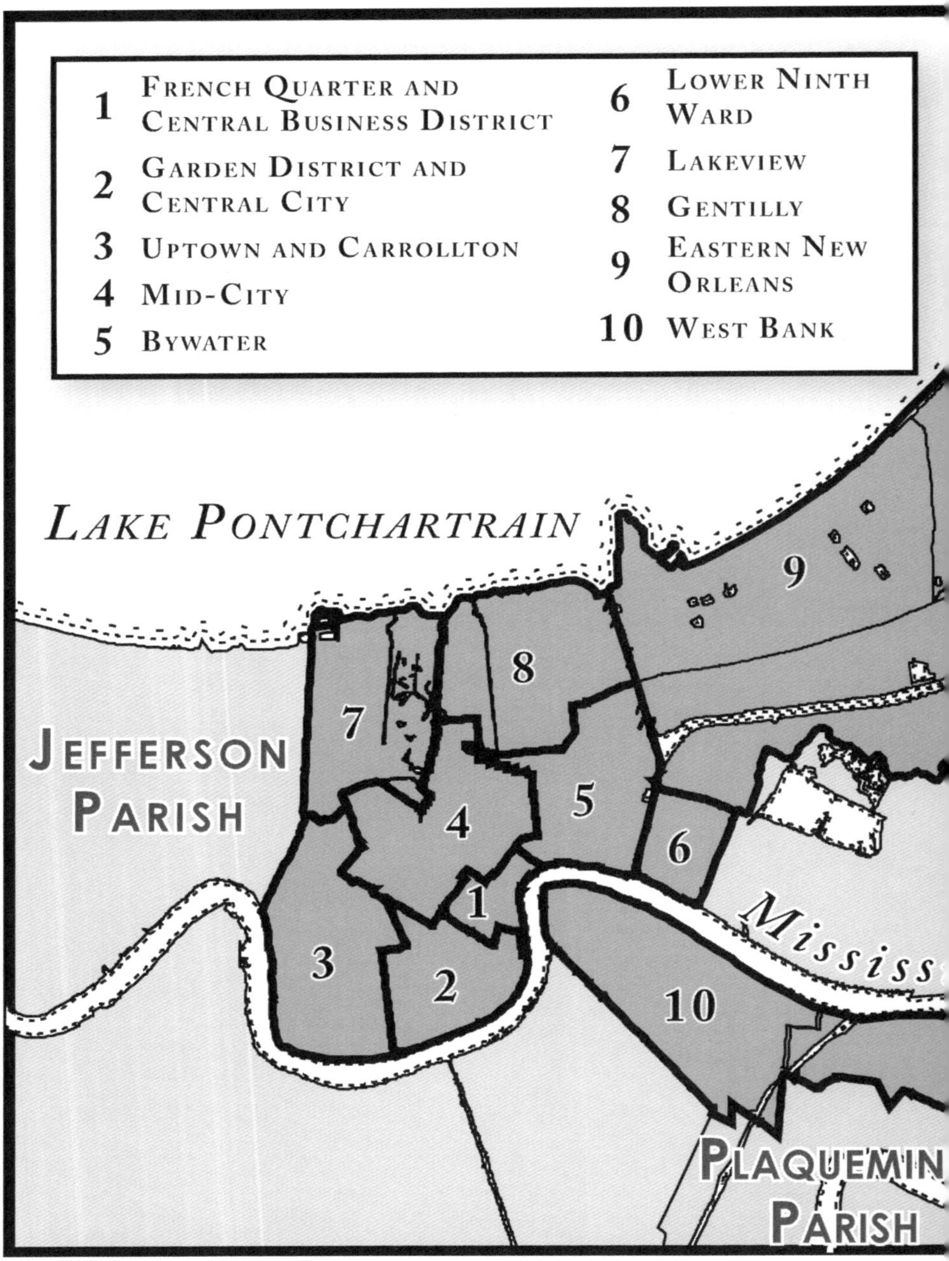

Adapted from a map by Ray Whitlow.

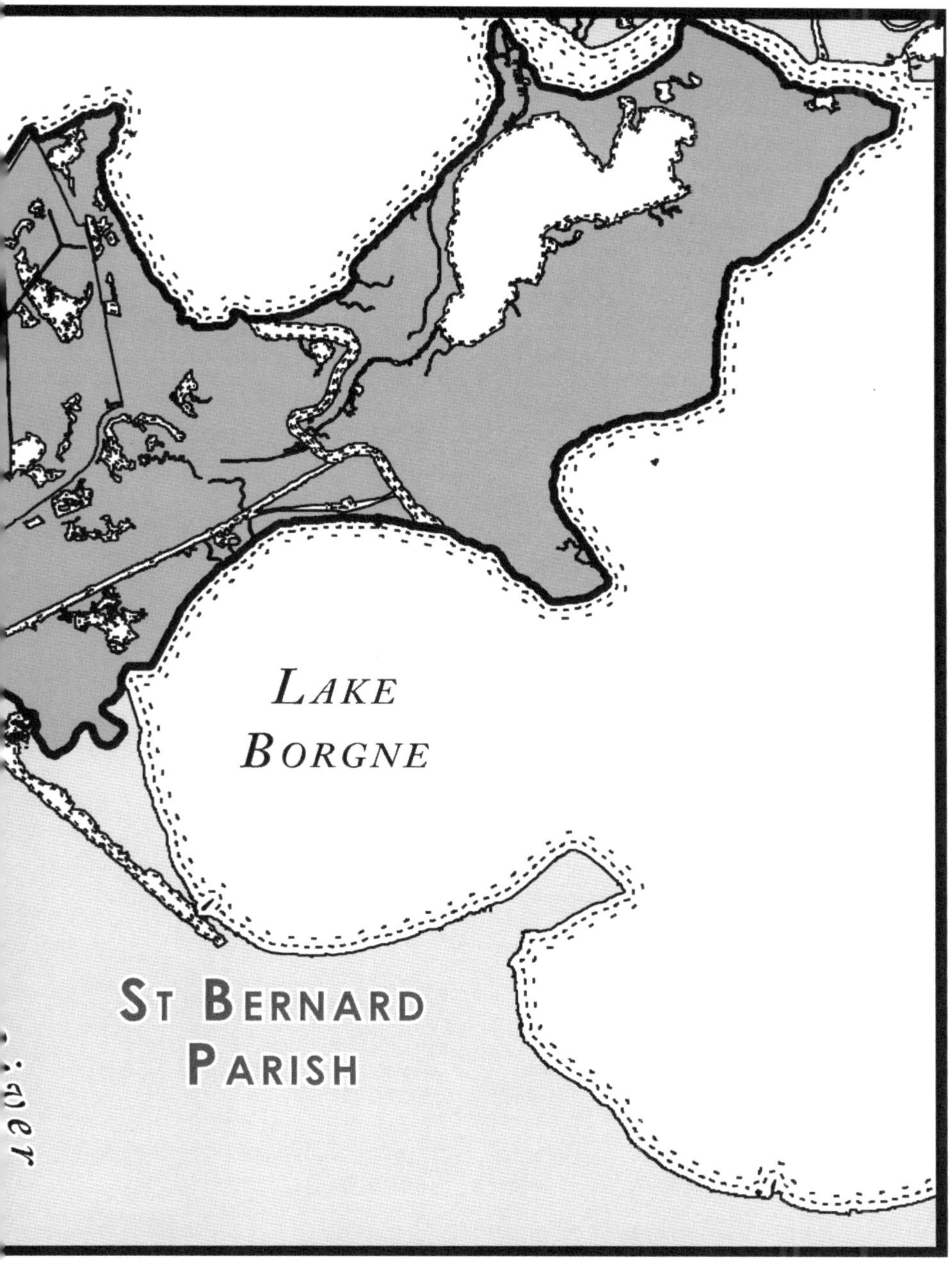
LAKE BORGNE
ST BERNARD PARISH

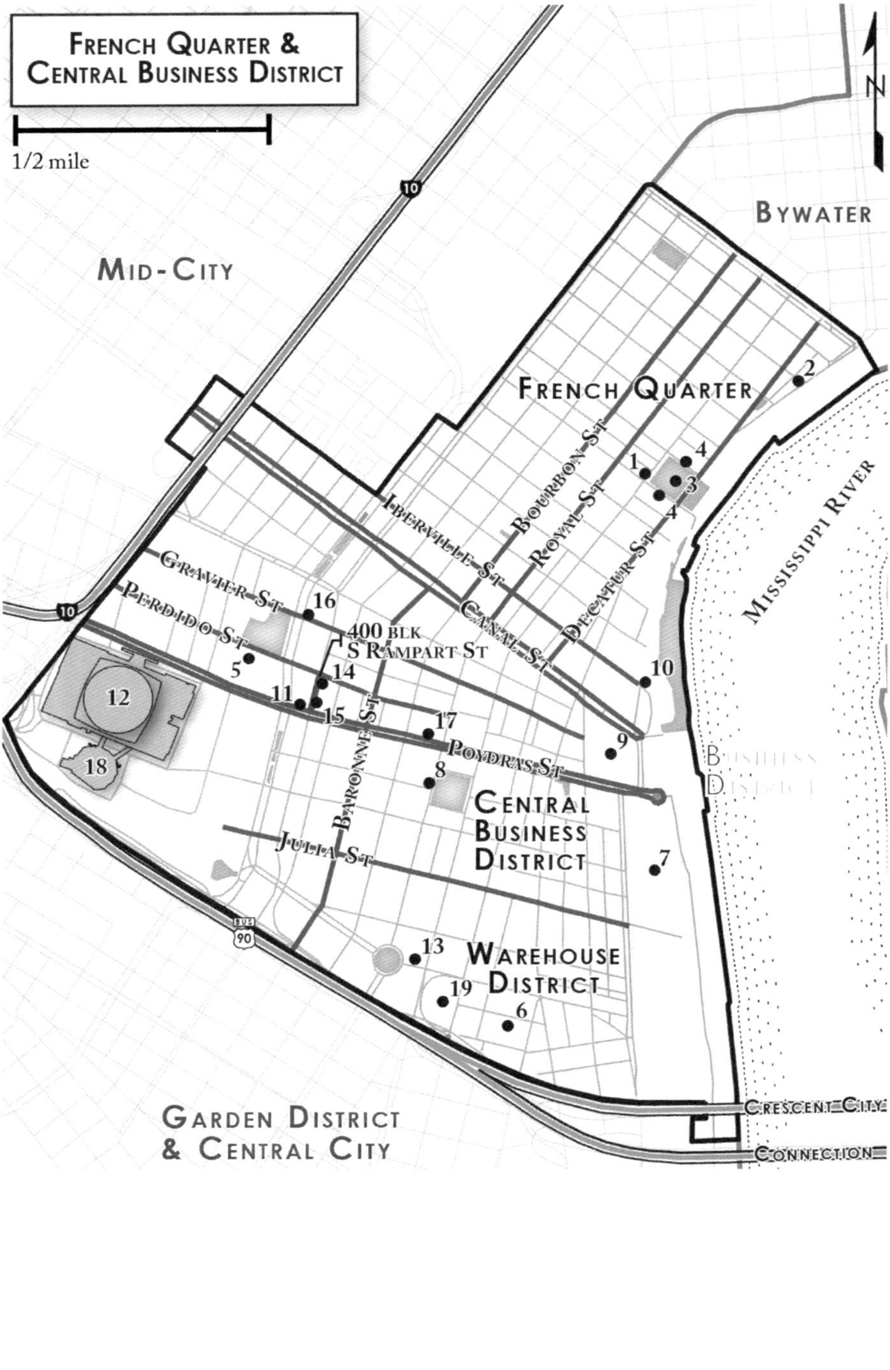
French Quarter &
Central Business District
1/2 mile
N
Bywater
Mid-City
French Quarter
Mississippi River
Bourbon St
Royal St
Decatur St
Iberville St
Canal St
Gravier St
Perdido St
400 blk
S Rampart St
Baronne St
Poydras St
Julia St
Central
Business
District
Warehouse
District
Garden District
& Central City
Crescent City
Connection
10
90
1
2
3
4
4
5
6
7
8
9
10
11
12
13
14
15
16
17
18
19

Chapter 1

French Quarter and Central Business District

MAP KEY

French Quarter
1. Cabildo
2. French Market
3. Jackson Square
4. Pontalba Buildings

Central Business District
5. City Hall
6. Cotton Mill
7. Ernest N. Morial Convention Center
8. Gallier Hall
9. Harrah's Casino
10. Liberty Place Monument
11. Little Gem Saloon
12. Mercedes-Benz Superdome
13. Ogden Museum of Southern Art
14. Old Eagle Saloon
15. Old Iroquois Theater
16. Old Pythian Temple
17. One Shell Square
18. Smoothie King Center
19. World War II Smithsonian Museum

FRENCH QUARTER

A Note on Identity

Jean-Baptiste Le Moyne de Bienville founded New Orleans in the present-day French Quarter in 1718. In the 1800s, as Americans settled upriver of today's Canal Street, the Quarter was often called the "old city" or "Creole Quarter." Its nostalgic "Vieux Carré" (or "old square") moniker was popularized at the turn of the twentieth century.[10]

The Vieux Carré Commission (VCC), which has been responsible for preserving the French Quarter's architecture and character since 1936, oversees the area bounded by Iberville Street, North Rampart Street, Esplanade Avenue and the Mississippi River. The city and the U.S. Department of the Interior have slightly different boundaries for the neighborhood.

At the Heart of It

Color is at the heart of New Orleans' French Quarter, where Bienville's men cleared the forest in 1718. From the neon on Bourbon and Canal Streets to the red brick and bright shutters that line its narrow "rues," the French Quarter's colors are many and meaningful. They reveal history, brand immortal establishments and even guide the VCC's preservation practices.

In the late 1700s, the French Quarter had two fires that destroyed almost all of its early architecture. What we see today, therefore, was mostly built while the city was under Spanish rule (1762–1803) and part of the United States, beginning in 1803 after the Louisiana Purchase was signed in the Cabildo. The Quarter's buildings have been altered and changed throughout its long history. In the 1840s, for instance, Italianate-style details were sometimes added to Creole cottages built thirty years earlier. That same decade, the neighborhood's famous iron lace galleries (or big, second-story balconies) were first introduced with the completion of the Pontalba Buildings next to Jackson Square.[11]

The VCC rates privately owned structures in the Quarter, like the Pontalba Buildings, by color. For example, buildings with a purple rating have national architectural and historical importance, green indicates local importance and yellow buildings "contribute to the character of the District." These seemingly vague descriptions, along with the fact that new details have been layered onto historic structures for more than two hundred years, make it easy to wonder what, exactly, is being preserved. The answer is the *tout ensemble*, or "all [of it] together." A phrase coined by a Louisiana Supreme Court judge in a 1941 preservation case, *tout ensemble* might seem impossible to define. But that is exactly the point.

As VCC director Lary Hesdorffer put it, "The *tout ensemble* term makes much more sense when you think about what the district would look like if you didn't have those yellow-rated buildings. Even though they aren't the highest-rated, they are extremely important to Vieux Carré's charm, interest and fascination." As for what time periods are preserved, Hesdorffer said that the VCC doesn't pick and choose. "If you do that, you're acting like a museum," he said, "and the French Quarter is hardly that. The French Quarter is a living part of the community."

Hesdorffer believes that when the neighborhood's soft red brick finally crumbles, the city should welcome modern design that is appropriate in the Quarter's context. "The easy way out for whoever develops new buildings would be to try and build exactly what was there before," he said. "The great challenge will be to create something in twenty-first-century style that is compatible, appropriate and garners enough favor to pass. It will be tough, but it won't be impossible."

Human hues and the politics of skin color have also long defined the French Quarter. During its first two centuries, the neighborhood was one of America's most culturally diverse. Just after it was founded in 1718, French, German and Swiss settlers were recruited to the colony with advertisements that portrayed the mosquito-infested swamp as "a new Eden."[12] Spanish rule brought new culture here in the late 1700s, while thousands of slaves were forced to New Orleans' port from Africa. Free people of color, most of them Catholic and of mixed French or Spanish descent, were (roughly) equally numbered to enslaved blacks in the French Quarter.[13] There was a three-tiered Caribbean racial structure here.[14] "A class of marginal status and frequently mixed origin was inserted between blacks and whites."[15]

In the early 1800s, when the French Quarter was known as the Creole Quarter, the term *Creole* was likely synonymous with *native*, or having ancestry here that dated back to the city's colonial rule.[16] Creoles included whites, free people of color and sometimes even black slaves. Racial division and tension would change who was associated with the word throughout time, but until the Civil War, *Creole* was wide-encompassing, and life in the Creole Quarter remained vastly different from life across Canal Street. The American Sector operated within a strict "white-or-black racial caste system."[17]

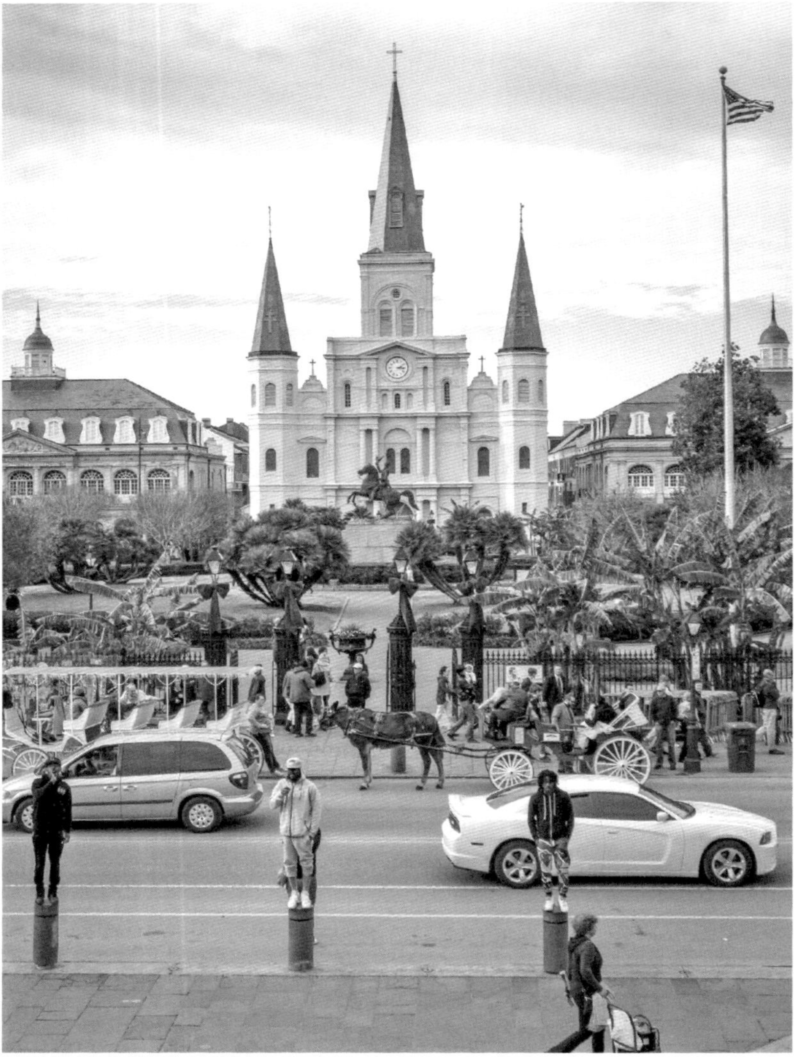

Street artists perform in front of Jackson Square. *Photo by Bruce Cervini.*

As the Civil War drew nearer and racial tensions grew, the rights of free people of color in the Creole Quarter were shaved away. This continued after the Civil War, when segregation—a ruling with its roots in New Orleans, where Homer Plessy was from—stripped all that was left of their "marginal status." Segregation drove some Creoles of color to leave for Mexico, Cuba, Haiti and France.[18] Many white Creoles, who distanced themselves from

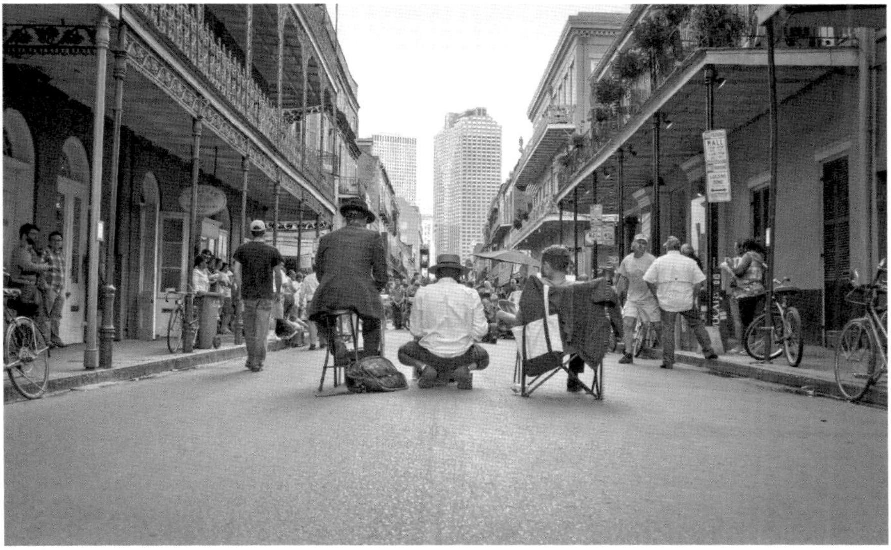

Pop-up poets write haikus for tourists on Royal Street in the French Quarter. *Photo by Bruce Cervini.*

the word in Jim Crow Louisiana, left for the garden suburbs of Esplanade Avenue and the lower faubourgs.[19] As Creoles departed from the French Quarter during the turn of the century, thousands of olive-skinned Sicilians arrived by ship at the corner of Elysian Fields and Esplanade Avenues.[20] They clustered around today's Decatur Street, then sometimes called "Dago Street," creating a "Little Palermo."[21]

The Sicilians were met with hostility. Living mostly in the subdivided homes of their Creole predecessors, they were criticized for their poverty and blamed for the city's last major yellow fever epidemic in 1905.[22] Still, many thrived at New Orleans' French Market and on the nearby docks, where they launched the country's tropical fruit industry—a colorful commercial venture, indeed.

Today, Little Palermo is unrecognizable. Many of the Sicilians left for the suburbs in the mid-twentieth century. The French Market has transformed from a robust food bazaar to a place mostly populated by shopping tourists. While most residents of the French Quarter are white and wealthy, its tourists remain diverse. In 2014, New Orleans welcomed 9.52 million visitors from all over the world, and most of them, undoubtedly, explored the French Quarter.[23]

Festivals and Events

Festivals abound in the French Quarter and include Satchmo Summerfest, the Tennessee Williams Literary Festival and French Quarter Festival. Now nearly as popular as Jazz Fest, the latter hosts more than 1,700 musicians on five stages over four days.

In August, wearing a red dress, or less, is an absolute requirement at the annual Red Dress Run. On the heels of that event is Labor Day Weekend's Southern Decadence Festival—an around-the-clock dance party and the city's largest gay event.

CENTRAL BUSINESS DISTRICT

A Note on Identity

Most people refer to New Orleans' Central Business District as "the CBD." A national historic district, the CBD encompasses four local historic districts: Lafayette Square, Picayune Place, Canal Street and the Warehouse District. The Data Center includes the Warehouse District in the Lower Garden District neighborhood, but it will be treated as part of the CBD here.

The CBD was New Orleans' first American neighborhood. In 2003, the Preservation Resource Center of New Orleans' board voted to officially call the CBD the "American Sector," a name it agreed "would complement 'The French Quarter' and help explain the development of New Orleans after the Louisiana Purchase."[24]

At the Heart of It

Today's Central Business District was founded in 1788 as New Orleans' first suburb, called Faubourg St. Marie (later Faubourg St. Mary). After the Louisiana Purchase, the neighborhood became home to thousands of American newcomers who soon erected the city's first Protestant churches, the first English-language theater and the luxurious St. Charles Hotel.[25] By the 1850s, the city's cultural compass clearly pointed to the new American Sector. The local government moved to the impressionable GALLIER HALL, while "Newspaper Row" and the "Cotton District" both developed nearby.[26] Retailers abandoned the Creole Quarter for Canal Street's broad, well-lit spaces, and commercial activity along the river helped keep the neighborhood's financial pulse strong.[27] Indeed, wealth and consumerism have long been at the heart of today's CBD.

Fundamental to those values was the exploitation of the poor and enslaved. In the early 1800s, thousands of Irish and German immigrants settled in today's CBD to work low-paying jobs on the docks, in warehouses and in the canal trenches, where many died from yellow fever. Unlike in the downriver Creole neighborhoods, where free people of color were either equal to or outnumbered enslaved blacks, the American side of town operated within a strict "white-or-black racial caste system."[28] Today's CBD was central to the slave trade. In 1861, the last year that slave dealerships existed, fifteen were located around the Gravier Street/Baronne Street intersection.[29]

Not surprisingly then, racial tensions erupted here after the Civil War, culminating in the Battle of Liberty Place. In 1874 on Canal Street, militant conservative Democrats known as the "White League" launched a strategic attack on the Federalists, subsequently returning to power and ending Reconstruction.[30] In 1891, the thirty-five-foot-tall Liberty Place Monument was erected here to honor the White League combatants.[31] Meanwhile, poverty and segregation were forced on the neighborhood's black "backatown" residents, who over the next few decades would create, grow and popularize American jazz.[32]

The 400 block of South Rampart Street would prove especially important to the development of this American art form, as Buddy Bolden, who is credited as jazz's inventor, played at the Little Gem Saloon and former Eagle Saloon with his legendary contemporaries.[33] A young Louis Armstrong lived nearby then, and as a teenager he won a talent show at Rampart's Iroquois Theater with his face covered in flour—the expected minstrel uniform.[34] Although criticized throughout his career as an Uncle Tom, Armstrong was a victim of Jim Crow terrorism and later publicly boycotted his home city when it banned integrated bands in 1956.[35]

Other distinctly black New Orleanian cultural traditions are rooted in this area. In 1909, the Knights of Pythias fraternal order constructed the seven-story Pythian Temple, which the *Daily Picayune* called the "biggest business enterprise ever attempted by the colored race in the United States."[36] The Pythian housed offices for local black businesses, a banquet room and a roof garden, where New Orleans' earliest jazz greats played.[37] Soon after the Pythian Temple opened, a group of laborers called The Tramps saw a comedy skit here about the African Zulu tribe. Inspired, the group changed

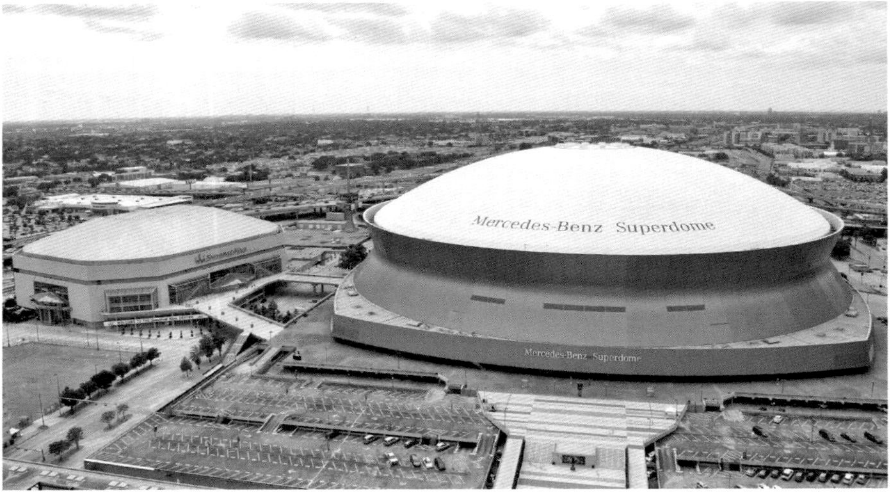

New Orleans' SMOOTHIE KING CENTER, home to the Pelicans, and the Mercedes-Benz Superdome, the capital of Who Dat Nation. *Photo by Mitchell Mendis.*

its name, and today's famed Zulu Social Aid and Pleasure Club soon began parading down South Rampart Street.[38]

In the second half of the twentieth century, the face of the Central Business District drastically changed. CITY HALL moved to its current office building on Perdido Street, and new skyscrapers honored the Big Easy's growing Big Oil credence. On a widened, commercial Poydras Street, ONE SHELL SQUARE was erected in 1972 as the city's tallest building—a title it keeps today.[39] Completion of the MERCEDES-BENZ SUPERDOME in 1975 marked the peak of this development, all of which was at the expense of nineteenth-century warehouses and much of the historic backatown.[40] Nonetheless, the Dome has since seen New Orleans through thick and thin—Saints wins and Hurricane Katrina, when more than twenty thousand people sought refuge here during the storm.

Rather than oil or shipping, today's Central Business District thrives on tourism. Its more than 1-million-square-foot ERNEST N. MORIAL CONVENTION CENTER is insulated by countless hotels, HARRAH'S CASINO and a host of museums—including the WORLD WAR II SMITHSONIAN and the OGDEN MUSEUM OF SOUTHERN ART—as well as smaller galleries lining Julia Street. The city has marketed the area to transplants, too, putting forth great effort to convert historic stalwarts like the block-long COTTON MILL and, beginning in 2015, the Pythian Temple into swanky lofts. Meanwhile, other important backatown buildings have become hollow, crumbling shells. The old Iroquois Theater and Eagle Saloon are vacant and unrecognizable. And while the city honors Louis Armstrong with a park and the airport in his name, his childhood home is now a parking lot.[41]

Festivals and Events

Every summer, horned Big Easy Rollergirls chase runners through the CBD streets with plastic bats at New Orleans' version of Running of the Bulls. Every first Saturday of the month, Julia Street galleries participate in an Art Walk, hosting free exhibitions and openings with refreshments. The first Saturday of August is always White Linen Night, where thousands of browsing patrons peruse the galleries in, of course, white linen.

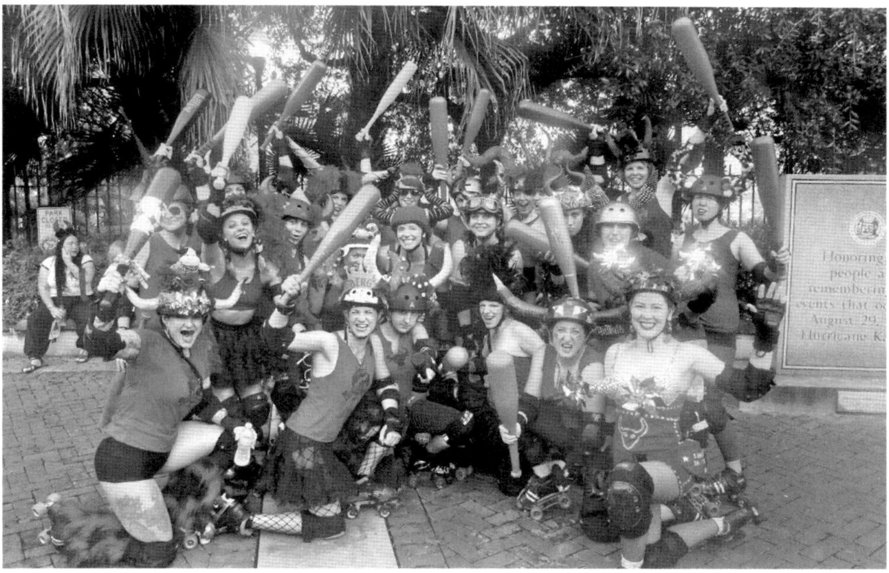

The Big Easy Rollergirls gear up for Running of the Bulls, 2014. *Photo by John Haffner.*

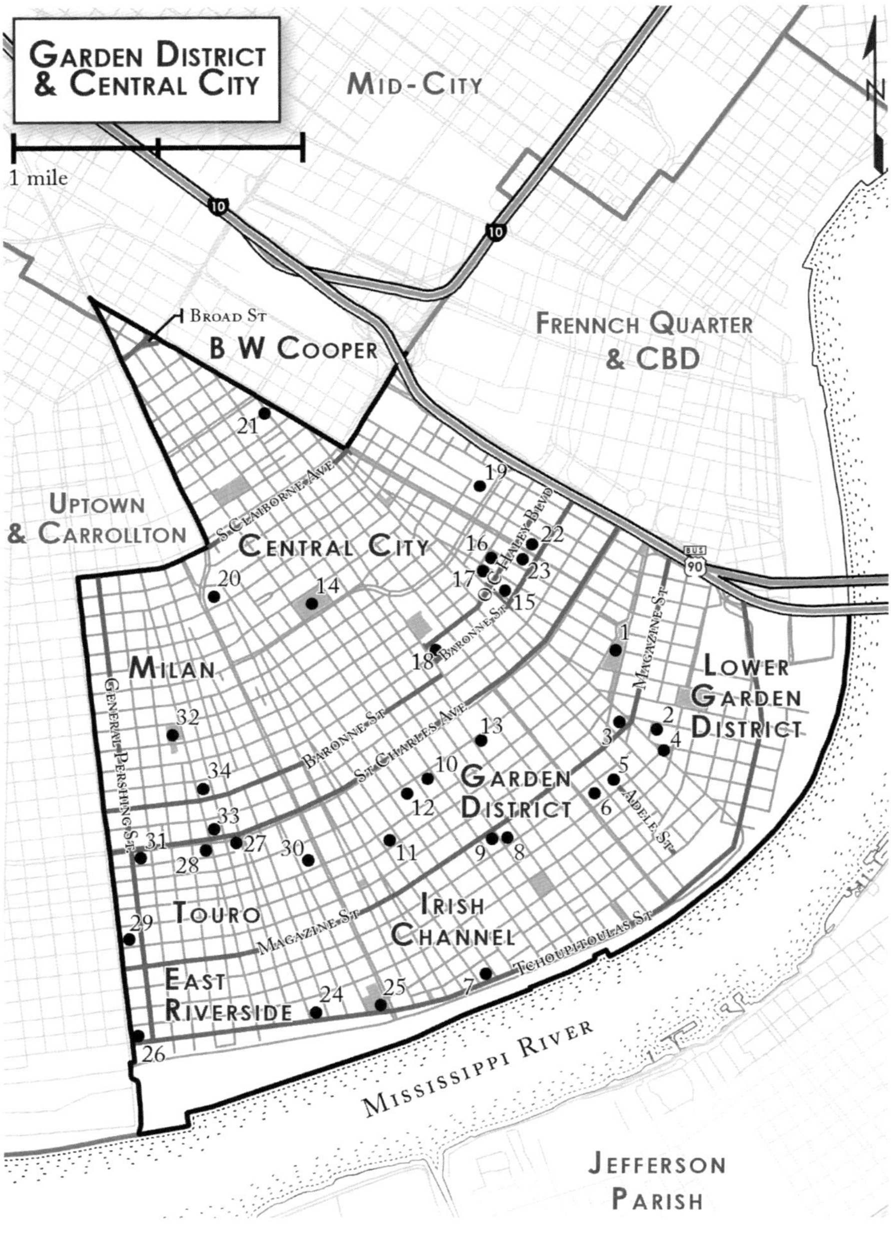
Garden District & Central City
1 mile
Mid-City
Broad St
B W Cooper
Frennch Quarter & CBD
Uptown & Carrollton
S Claiborne Ave
Central City
O C Haley Blvd
Baronne St
Milan
General Pershing St
St Charles Ave
Magazine St
Lower Garden District
Garden District
Adele St
Touro
Irish Channel
Tchoupitoulas St
East Riverside
Mississippi River
Jefferson Parish

Chapter 2

Garden District and Central City

MAP KEY

Lower Garden District
1. Coliseum Square
2. Kingsley House
3. Lily's Café
4. River Garden Apartments
5. St. Alphonsus Church
6. St. Mary's Assumption

Irish Channel
7. NOLA Brewing Company
8. Parasol's Bar & Restaurant
9. Tracey's

Garden District
10. Commander's Palace
11. George Washington Cable House
12. Lafayette Cemetery No. 1
13. Toby's Corner

Central City
14. A.L. Davis Park
15. Ashé Cultural Arts Center
16. Café Reconcile
17. Casa Borrega
18. Dryades YMCA
19. Guste Apartments
20. Harmony Oaks Apartments
21. Marrero Commons
22. New Orleans Jazz Market
23. Southern Food and Beverage Museum

East Riverside
24. Global Maritime Ministries
25. John P. Lyons Memorial Center
26. Tipitina's

Touro
27. New Orleans Musicians' Clinic
28. Rayne Memorial Methodist Church
29. St. Stephen's Church
30. Touro Infirmary
31. Touro Synagogue

Milan
32. Atkinson-Stern Tennis Center
33. Columns Hotel
34. Martin's Wine Cellar

LOWER GARDEN DISTRICT

A Note on Identity

This neighborhood got its name when the nonprofit Friends of the Cabildo published *New Orleans Architecture*, volume 1, *The Lower Garden District*, in the 1970s. Neighborhood residents welcomed this new brand as a way to disassociate from the area's high-crime St. Thomas public housing development.

The city map still identifies St. Thomas, which was torn down and replaced with the RIVER GARDEN APARTMENTS, as its own neighborhood. Engulfed by the Lower Garden District and historically linked to it, the development's history is included in this essay.

At the Heart of It

In the Lower Garden District, triumphant examples of preservation are interspersed with despairing decay. Mansions nearly two hundred years old are both newly renovated and buckling under the weight of vines here. The history of this neighborhood dates back to 1806, when Barthélémy Lafon began designing the former plantation land with parks, basins, fountains and canals—some of New Orleans' earliest expressions of Greek Revival–style planning.[42] Soon, wealthy Americans moved around COLISEUM SQUARE on streets named for the nine Greek muses.

In the 1840s and '50s, thousands of Irish and German immigrants settled along the Mississippi River in today's Lower Garden District to work in warehouses and stockyards and on the docks. Impressionable churches were built for them. The Irish attended ST. ALPHONSUS, with its painted ceilings and finely detailed high altar, while the Germans held mass at ST. MARY'S ASSUMPTION, with its intricate brickwork in German Baroque Revival style.[43] In the 1890s, the KINGSLEY HOUSE opened here as the first settlement house in the South. Settlement homes were meant to integrate poor immigrants with wealthier neighbors to help them overcome language and cultural and social barriers.[44] Both the churches and the Kingsley House are still open today.

When the Great Depression hit, few in the Lower Garden District were wealthy anymore. The neighborhood's mansions were divided into boardinghouses and apartments, and in 1937, President Franklin D. Roosevelt signed the loan that would commence the construction of the city's St. Thomas and Magnolia housing developments—the first public

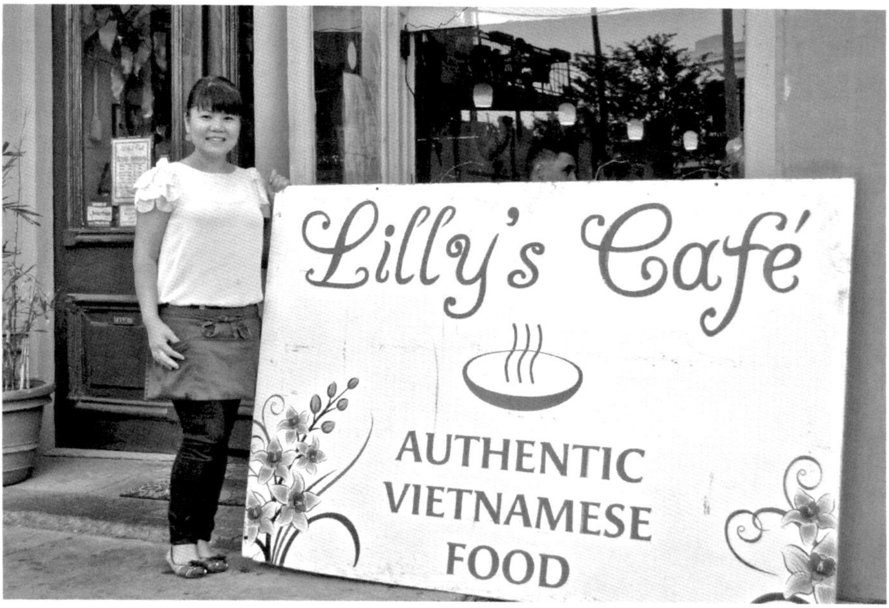

Lilly Vuong in front of her famed Magazine Street eatery, Lilly's Café. *Photo by author.*

housing projects in the country—as part of the New Deal.[45] When St. Thomas opened as an all-white development, it saved 1,500 families from squalor. Two decades later, when the projects were racially integrated, these low-income white residents had options in the suburbs.[46] African Americans did not, and they promptly replaced the whites who left.

Long a place where wealth and poverty have collided, the Lower Garden District's challenges grew in the 1970s. City neglect and mismanagement led to ubiquitous poverty and crime in St. Thomas, while residents of the surrounding area made efforts to disassociate from the development. By the turn of the century, the city had voted to demolish St. Thomas, and in 2004, the mixed-income River Garden Apartments—with only 182 public housing units compared to St. Thomas's 1,500—opened near the development's former site. Because the Lower Garden District is on high-lying land along the Mississippi River, it avoided major flooding during Hurricane Katrina. Since the storm, however, it is one of the most rapidly gentrifying neighborhoods in the city.

Today, evidence of Lower Garden District's twentieth-century hardships and post-Katrina growth are layered atop its original foundation. Antique shops, corner stores and new boutiques and restaurants alternate along

Magazine Street. People of all backgrounds greet one another by name on the sidewalks. To transplants, many of whom have settled here, the Lower Garden District likely feels genuine and local. To natives, many of whom have been displaced, it may feel quite the opposite. In 2013, after months of organizing, crowds with signs that said, "Jim Crow Can't Live Here Anymore" protested against the River Garden Apartments' management for allegedly harassing and intimidating public housing residents.[47] The Lower Garden District still faces challenges in reconciling old and new, wealthy and poor.

Festivals and Events

The Coliseum Square Association hosts guided house tours each fall and spring. The Lower Garden District is central to many St. Charles Avenue Mardi Gras parades. The St. Patrick's Day Parade also passes through part of the neighborhood.

IRISH CHANNEL

A Note on Identity

There are competing theories about how, when and where the Irish Channel neighborhood came into existence. Many say that the Irish Channel name was first given to Adele Street in today's Lower Garden District.[48] When the city cleared Adele to erect the St. Thomas public housing development in the late 1930s, it muddied perceptions of where the Channel was located.[49] In the 1970s, planners who drew neighborhood boundaries moved the Irish Channel upriver. "Official" borders, while excluding areas long perceived as part of the Irish Channel, neatly align with ward and municipal district boundaries.[50]

At the Heart of It

Diversity and pride are at the heart of today's Irish Channel, which encompasses a great expanse of culture, architecture and housing stock. Although the Irish have stolen the neighborhood's historical spotlight, thousands of Germans also settled here between the 1830s and 1850s.[51]

Near both the bountiful Garden District and the wharf, these immigrants took up jobs as warehouse and stockyard hands, dockworkers and domestics.

In the mid-twentieth century, descendants of the neighborhood's original Irish and German settlers began moving to new, exclusively white lakeside suburbs.[52] While the two world wars had devastated the local German population and shamed all public displays of German tradition and culture, New Orleans' Irish remained proud.[53] In 1947, the city's St. Patrick's Day Parade tradition began, and in 1952, the neighborhood's famous Irish-themed bar and restaurant, PARASOL'S, opened.[54]

Meanwhile, Latinos and African Americans started replacing the whites who were leaving the neighborhood. At first, new residents resisted encroaching realities of poverty and crime, but redlining and discriminatory housing practices proved to be powerful foes. In twenty years, the Irish Channel's population dropped by 38 percent—double the rate of the city.[55] By 1990, one in four neighborhood homes here were vacant.[56]

Brave residents who were tired of crime decided to organize. They brought the old neighborhood association back to life and lobbied police officials to step up their efforts.[57] The Irish Channel's revival accelerated after Hurricane Katrina. Quaint shotguns and new shops and restaurants

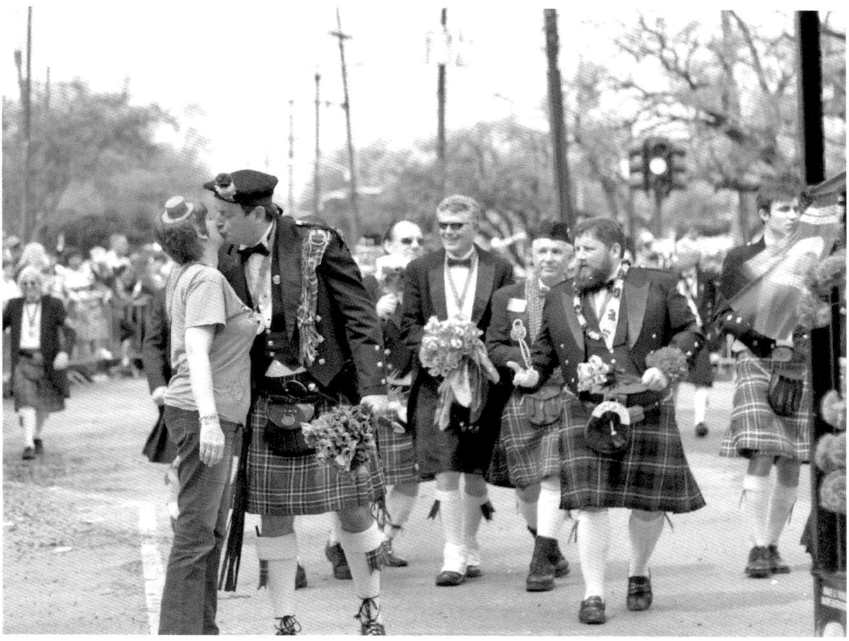

A St. Patrick's Day Parade marcher steals a kiss in the Irish Channel. *Photo by Lindsay Arvin.*

along Magazine Street have helped lure young professionals here. From 2000 to 2010, poverty decreased by almost 20 percent.[58]

Today, the Irish Channel is again home to people of a variety of backgrounds, except in March, when everyone here is Irish. For nearly a full month, streets are flooded with revelers in green, and bars transform from local dives to tourist destinations. Parasol's hosts an annual block party on St. Patrick's Day weekend, following the local parade. Nearby, TRACEY'S competes for the "Best Roast Beef Po-Boy" title.

Like the local Irish and Germans before them, today's Irish Channel residents celebrate beer. NOLA BREWING COMPANY, the city's largest brewery and its only one for several years after Hurricane Katrina, sits on Tchoupitoulas Avenue. An outfit driven by pride, owner Kirk Coco opened it after learning that Hurricane Katrina forced the once New Orleans–brewed Dixie Beer to Wisconsin. His experience with brewing was limited, but his bravado was unbounded: "You can't be a real city unless you have a beer," he told the *Times-Picayune*.[59] Today, the brewery's selection plays tribute to its neighborhood with names like Hopitoulas IPA, 7th Street Wheat and Irish Channel Stout.

Festivals and Events

Whole cabbages are thrown from floats, and paraders hand out flowers in exchange for a kiss on the cheek at the annual St. Patrick's Day Parade. Following the show, Parasol's neighborhood block party carries on into the night.

THE GARDEN DISTRICT

A Note on Identity

Travel writers named this neighborhood during the mid-1800s for its impressive English-style gardens.

At the Heart of It

The Garden District is home to more than two thousand families, some of whom have been in the neighborhood for generations.[60] Among the mansions that have been passed down for more than a century is

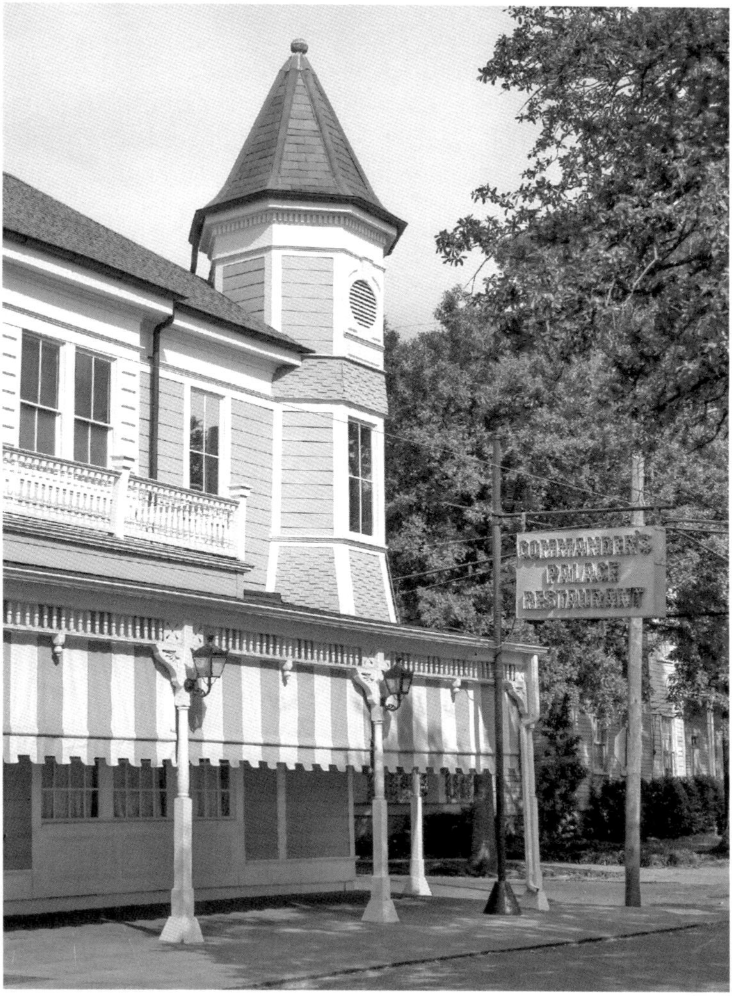

The Garden District's Commander's Palace restaurant dates back to 1880. *Photo by Bruce Cervini.*

"TOBY'S CORNER." Built in the 1830s for Philadelphia businessman Thomas Toby and soon after sold to the Westfeldt family, it is thought to be the neighborhood's oldest estate still standing.[61] Preservation and rich tradition are very much at the heart of today's Garden District.

In 1832, much of the plantation land that made up today's Garden District was subdivided for development.[62] American merchants—many from the North—came to the new neighborhood chasing fortune in the cotton, sugar, insurance and shipping industries. They looked down on Creole architecture and broadcast their wealth with Italianate- and Greek Revival–style mansions. Settlers commissioned international artists to paint murals and portraits for their high-ceilinged interiors, bestrewn with detailed marble and stained glass. Outside, English-style gardens presented "romanticized natural settings" that defied formal French design.[63]

In 1860, three-fourths of the Garden District's professional gardeners were German or Irish, and most of them lived in the neighborhood's riverfront periphery.[64] Hiring immigrant workers proved cheaper than owning slaves, who lived in attached slave quarters, and was often preferred.[65] Nevertheless, Americans introduced a strict "white-or-black racial caste system" to the city.[66] While living in the Garden District in the late 1800s, writers Kate Chopin and George Washington Cable explored the chafing racial philosophies of the French Quarter and burgeoning American Sector. Cable wrote *Old Creole Days* (1879) and *Grandissimmes* (1880) at 1313 Eighth Street, where he also often hosted Mark Twain.[67]

The Garden District's social scene was robust in the late nineteenth century. Elite politicians, military generals, musicians and artists came together in its many estates. Emile Commander established the neighborhood's first restaurant in 1880, and more than 130 years later, the world-renowned Commander's Palace is still named for him.[68] Owned by New Orleans' famed restaurant family, the Brennans, Commander's has won countless culinary awards under the leadership of Executive Chefs Paul Prudhomme, Emeril Lagasse and Tory McPhail.

Across the street from Commander's, Lafayette Cemetery No. 1 (est. 1833) draws an after-lunch crowd. Tourists and locals alike weave around aboveground tombs and recall scenes that were filmed here from the movies *Double Jeopardy* (1999) and *Dracula* (2000). Not surprisingly, the Garden District continues to be a transient place for present-day icons and celebrities. New Orleans' quintessential American neighborhood, it has been featured in countless books, films and television shows throughout the twentieth century. Homes here remain awe-inspiring and beget admiration from organized walking tours daily.

Festivals and Events

Each year, a Garden District Association board member hosts Jazz & Juleps at his or her home. The ticketed event features music, a southern supper and New Orleans' favorite springtime cocktail.

After trick-or-treating in the early evening, local families join for the neighborhood's annual Halloween Under the Oaks party.

CENTRAL CITY

A Note on Identity

The city puts the B.W. Cooper development (formerly the Calliope project) in the Mid-City District. This development was demolished in 2008 and replaced by the Marrero Commons. Many sources, from residents to the *Times-Picayune*, refer to the Commons as being part of Central City. It is treated as such here.

The neighborhood's Magnolia project and Melpomene project were later named the C.J. Peete Apartments and the Guste Apartments, respectively. Today, the Harmony Oaks Apartments have replaced C.J. Peete.

The area of Central City above Claiborne Avenue is known as "Hoffman Triangle." The northernmost part of Hoffman Triangle, above Broad Street, is part of "Zion City."

At the Heart of It

At the heart of Central City is its long history of overcoming adversity. From Jim Crow laws and public housing neglect to redlining and today's discriminatory bank practices, hardship has been forced on this community for more than a century. Oretha Castle Haley Boulevard has long sustained the pulse of Central City. Today, it is home to cultural centers, restaurants and nonprofits that are dedicated to supporting the neighborhood.

In the late 1800s, when Oretha Castle Haley Boulevard was known as Dryades Street, Orthodox Jews from Russia and Poland settled here. Throughout the early twentieth century, it was a bustling commercial corridor and a center for Jewish social life. At the time, Dryades was one of the only places in the city where African Americans could shop without being harassed. In 1905, the Colored Young Men's Christian Association (today's Dryades YMCA) opened on the street, and by 1928, its School of Commerce was offering accounting, bookkeeping, office management and other skills classes to African Americans.[69]

Central City became home to African American businessmen, doctors, nurses, artists and musicians. Despite their many contributions to New Orleans' rich culture, segregation and poverty remained powerful predators. In the 1940s, many Central City residents moved to the new Magnolia and Calliope projects—the latter was built on a former city dump.[70] In fact, America's "projects" began here: Magnolia was the first all-black public housing development that President Franklin Delano Roosevelt signed into existence during the New Deal. Its all-white counterpart, St. Thomas, was erected in the Lower Garden District at the same time.[71]

About fifteen years after the projects were built, civil rights activism erupted in Central City. Meetings at the Y gave birth to the Consumers' League of Greater New Orleans, and in 1960, the group led a "Don't Buy Where You Can't Work" campaign on today's O.C. Haley Boulevard.[72] Among the boycotters was Oretha Castle herself. Then a student at Southern University of New Orleans, Castle emerged as a leader at protests, demonstrations and sit-ins.[73]

Despite civil rights gains, in 1964 the Melpomene project opened in the neighborhood, meeting poverty's increasing demands.[74] Over the next few decades, Central City's three public housing developments became home to thousands of New Orleans' most destitute African American families. By the turn of the century, the neighborhood was the city's poorest.[75]

In the years leading up to Hurricane Katrina, community members again organized against harsh realities. Arts activists who were focused on positively portraying people of African descent opened the Ashé Cultural Arts Center on O.C. Haley Boulevard in 1998.[76] Nearby, a pastor's effort to develop a business where at-risk youth could work and grow gave way to Café Reconcile, which offers a culinary training and life skills development program.[77]

When Hurricane Katrina hit, flooding in Central City ranged from eight feet of water near Claiborne Avenue to less than two feet near St. Charles.[78] Having already withstood half a century of neglect and mismanagement, Central City's projects also withstood the storm. Despite lawsuits, protests and thousands of displaced residents, the first white-majority city council in more than two decades voted unanimously to raze "the bricks."[79] The B.W. Cooper and C.J. Peete developments faced the wrecking ball in early 2008.

While parts of Central City crumbled after the storm, its O.C. Haley Boulevard flourished. New arts and community-based organizations settled here, as did Casa Borrega, a restaurant that hosts many events for the local Latino community. In 2014, the Southern Food and Beverage Museum, which incorporates the Museum of the American Cocktail, opened on the

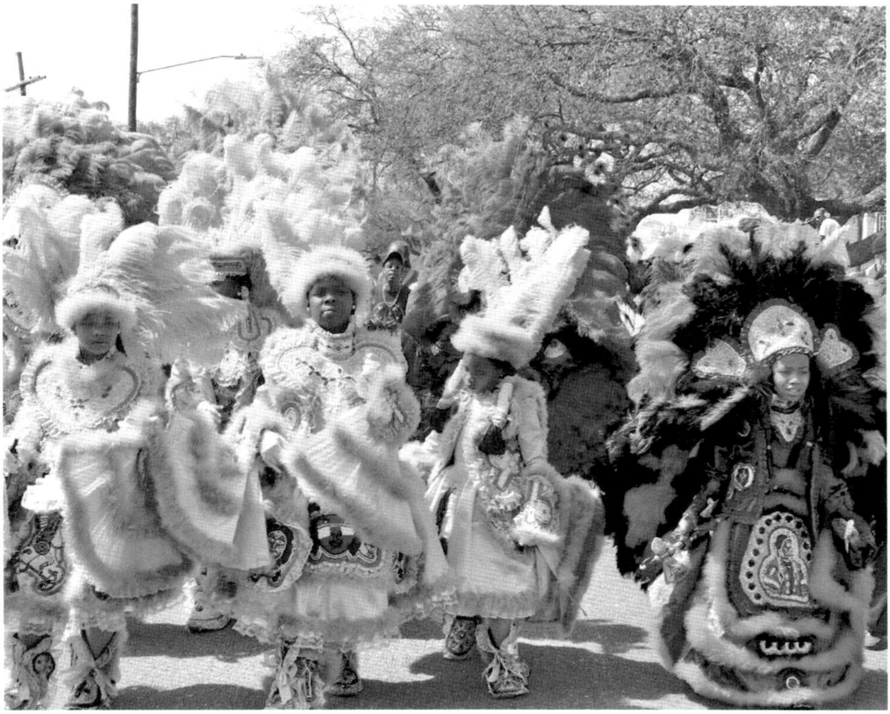

Mardi Gras Indians show off their suits of beads and feathers on Super Sunday in Central City. *Photo by author.*

corridor. A year later, the New Orleans Jazz Market—a performing arts venue, jazz community center and archive—joined its food-and-beverage contemporary here.

From paintings on boarded-up doors of abandoned homes to commissioned murals scaling the sides of buildings, Central's City vast range of public art exposes its challenges and triumphs. While the neighborhood has much to celebrate, its dramatic population decline since Hurricane Katrina is a stark reality. From 2000 to 2010, the number of people living here dropped from more than twenty-three thousand to twelve thousand.[80] New pastel-colored town homes that have replaced the projects make displacement easy on the eyes, but the numbers beg the question: where did all the people go? They are in Houston, Atlanta and Jackson; some are under New Orleans' bridges, and others are in dilapidated shotguns subject to still-rising rents.[81]

Festivals and Events

Central City's most famous festival is Super Sunday, held on St. Joseph's Day in March each year. Since the 1970s, Mardi Gras Indian gangs have danced through the neighborhood to call-and-response rhythms, competing for local attention and praise. The festival starts and ends at A.L. Davis Park.

Each year on the Sunday before Martin Luther King Day, Ashé Cultural Arts Center hosts the Lift Every Voice & Sing concert, featuring freedom songs from the civil rights era.

The O.C. Haley Boulevard Merchants and Business Association organizes the annual Central City Festival, complete with a health fair, food and crafts vendors, live music and Mardi Gras Indian performances. In 2014, Big Freedia's audience set the twerking Guinness World Record here.

EAST RIVERSIDE

A Note on Identity

East Riverside residents often just say they live "uptown off Tchoupitoulas" or "uptown off Magazine."

At the Heart of It

Like all neighborhoods in the Garden District and Central City Planning District, East Riverside began as plantation land. It developed between 1807 and 1850 and became incorporated as part of New Orleans in 1870.[82] Since then, the neighborhood's many resources have served the broader city. From the late 1800s to the 1940s, it was sought out for its Jefferson City Market, which sat at the corner of present-day Magazine and General Pershing Streets and sold imports straight from the river.[83]

In 1948, the John P. Lyons Memorial Center became the neighborhood's newest popular gathering place. Complete with air conditioning and a pool, the *Times-Picayune* touted it as "the finest youth recreational center in the South and perhaps one of the finest in the nation."[84] Further easing life along the river, in 1963 the Baptist Seamen's Service opened on Tchoupitoulas Avenue as a ministry for visiting seafarers. This organization has evolved into today's GLOBAL MARITIME MINISTRIES INC. (GMM), where more than ten thousand port employees come each year to regroup, contact their families using the center's computers and seek counseling and Christian fellowship.[85]

In the late 1970s, a group of young music fans established East Riverside's most famous venue, TIPITINA'S. The club was dedicated to a single musician, R&B legend Professor Longhair (Henry Roeland Byrd), as a place for him to play during his final years.[86] Now, decades after Professor Longhair passed away, Tipitina's patrons still line up along Napoleon Avenue to see performances by many of the musicians he influenced. The venue's nonprofit arm, Tipitina's Foundation, offers a jazz performance internship program for youth; Sunday Youth Music Workshops, where New Orleans' most

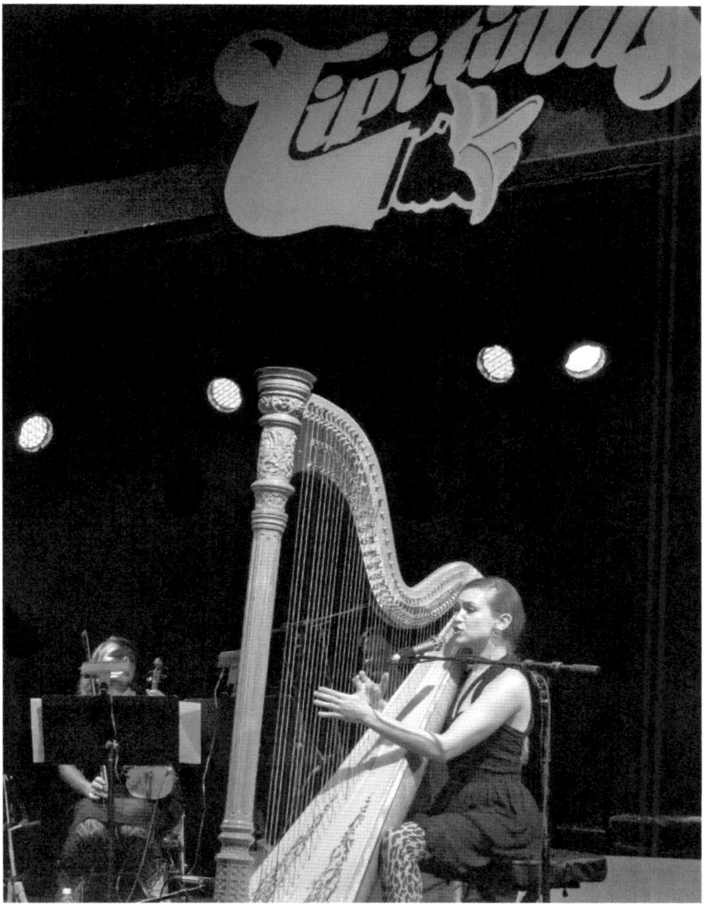

Joanna Newsom performs at Tipitina's. *Photo by Bruce Cervini.*

experienced musicians tutor the aspiring; and fully equipped "co-op" workspaces, where musicians can team with other industry professionals.

Located on the city's natural levee, East Riverside did not suffer extensive flooding during Hurricane Katrina, although the storm did force the Lyons Center to close.[87] The center reopened in 2013 after a $4.9 million renovation.[88] Today, it offers updated indoor and outdoor athletic space, as well as a computer lab, multipurpose rooms and a dance studio. It is home to the New Orleans Ballet Association and is usually teeming with people of all ages in leotards and basketball uniforms.

Festivals and Events

Every summer, locals swarm to Tipitina's Foundation Free Fridays, a concert series featuring everyone from local icons to national Hall of Famers. In September, the Foundation's Rhythm & Blues 5K supports programs in music education and development. Runners gather at the event's outdoor festival after the race.

The Lyons Center has a rotating calendar of exercise and dance classes, piano lessons and painting workshops.

GMM's annual GlobalFest is a fundraising event that includes dinner, music and a silent and live auction.

TOURO

A Note on Identity

Touro residents often say that they live "uptown off Magazine Street" or "uptown off St. Charles." The neighborhood is named for Judah Touro, a famed New Orleans philanthropist.

At the Heart of It

Touro's patchwork skyline of high-rise healthcare facilities, impressive religious sanctuaries and large estates make the neighborhood feel distinctly different from the rest of New Orleans. The area as we know it today began to take shape after it was incorporated as part of the city in 1870.[89]

Before the turn of the century, two of New Orleans' historic churches—St. Stephen's and Rayne Memorial Methodist—were built here in Gothic Revival style.[90] In 1882, Touro Infirmary moved to its current location and began offering free services to the city's indigent.[91]

The neighborhood's namesake, Judah Touro, was a Jewish merchant who lived in New Orleans for most of his life. One of the most influential philanthropists of the late 1800s, Touro's generosity touched a diverse range of organizations nationwide—including many Christian ones.[92] Here, he is the beneficiary of both Touro Infirmary and the Touro Synagogue, which was dedicated in 1909.[93] The synagogue's roots trace back to New Orleans' first and the country's sixth, Congregation Gates of Mercy, which was founded in 1828 near the French Quarter.[94]

Touro Infirmary has long been a medical trendsetter. In the 1920s, it bought the first incubators in New Orleans and became one of fifteen hospitals to receive funding for insulin testing nationwide.[95] That same decade, Touro opened the city's first physical therapy department.[96] Its growth attracted other health services to the neighborhood throughout the twentieth century. The infirmary continued its leadership after Hurricane Katrina as the first hospital to reopen, just twenty-eight days after the storm.[97]

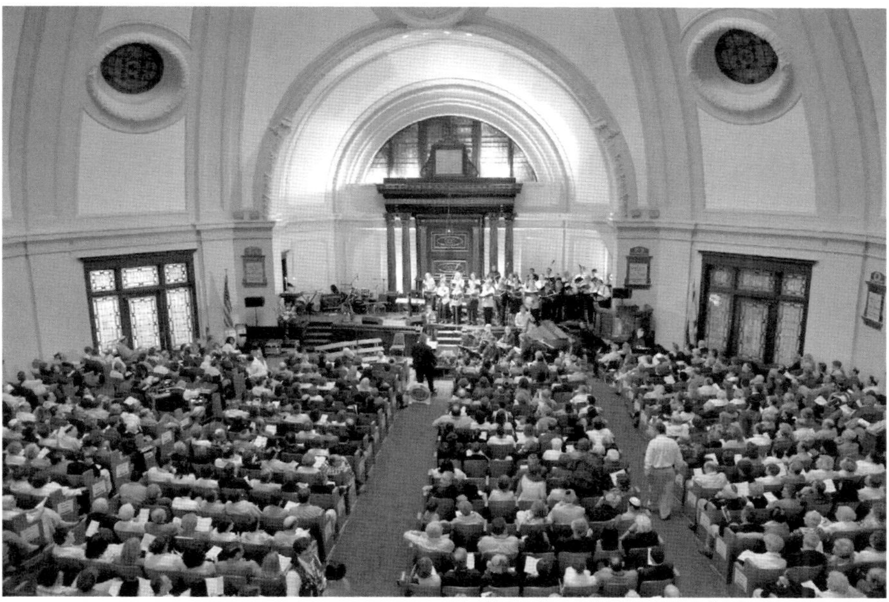

Inside Touro synagogue, a neighborhood landmark since 1909. *Photo by Scott Saltzman.*

At the heart of the Touro neighborhood today is a deeply rooted commitment to the well-being of the city's diverse population. Its many institutions honor the importance of community, openness and New Orleans traditions. The historic Rayne Memorial Methodist, for example, welcomes persons of any sexual orientation, gender identity, race, faith background, marital standing and family structure.[98] Nearby, the NEW ORLEANS MUSICIANS' CLINIC keeps "performers alive in body, mind, and spirit" through comprehensive healthcare and social services.[99] Some of the musicians who seek services here may even play at Touro Synagogue's annual Jazz Fest Shabbat, when worship is kicked up a notch to the sounds of New Orleans' brass.

Festivals and Events

Bagels are fresh and all are welcome to Touro Synagogue's Saturday morning Torah study. In addition to Jazz Fest Shabbat, the synagogue has a monthly Family Shabbat.

Touro Infirmary has a full calendar of health screening events, classes and support groups for community members.

MILAN

A Note on Identity

Milan residents often say they live "uptown off St. Charles" or "uptown off Claiborne." Those who do refer to the neighborhood's official name usually call it "the Milan."

At the Heart of It

A mostly residential neighborhood, the Milan is home to a diverse group of people, including many Latino families.[100] Along and near St. Charles Avenue, Italianate, East Lake, Queen Anne and Colonial Revival mansions—many built in the late 1800s—are often divided into apartment units. Perhaps the most famous of these estates is the COLUMNS HOTEL, where locals and tourists alike can almost always be found drinking Pimm's Cup cocktails on the porch.

Moving back toward Claiborne Avenue, street blocks get tighter, elevation gets lower and homes get smaller—most are bungalows and shotguns. Few settled in this part of the Milan until the turn of the twentieth century, when a new drainage system helped spur the area's development.[101] Despite efforts, the Milan's low elevation has made flooding a perpetual issue here.[102] Hurricane Katrina left more than 90 percent of the neighborhood's homes damaged and forced local businesses like MARTIN'S WINE CELLAR, which opened here in 1946, to relocate.[103] Martin's returned to the Milan in 2015 with an expanded deli and seating for 120 people.

Organizations like the Delachaise Neighborhood Association and the Milan Focus Group welcome neighborhood business development, which is picking up on and around Baronne Street. These groups meet at what is perhaps the Milan's most coveted community resource: the ATKINSON-STERN TENNIS CENTER. With nine state-of-the-art tennis courts (seven doubles and two singles), it is named for both its predecessor's beneficiary, Edgar Bloom Stern, and Nehemiah Atkinson, who served as director of the Stern Center for more than twenty years and inspired many local African Americans to play tennis.[104]

Festivals and Events

The Atkinson-Stern Tennis Center hosts local school matches, an after-school program, summer camp and clinics for all ages and abilities.

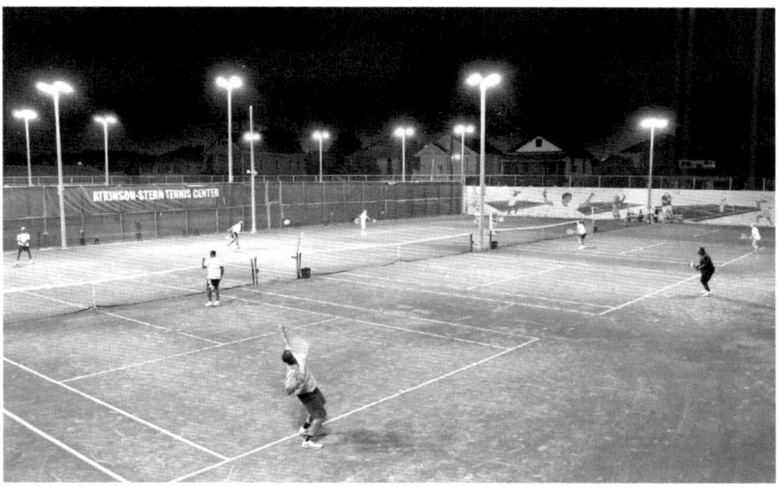

Atkinson-Stern Tennis Center is always teeming with locals from the Milan neighborhood. *Photo by author.*

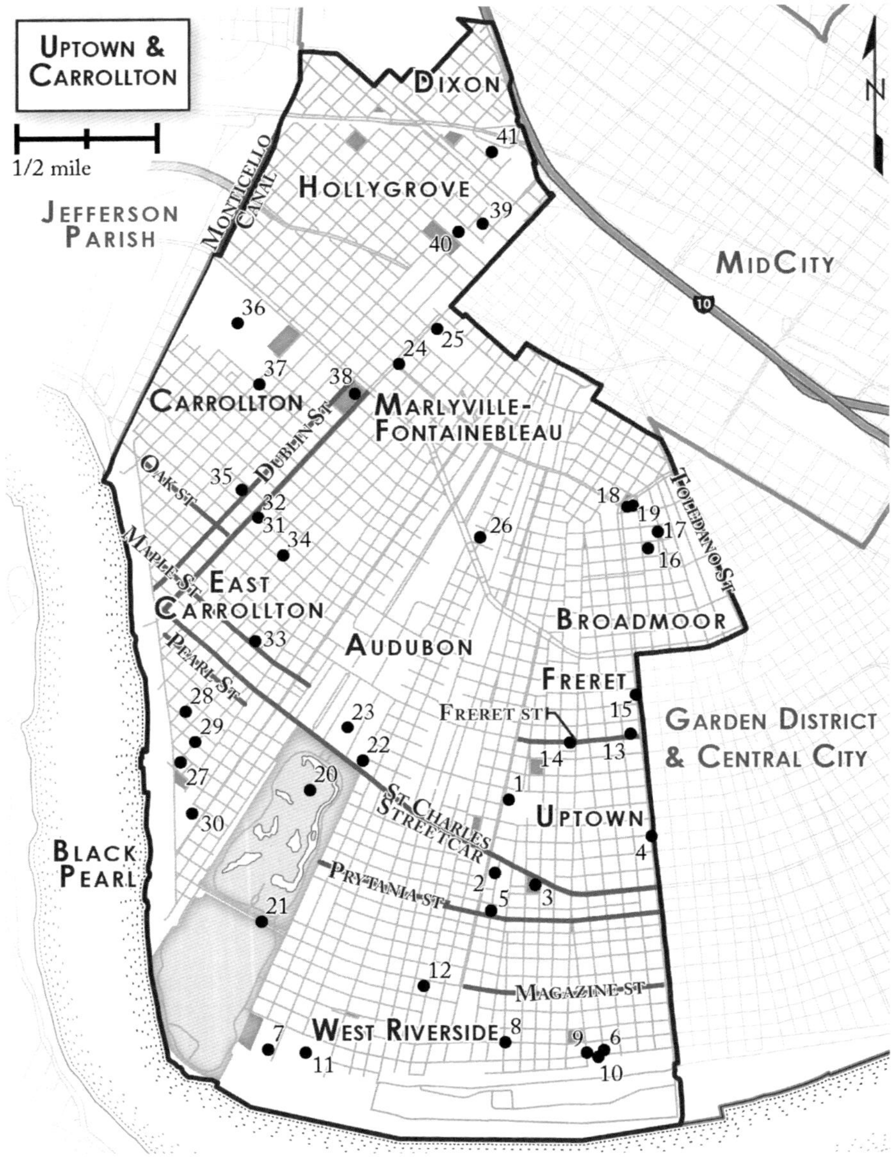
Uptown & Carrollton
1/2 mile
N
Dixon
Hollygrove
Jefferson Parish
Monticello Canal
MidCity
10
Carrollton
Marlyville-Fontainebleau
Dublin St
Oak St
Maple St
East Carrollton
Pearl St
Audubon
Broadmoor
Toledano St
Freret
Freret St
Garden District & Central City
Uptown
St Charles Streetcar
Prytania St
Magazine St
Black Pearl
West Riverside
1
2
3
4
5
6
7
8
9
10
11
12
13
14
15
16
17
18
19
20
21
22
23
24
25
26
27
28
29
30
31
32
33
34
35
36
37
38
39
40
41

Chapter 3

Uptown and Carrollton

MAP KEY

UPTOWN
1. Isidore Newman School
2. Jewish Community Center
3. Milton H. Latter Library
4. Pascal's Manale
5. Prytania Theatre

WEST RIVERSIDE
6. Hansen's Sno-Bliz
7. Children's Hospital
8. Domilise's Po-Boy & Bar
9. F&M Patio Bar
10. Public Belt Railroad
11. Old U.S. Marine Hospital
12. Whole Foods Arabella

FRERET
13. Freret Market
14. Gasa Gasa
15. Oschner Baptist Medical Center

BROADMOOR
16. Andrew H. Wilson School
17. Broadmoor Arts and Wellness Center
18. Broadmoor Community Care
19. Rosa F. Keller Library and Community Center

AUDUBON
20. Audubon Park
21. Audubon Zoo
22. Loyola University
23. Tulane University

MARLYVILLE-FONTAINEBLEAU
24. Beaux Arts Arch
25. Notre Dame Seminary
26. Ted's Frostop

BLACK PEARL
27. Mount Moriah Baptist Church
28. Plymouth Rock Baptist Church
29. Singleton's Po-Boys & Mini Mart
30. University Square

EAST CARROLLTON
31. Anthony Bean Community Theater
32. Central St. Matthew
33. Maple Street Books
34. Plum Street Snoballs

CARROLLTON
35. Carrollton Streetcar Barn
36. Carrollton Water Plant
37. Community Commitment Education Center
38. Palmer Park

HOLLYGROVE-DIXON
39. AARP
40. Hollygrove Market and Farm
41. Trinity Christian Community Center

UPTOWN

A Note on Identity

Most New Orleanians think of "uptown" as the area that spans from the Lower Garden District to Carrollton. As historian and geographer Richard Campanella put it, when the city named a specific neighborhood here "Uptown," it was "a little like renaming Wyoming the West."[105]

At the Heart of It

Before the 1830s and '40s, today's Uptown neighborhood was plantation land. The New Orleans and Carrollton Railroad initiated development here when it began rolling down St. Charles Avenue in 1835. Among the neighborhood's early settlers were German Jews, who arrived in New Orleans after their Orthodox eastern European counterparts.[106] By 1887, they had opened a Jewish orphanage here, and in 1903, the ISIDORE NEWMAN SCHOOL was founded to educate the orphan boys.[107]

Many of Uptown's famed institutions trace their history to the early twentieth century. The Italianate Beaux Arts mansion that serves as today's MILTON H. LATTER PUBLIC LIBRARY, for example, was erected in 1907 and eventually became home to silent-screen movie star Marguerite Clark.[108] By 1915, locals were eating raw oysters at PASCAL'S MANALE RESTAURANT and going on dates at New Orleans' first movie theater, the PRYTANIA.[109] All the while, the neighborhood stayed connected to its Jewish roots. In 1948, the old orphanage was reinvented as the city's JEWISH COMMUNITY CENTER.[110]

At the heart of Uptown today are these same historic institutions and services. The New Orleans and Carrollton Railroad is now the St. Charles Avenue Streetcar—the oldest continually operating streetcar in the world.[111] Pascal's most popular dish is its buttery barbecue shrimp, and the single-screen Prytania Theatre maintains its century-old charm. Just two blocks away, Isidore Newman School has a nationally renowned athletics program. All three Manning brothers—Cooper, Peyton and Eli—played football here in the 1990s.

In addition to aged fortresses, Uptown offers many modern surprises. Locally owned shops, restaurants and beauty services pepper the neighborhood, especially on Prytania and Magazine Streets. Best of all, according to many residents, is the neighborhood's walkability. "It's really

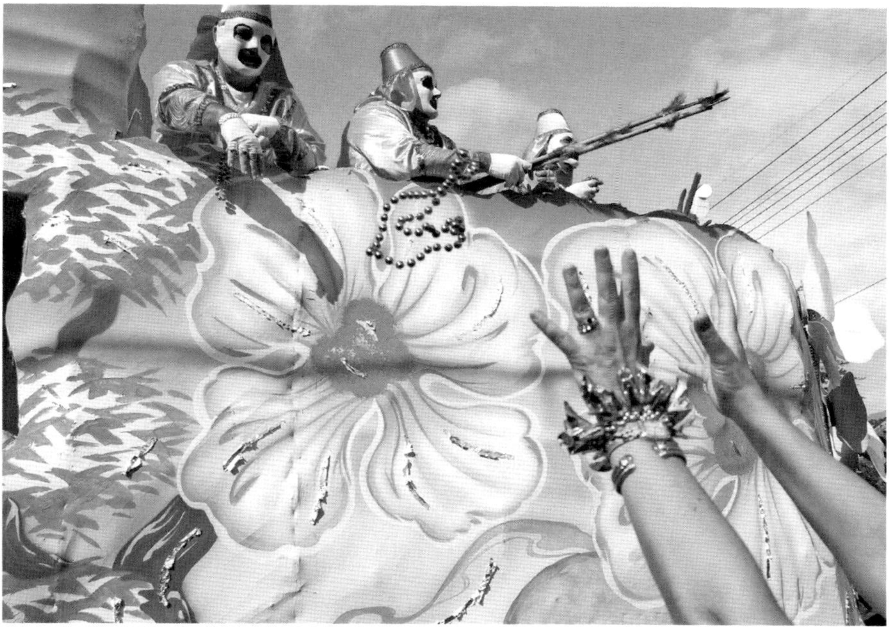

A Mardi Gras parade on the Uptown route. *Photo by Sally Asher.*

urban life at its best," said Bouligny Improvement Association board member Judy Jurisich. "It's comfortable and has gracious homes and lots of greenery. We can easily walk to just about any kind of activity, store or restaurant."

Festivals and Events

Since the 1970s, Uptown has hosted countless Mardi Gras parades. Many start on the neighborhood's border, Napoleon Avenue, before turning onto St. Charles to head downtown.

The Prytania Theatre hosts the New Orleans Film Festival, French Film Festival and an Oscar Party each year.

The Jewish Community Center has several annual events that are open to the public, including Adloyadah carnival, which celebrates the Purim holiday with sno-balls and hamantaschen; an a capella concert on Chanukah; and a Holocaust memorial event.

West Riverside

A Note on Identity

West Riverside residents often say that they live "uptown off Tchoupitoulas" or "uptown off Magazine."

At the Heart of It

Industry and invention are at the heart of West Riverside, where residents have long affected the culture and commerce of Greater New Orleans. This started as early as 1795, when cane sugar was first granulated on the plantation of the city's earliest mayor, Jean Étienne de Boré, just downriver from Audubon Park.[112] Crystallized sugar helped launch the South's plantation economy, which enriched the region for 150 years while also entrenching slavery here.[113]

In the late 1800s, the United States Marine Corps bought Boré's old lot and erected a Marine Hospital in today's West Riverside. The campus was impressive, boasting more than one thousand orange trees, the surgeon's Italianate-Victorian mansion and the overseer's Creole cottage, which dated back to the early 1830s.[114] American merchant seamen paid forty cents per month for care at the Marine infirmary, while consuls representing foreign seamen were charged seventy-five cents per day.[115]

Meanwhile, others in West Riverside focused on rail transportation. In 1893, construction began on Magazine Street's Arabella Bus Barn, a block-long facility where new electric streetcars were stored and maintained.[116] In 1908, the neighborhood celebrated the opening of the Public Belt Railroad. For the first time in New Orleans' history, ships could unload goods onto locomotives that serviced twenty miles of land along the port.[117]

New activity along the Mississippi River created a market for refreshments on Tchoupitoulas Avenue. In the 1930s, Ernest Hansen invented the city's first ice-shaving machine and founded Hansen's Sno-Bliz here.[118] Nearby, Domilise's Po-Boys & Bar and Fump and Manny's, today's F&M Patio Bar, also emerged as neighborhood mainstays.[119]

In the mid-1970s, the New Orleans Children's Hospital opened next door to the Marine infirmary, which closed just a few years later when its federal public funding was cut. More than three thousand people mourned the "death" of the Marine Hospital with a jazz funeral, second-lining on

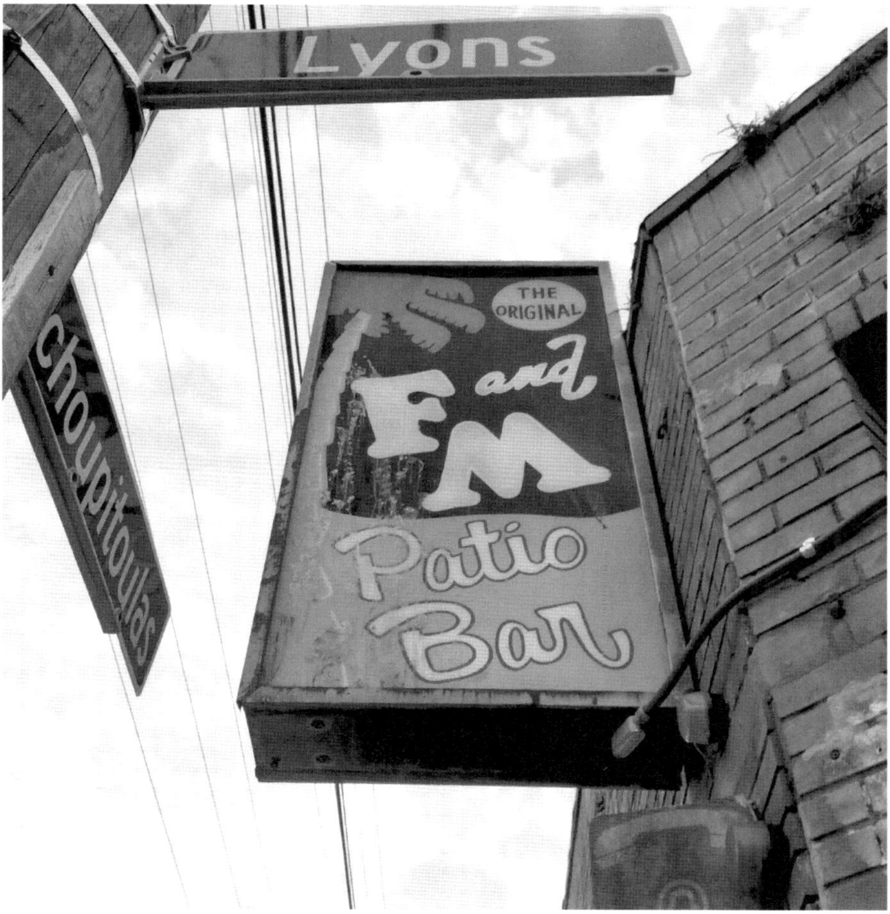

F&M's on Tchoupitoulas Street has been a college student hangout since it opened its dance hall in the 1930s. *Photo by Drew Handwerk.*

nearby streets before coming back to the grounds for red beans and rice.[120] In 2014, Children's Hospital bought the former military property, although efforts to update the historic campus are costly and slow. Many are advocating for the renovation and use of the former surgeon's mansion and the Creole cottage—likely the oldest building in the broader uptown area today.[121]

On Magazine Street, a preservation success story unfolded at the old Arabella Bus Barn in 2002, when a WHOLE FOODS MARKET breathed new life into what had become a vacant neighborhood eyesore.[122] A movement to repair and sell abandoned homes in West Riverside is also gaining momentum as the area increasingly becomes a destination for families.[123]

Still, on Tchoupitoulas Avenue, F&M Patio Bar keeps the neighborhood a college student hangout. Nearby Hansen's sno-balls and Domilise's po-boys haven't changed for nearly eighty years—thank goodness.

Festivals and Events

Events at Whole Foods Arabella frequently change, although yoga and cooking classes are always on its calendar.

FRERET

A Note on Identity

The Freret neighborhood's main artery is Freret Street. It is named for William Freret, who served as mayor of the city from 1840 to 1842 and again from 1843 to 1844.[124]

At the Heart of It

Once in the back of various plantations, today's Freret neighborhood developed between 1834 and 1850. During this time, William Freret served as the city's mayor, although Freret Street was not named for him until after he died in 1864.[125] Still made of cobblestone in the early twentieth century, Freret Street boomed in the 1920s, when it got its own streetcar. Jewish and Italian merchants opened businesses here and often lived above or near their stores. By the late 1930s, about eighty businesses called Freret Street home.[126] It was one of the city's most bustling commercial corridors.

In 1952, Freret's local elementary school changed from an all-white to an all-black school, initiating the neighborhood's white flight to the suburbs.[127] Freret's decline was slow but steady. In the 1960s and '70s, it was still a diverse community, and many who lived in the neighborhood worked here. As the century wore on, this vibrant neighborhood grew poorer and earned a reputation for violent crime. By 1994, only thirty-four businesses remained on Freret Street.[128]

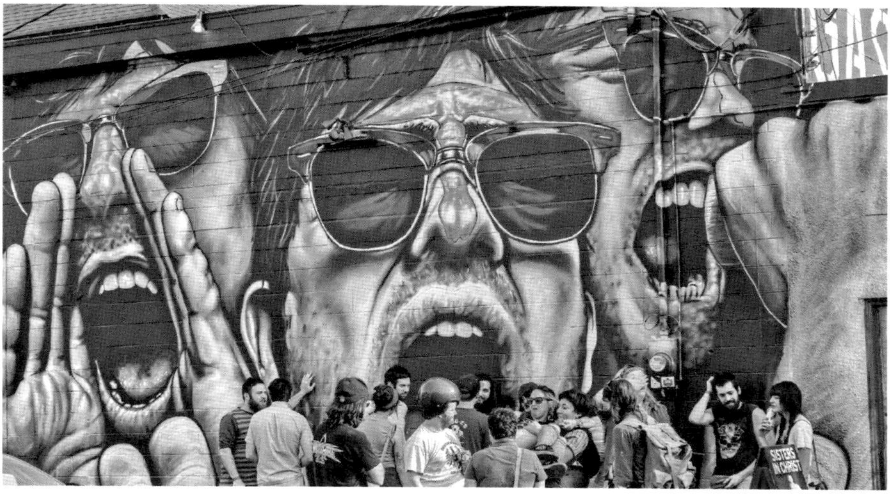

Freret Street's Gasa Gasa music venue has a façade-sprawling mural by French graffiti artist MTO. *Photo by Bruce Cervini.*

Interest in Freret's revival began in 2001, when the city partnered with the National Trust for Historic Preservation's Main Street Program and pledged $300,000 to the Freret Street corridor.[129] Despite this effort, progress was slow. After Hurricane Katrina, which flooded the neighborhood with nearly seven feet of water at its northern border, redevelopment gained some traction.[130] In 2008, Freret Street became a recognized cultural district, which allows for tax-free sales of original artwork produced here and places a premium on historic restoration.[131]

Today, Freret Street again boasts more than sixty-five local businesses.[132] Whether seeking live music, craft cocktails or casual cuisine turned up a notch, the neighborhood has it all. Among the organizations that have led Freret into its new era is the Freret Business and Property Owners Association. Volunteer members of this group promote Freret Street to shoppers, diners and business owners who may have interest in relocating here.

Health and wellness services in Freret include a gym, a yoga studio and a massage therapy and acupuncture specialist. Oschner Baptist Medical Center (established in 1926) features a state-of-the-art Women's Pavilion, which aims to connect women to expert care through all life stages.

Festivals and Events

Every year, Freret Street Festival helps kick off the festival season with live music, food, artwork and activities for all ages.

The FRERET MARKET, complete with "food, art and flea," is held the first Saturday of every month, from September through June.

BROADMOOR

A Note on Identity

The city, Historic District Landmarks Commission and Broadmoor Improvement Association have different boundaries for Broadmoor. The neighborhood runs roughly from Nashville Avenue to Toledano Street and from South Jefferson Davis Parkway to South Claiborne Avenue.

At the Heart of It

When Bienville founded New Orleans in 1718, today's Broadmoor was swampland and even had a twelve-acre lake.[133] In 1834, city planner Charles Zimpel labeled the area "vacant land" on his *Topographical Map of New Orleans*.[134] The neighborhood did not begin to develop until a new drainage system was implemented here around the turn of the twentieth century. ANDREW H. WILSON SCHOOL was built in 1922, and soon, Spanish- and Mission Revival–style homes, which were popular during that time, sprang up around it.[135]

Broadmoor grew until the mid-1900s, when white flight and discriminatory bank practices hurt neighborhoods citywide. In 1970, residents incorporated the Broadmoor Improvement Association (BIA) to help the neighborhood cope with population decline.[136] Almost forty years later, when Hurricane Katrina hit, this group was pivotal to the neighborhood's survival. Today, Broadmoor may hold New Orleans' title for the best neighborhood comeback.

During the storm, 100 percent of homes in Broadmoor were flooded with between six and ten feet of water.[137] When the city released its rebuilding plan after Katrina, a big green dot covered the neighborhood, meaning it would

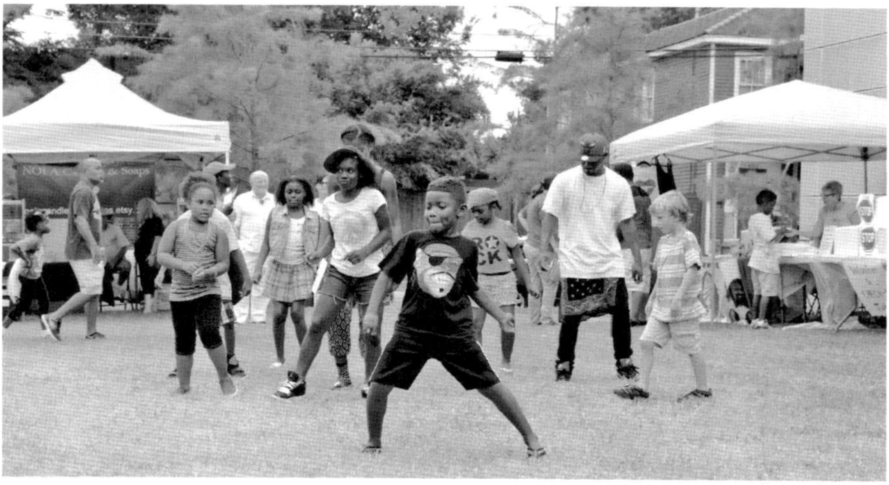

Neighbors line-dance at the Broadmoor Art Market. *Photo by author.*

potentially be leveled and made into a park.[138] Three days after news of the dot broke, residents huddled under a generator-lit tent at the "Broadmoor Lives!" rally. After much collaboration, the community delivered a three-hundred-page document to city council that detailed a holistic approach to rebuilding.[139]

Today, the Broadmoor Education Corridor is evidence of the community's success. Its ANDREW H. WILSON CHARTER SCHOOL hosts countless events and programs, including an after-school basketball club for at-risk youth. BROADMOOR COMMUNITY CARE is the social services arm of the corridor and offers counseling, parenting workshops and clinical support to Wilson students. In 2015, the corridor welcomed the BROADMOOR ARTS AND WELLNESS CENTER, which features studio space for practicing artists, as well as classes for the aspiring. Perhaps the neighborhood's most prized resource of all, however, is its state-of-the-art ROSA F. KELLER LIBRARY AND COMMUNITY CENTER. The menu at the center's Green Dot Café is a poignant and delicious representation of the power of people working together.

Festivals and Events

The Rosa F. Keller Library and Community Center hosts groups and classes—from zumba to a citizenship class—almost every evening. Every third Tuesday of the month neighbors come together at its "Eatmoor in Broadmoor" event, complete with food trucks and music.

AUDUBON

A Note on Identity

There are at least seven unique neighborhood associations that claim boundaries within the city's Audubon. Many refer to this broad area as "Audubon-University."

At the Heart of It

A prestigious place to call home today, Audubon's early history was full of neglect and cronyism. From the 1830s to the 1850s, as downriver plantations were being subdivided into faubourgs, Pierre Foucher's tract—today's Audubon neighborhood—remained a long, solid lot. Fleeing for France before the Civil War, Foucher's son abandoned the family land, and the city took the liberty of using it.[140] Throughout the war, today's Audubon Park played host to both a Confederate camp and a Union hospital. When the war was over, it became the activation site for the Ninth Calvary Buffalo Soldiers, whose members were among the country's first black troops in the peacetime regular army.[141]

In 1871, Foucher's widow sold the lot to swindling developers. They lobbied the state to create a park here and then sold the land to the city at an inflated rate.[142] Upper City Park was established in 1879, but it remained a cow pasture until it was chosen to host the World's Industrial and Cotton Centennial Exposition in 1884–85.[143] A few years later, it was renamed to honor artist and naturalist John James Audubon.[144]

Around the turn of the century, both Tulane University and the Jesuit-run Loyola College (now Loyola University) opened their doors across St. Charles Avenue from the park. For more than one hundred years, Tulane and Loyola have attracted thousands of students to New Orleans from across the United States. Their leadership, and the leadership at the park and its Audubon Zoo, is at the heart of the neighborhood today. Research and programs at these institutions often aim to have a positive impact on the Greater New Orleans community.

While Hurricane Katrina spared the Audubon Park and Zoo major damage, it flooded South Claiborne Avenue with more than eight feet of water and caused Tulane and Loyola to close during the fall 2005 semester.[145] The storm created incredible challenges for Tulane and Loyola but also gave their administrations a reinvigorated and powerful sense of purpose—New Orleans needed their scholarship and guidance more than ever before. At Tulane, former president Scott Cowen created the Center for Public Service as part of the university's renewal plan and made service learning a requirement for all students to graduate. Programs like Tulane City Center and URBANbuild followed, which have since resurrected local landmarks and rebuilt homes in New Orleans' most underserved neighborhoods.

Festivals and Events

Each year, twelve thousand students and community members come together for Tulane University's Crawfest, featuring more than eighteen thousand pounds of crawfish, live music and local art vendors.

The Audubon Zoo celebrates African American culture with Soul Fest each March and hosts the Asian Pacific American Society Heritage Festival every April. Throughout the year, it hosts several other events, including Zoo Camp and the ZOOvie outdoor movie series.

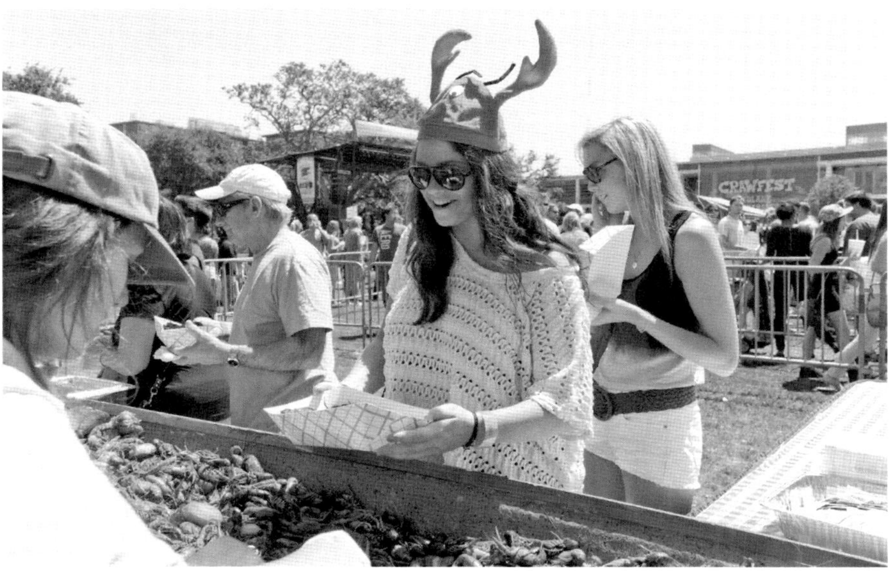

Tulane treats students and locals alike to more than eighteen thousand pounds of crawfish at its annual Crawfest. *Photo by Sally Asher.*

MARLYVILLE-FONTAINEBLEAU

A Note on Identity

The Marlyville-Fontainebleau neighborhood is named for free person of color and former landowner here Pierre Marly, as well as for its main thoroughfare, Fontainebleau Drive.[146]

At the Heart of It

In the 1700s and early 1800s, today's Marlyville-Fontainebleau made up the "woods end" of several plantations. The outlines of these colonial-era farms can be seen in the many streets that angle back from the river and converge in the neighborhood today. Recorded as "vacant land" in 1855 and "unimproved Palmetto lands" in 1894, Marlyville-Fontainebleau did not develop until the turn of the twentieth century.[147] In 1912, the New Orleans Architectural Club held a design contest for a gate to its Fontainebleau Drive.[148] More than one hundred years later, the winning Beaux Arts arch still welcomes people to the neighborhood.

In 1922, the Notre Dame Seminary Graduate School of Theology built its handsome chateau-styled campus on Carrollton Avenue.

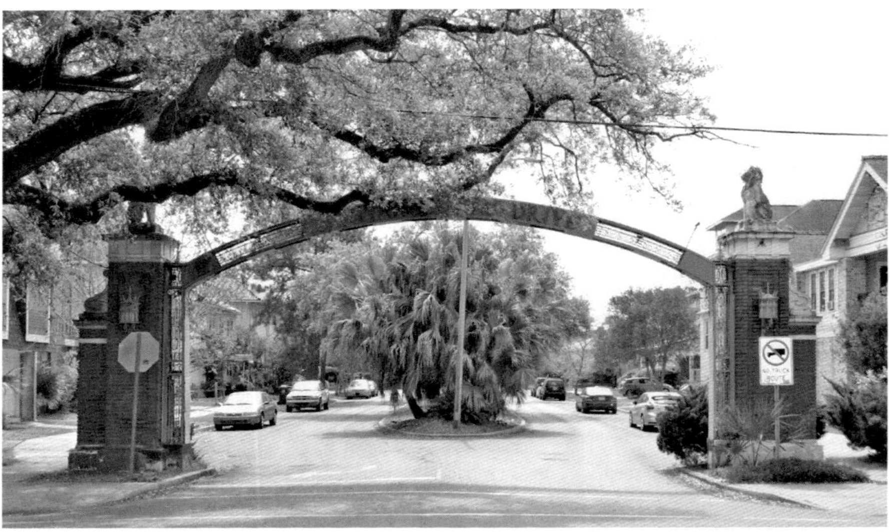

Fontainebleau Drive's Beaux Arts arch was designed in 1912. *Photo by Mitchell Mendis.*

Development picked up in the neighborhood around this time, and by 1949, it was mostly complete. As an almost entirely residential neighborhood that was established later in New Orleans' history, Marlyville-Fontainebleau is defined by its architecture, much of which reflects the Craftsman movement. Its shaded streets are lined with canopy oaks, California bungalows and Mission Revival–style homes. The convergence of streets here creates a disorderly arrangement of one-block courts and novel, narrow alleyways that line the backs of many homes.

During Hurricane Katrina, flooding on Marlyville-Fontainebleau's east side reached eight feet—almost twice as high as in the rest of the neighborhood.[149] Residents joined forces with the bordering Broadmoor neighborhood in their efforts to rebuild.

Festivals and Events

Monday is date night at the neighborhood's TED'S FROSTOP diner, where a different guest chef prepares the dinner menu each week.

BLACK PEARL

A Note on Identity

The city's Black Pearl has had many monikers throughout the last century. Today, many call it "the Black Pearl" or "Uptown Triangle."

At the Heart of It

Freight train clamor and riverboat bellows compete for attention from opposite sides of today's Black Pearl levee. There's a unique easiness here, where chickens walk the streets and rows of bungalows and single shotgun houses are reminiscent of the neighborhood's humble beginnings. Formerly plantation land, the Black Pearl first developed in the late 1800s.[150] African American residents—many of them freed slaves—worked as domestics in mansions lining St. Charles Avenue, while local Irish, Italian and German immigrants ran groceries and barrooms or worked the wharves.[151]

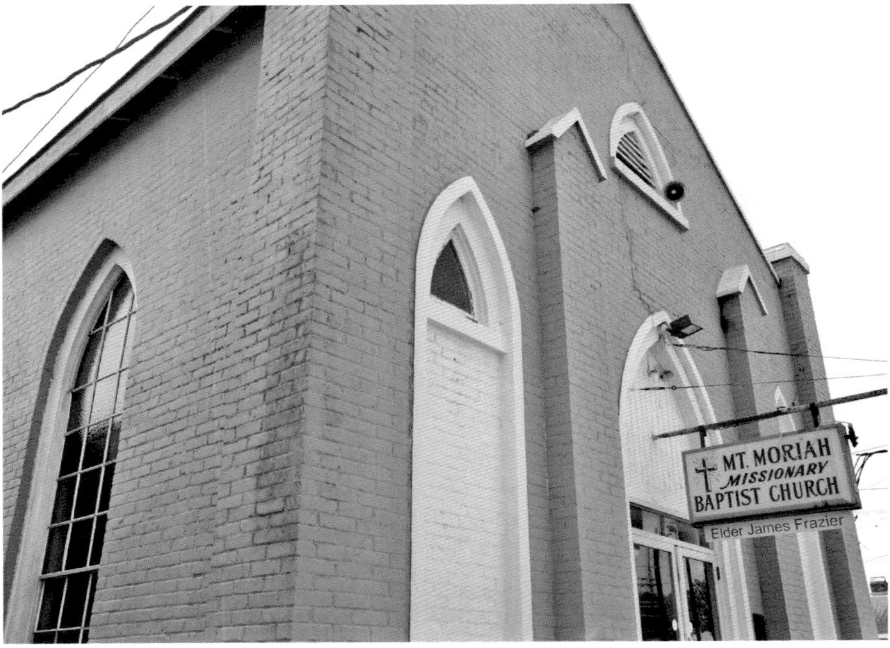

Gospel queen Mahalia Jackson grew up singing in the Black Pearl's Mount Moriah Baptist Church. *Photo by Mitchell Mendis.*

In 1911, queen of gospel Mahalia Jackson was born in the Black Pearl. She lived in a single shotgun house with twelve others and grew up singing in two local churches: Mount Moriah Baptist and Plymouth Rock Baptist. Jackson's family and neighbors called their area "Pinching Town," implying that unlike the comfortable residents of nearby "Pension Town" (in today's Carrollton), they instead were pinching pennies.[152] Others in Jim Crow New Orleans called the neighborhood "N-word Town." It was from this foundation that Jackson sprang to the frontlines of the civil rights movement.

Jackson became a close friend of Dr. Martin Luther King Jr., and in 1963, she sang at the March on Washington. Following her performance, when Dr. King began reading his prepared speech from the steps of the Lincoln Memorial, Jackson's shout changed history. The night before, King had followed advice to take out the "I had a dream" language from his address. Urging him to speak from the heart instead of reading his script, Jackson yelled, "Tell them about the dream, Martin!" And he did.[153]

In the 1970s, not long after Jackson passed away and was buried in New Orleans' Metairie Cemetery, federal and state government units hired the

Curtis and Davis architectural firm to draw a neighborhood map of the city for planning and fund allocation purposes.[154] At this time, only the outsider's moniker for the neighborhood had lived on. Finding no obligation to preserve it, and inspired by both the neighborhood's history and one of its central roads, Pearl Street, African American team member Pat Watts offered "Black Pearl" as a bold alternative.[155]

Today, the Black Pearl community is close-knit. On Saturdays, neighbors gather around a long table in the back of SINGLETON'S PO-BOYS & MINI MART to eat together. Some residents even grow their food together at the neighborhood's few community gardens. Commuters to Tulane's UNIVERSITY SQUARE offices join in this shared eating tradition on Tuesdays, when the Crescent City Farmers' Market has its weekly pop-up in the parking lot.

Festivals and Events

The Uptown Triangle Neighborhood Association organizes the Black Pearl's annual Halloween on Hillary Street, a block party meant to give children a safe area for trick-or-treating. The group also coordinates a biannual neighborhood cleanup day, as well as Pearls in the Pearl, a neighborhood-wide yard sale.

EAST CARROLLTON

A Note on Identity

The Central Carrollton Association's boundaries include much of the city's East Carrollton. No neighborhood organization bears the East Carrollton name.

At the Heart of It

East Carrollton has long been one of New Orleans' wealthier and more educated neighborhoods.[156] Once part of the Town of Carrollton, the area's first investors were also backers of the New Orleans and Carrollton Railroad, which enabled development here in the mid-1800s.[157] A blacksmith, tinsmith, bakery, doctor, druggist, dentist, gunsmith and many other professionals had businesses on Second Street (today's Maple Street) then.[158] Attracted to these

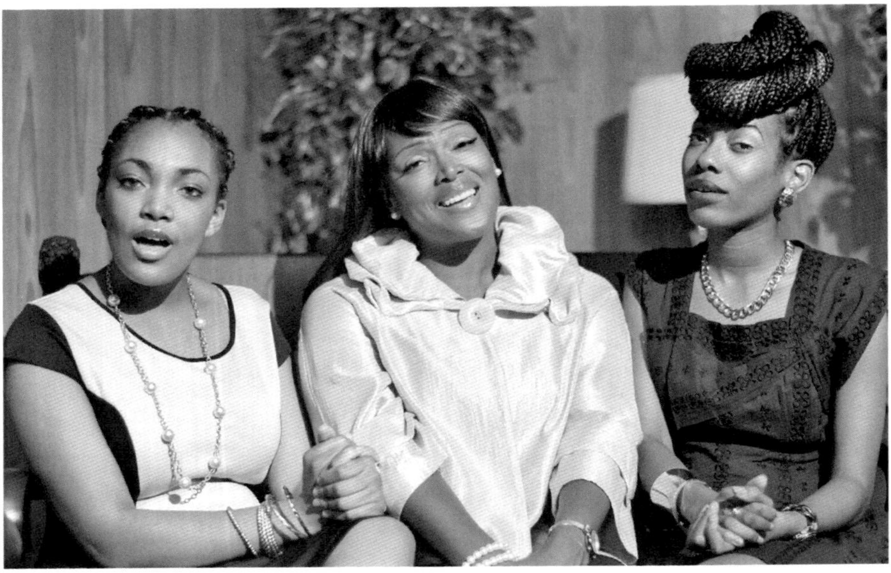

The Anthony Bean Community Theater's production of *Say Amen! Photo contributed by Anthony Bean Theater.*

amenities and the town's easy access to the city, many wealthy families built mansions here along St. Charles Avenue.[159] New Orleans annexed Carrollton in 1874, and most of the neighborhood had become developed by the turn of the twentieth century.

East Carrollton's brainy residents have historically included both professors and students of nearby Tulane and Loyola Universities. In the 1960s, John Kennedy Toole, late author of New Orleans' iconic novel, *Confederacy of Dunces*, lived here.[160] Just a block away, one of the city's oldest independently owned bookstores, Maple Street Books, opened in 1964.[161] Nearby, Plum Street Snoballs is also one of the oldest in its category. Its popularity has made it a staple at French Quarter Fest and Jazz Fest each year.

Progressive establishments continue to thrive in East Carrollton today. The Anthony Bean Community Theater and Acting School (established in 2000) is one of the Gulf South's few professional theater companies with an open enrollment for children and adults. In the theater's same building, Central St. Matthew United Church of Christ is "open and affirming," meaning it welcomes persons of every sexual orientation, gender identity, race, faith background, marital standing and family structure. Interim pastor Sharon Temple said that the church's growing congregation (about 150 people in 2014) is developing a mission of "bringing New Orleans together," often partnering with other churches and community groups to promote its vision of inclusivity and justice.

Festivals and Events

Anthony Bean Community Theater produces about seven plays annually. Its lineup is announced every November.

Every year in April, Maple Street Books acts as a pick-up location for World Book Night, when tens of thousands of people across the globe give out free paperbacks to their communities.

CARROLLTON (LEONIDAS)

A Note on Identity

The city's Leonidas is usually referred to as "Carrollton" or "West Carrollton." The area nearest the Mississippi River is often called "Riverbend," and the part of the neighborhood that borders Monticello Avenue is known as "Pension Town" and "Pigeon Town."

At the Heart of It

Across the city from New Orleans' French Quarter, today's Carrollton still feels like how it started—a town unto its own.[162] In 1845, the neighborhood made up a large part of the Town of Carrollton, where wealthy New Orleanians vacationed after making the long trip on the New Orleans and Carrollton Railroad.[163] They arrived at Dublin Street's elegant train station, which was located near a hotel, market, fire station and jail.[164]

New Orleans annexed Carrollton in 1874, and by the early 1900s, the neighborhood's infrastructure had expanded. Streetcars were built and maintained at the Carrollton Streetcar Barn, and the Carrollton Water Plant was erected to purify Mississippi River water for drinking.[165] The neighborhood also diversified: the area along its western border was nicknamed "Pension Town," likely for African American veterans who settled

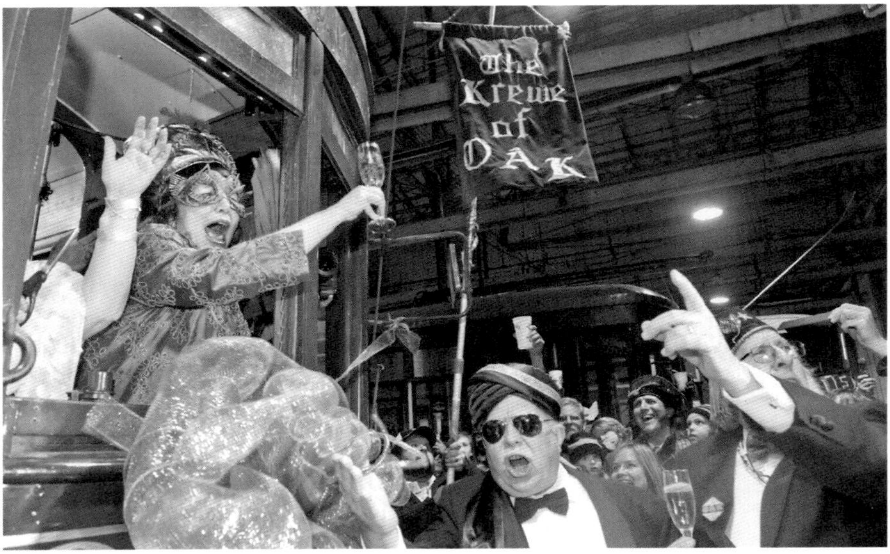

The Phunny Phorty Phellows kick off Mardi Gras each year with a streetcar ride that begins in the historic Carrollton Streetcar Barn. *Photo by Sally Asher.*

here after the Civil War and collected pensions.[166] How the neighborhood got its "Pigeon Town" name is uncertain. Some say it came from children's mispronunciations of "Pension Town," while others hold firm that it was named for the "pidgin" English spoken here by immigrants.[167]

As in many New Orleans neighborhoods, racism was prevalent in Carrollton throughout the twentieth century. Its PALMER PARK was not desegregated until 1977, after neighbors thwarted an earlier integration effort by advertising against making the park a "public disgrace" in the *Times-Picayune*.[168] Resource disparities continue to be an issue in the neighborhood today, but many passionate citizens are working to change that. Among them is Nicole Bouie, who founded the COMMUNITY COMMITMENT EDUCATION CENTER (CCEC) here after Hurricane Katrina. CCEC provides literary, computer and social skills training to locals. In 2015, it opened a coffee shop, Stella's, which supports its community programming.

Like Bouie, many of Carrollton's community leaders are independent thinkers and doers. Clamoring together to make a positive impact, some also resist being told what to do. In 2006, for example, the neighborhood's Oak Street joined several New Orleans commercial corridors in becoming a designated Main Street, supported by the National Trust for Historic Preservation. The partnership didn't last. Frustrated with "irrelevant standards and requirements," Oak Street merchants started their own group and a serious recruitment effort.[169] Today, the Oak Street Merchants, Residents and Property Owners Association is almost one hundred members strong, and the corridor is home to dozens of popular shops, restaurants and bars.

Perhaps Carrollton's boldest example of righteous independence is found in longtime resident Joseph Henry, who was shot on Mardi Gras day when he was twelve years old and has been in a wheelchair ever since. A natural leader who is unwilling to identify with his limitations, Henry has gone on to become team captain and point guard of the Rollin' Pelicans basketball team for many years. He also founded the Pigeon Town Steppers Social Aid and Pleasure Club in 1994.[170]

Festivals and Events

The Oak Street Po-Boy Festival in November features every type of po-boy a New Orleanian can dream of. The corridor's Krewe of Oak leads the Mid-Summer Mardi Gras parade and bar crawl every August.

Donned in pastel suits and alligator shoes, the Pigeon Town Steppers lead the neighborhood in a second-line celebration every Easter Sunday.

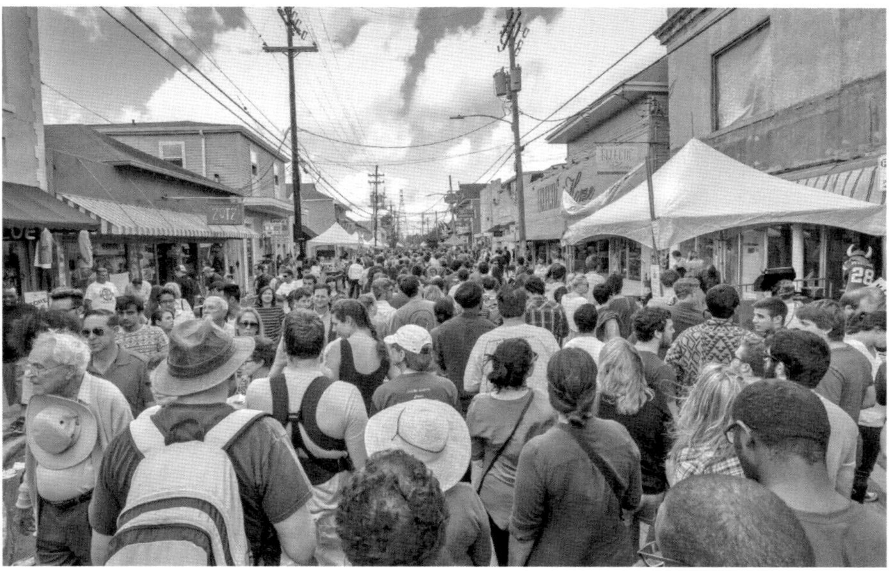

Nearly sixty thousand people visited Oak Street for its 2015 Po-Boy Fest. *Photo by Bruce Cervini.*

HOLLYGROVE-DIXON

A Note on Identity

In 2015, the *Times-Picayune* ran a story in its neighborhood series titled, "Is that Neighborhood Hollygrove? Or Dixon? Or Hollygrove-Dixon?" The article had no conclusive answer for what to call the area between Highway I-10, South Claiborne Avenue, South Carrollton Avenue and the Monticello Canal.

After Hurricane Katrina, residents in the southeast corner of Hollygrove, who owned some of the neighborhood's higher-valued real estate, started the Northwest Carrollton Neighborhood Association. As community activist Jarvain Bingmon put it, "In New Orleans, if you have the resources, you can create your own neighborhood."

At the Heart of It

Long a part of New Orleans' backswamp, today's Hollygrove-Dixon did not begin developing until 1920, when nearby draining systems were improved.[171] In just forty years, it became a robust residential working-class community—and one of musical genius.[172] The high note–hittin' R&B legend Johnny Adams lived in Hollygrove, as did Theryl DeClouet, who grew up jamming with the Neville Brothers and later played with New Orleans' famed Galactic band. Lil Wayne once called Hollygrove home, as well.

Despite its cultural buoyancy, Hollygrove-Dixon is below sea level, and flooding has plagued its entire existence. Hurricane Katrina took a violent toll on the neighborhood, and in the storm's aftermath, AARP hosted a six-month Livable Communities Workshop here. Residents learned how to organize, assigned "block captains" and formed committees on blight and safety.[173]

Today, a self-advocating spirit endures among those who participated in the workshop. The Hollygrove Seniors and the Hollygrove Neighbors Associations have successfully fought to rebuild the neighborhood's senior center, reopen the local elementary school and close a corner store that they believed was perpetuating crime.[174] All the while, the community's relationship with AARP grew so strong that the association moved its city headquarters to the neighborhood.

"People who come into Hollygrove all say the same thing: They've never seen a neighborhood work together like the people do here," said Bingmon, executive director of Hollygrove's Trinity Christian Community Center (TCC). "And I attribute that to our seniors. If you want to get something done in this neighborhood, the seniors will be your voice."

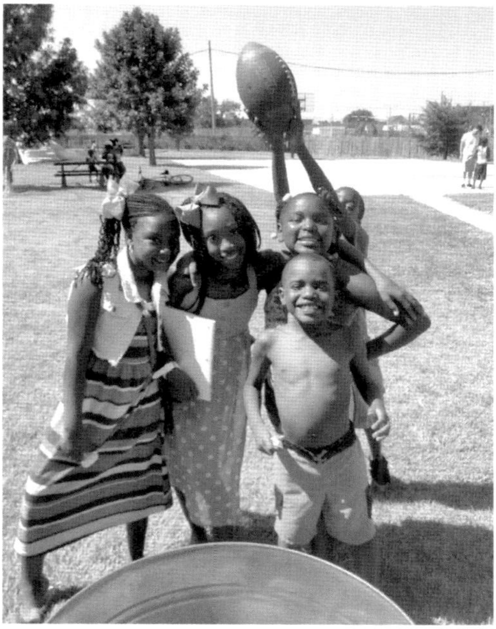

Hollygrove's Trinity Christian Community Center hosts a quarterly outreach barbecue. *Photo by Sandy Brown.*

In addition to the seniors, community groups and centers are at the heart of Hollygrove-Dixon. TCC has a library, computer lab, basketball court, playground and many multipurpose rooms that are available to local groups seeking space. The center hosts after-school programs, a summer camp and a U.S. Department of Health caseworker, who mentors local pregnant women and mothers on giving their babies a healthy start.[175]

Bingmon also oversees the Hollygrove Market and Farm, which he calls the "welcome center" of the neighborhood. "Years ago, Hollygrove was a food desert, and the market started with twenty-five-dollar boxes of produce every Saturday to help meet the community's needs," he recalled. Today, the market is open seven days a week and has a storefront full of local produce, an on-site urban farm and a community garden space. The twenty-five-dollar boxes remain an important part of its work.

Festivals and Events

All are welcome to the quarterly TCC outreach barbecue and the Hollygrove Seniors Monthly Luncheon.

The Hollygrove Market and Farm hosts an annual Party in the Garden fundraiser with catering by top New Orleans restaurants, live music and cocktails made with locally distilled spirits and seasonal fruits and herbs.

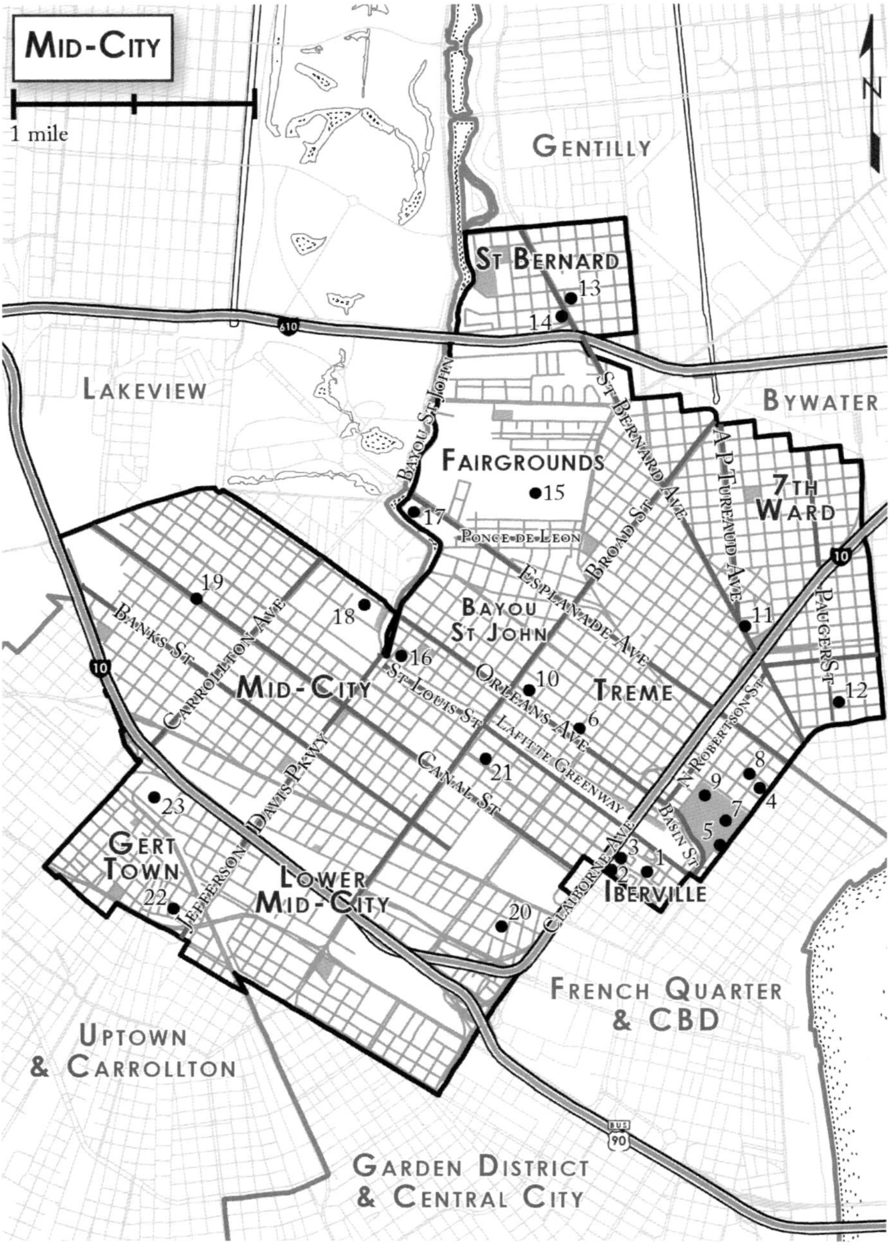

Mid-City
1 mile
Gentilly
St Bernard
13
14
610
Lakeview
Bywater
St Bernard Ave
Bayou St John
AP Tureaud Ave
Fairgrounds
15
7th Ward
17
Ponce de Leon
Broad St
10
Esplanade Ave
19
18
Bayou St John
11
Banks St
Carrollton Ave
16
Paugerst
10
Mid-City
St Louis St
Orleans Ave
10
Treme
12
6
Lafitte Greenway
N Robertson St
21
Canal St
Jefferson Davis Pkwy
8
9
4
23
7
Basin St
5
Gert Town
3
1
Claiborne Ave
2
Lower Mid-City
Iberville
22
20
French Quarter & CBD
Uptown & Carrollton
Bus 90
Garden District & Central City

Chapter 4

Mid-City

MAP KEY

IBERVILLE

1. Iberville Development
2. St. Louis Cemetery No. 1
3. St. Louis Cemetery No. 2

TREME

4. Backstreet Cultural Museum
5. Congo Square
6. Dooky Chase's Restaurant
7. Louis Armstrong Park
8. St. Augustine Church
9. Treme Community Center
10. Zulu Social Aid and Pleasure Club

SEVENTH WARD

11. Autocrat Social and Pleasure Club
12. The Porch 7th Ward Cultural Organization

ST. BERNARD

13. Columbia Parc
14. Fairview Baptist Church

BAYOU ST. JOHN

15. Fair Grounds Race Course
16. Parkway Bakery
17. Pitot House

MID-CITY

18. American Can Company Apartments
19. St. Patrick Cemetery No. 1

LOWER MID-CITY

20. LSU Medical Complex
21. Refresh Project

GERT TOWN

22. Blue Plate Artist Lofts
23. Xavier University of Louisiana

IBERVILLE

A Note on Identity

Iberville was once home to New Orleans' famed vice district, Storyville. In 1941, the Iberville public housing development replaced Storyville. The development was partially torn down in 2013.

At the Heart of It

At the heart of Iberville is its relationship with death, its history of debauchery and its recent redevelopment. By the early 1800s, the area had become home to St. Louis Cemeteries Nos. 1 and 2, both designed in traditional Spanish style with aboveground tombs. These cemeteries' location directly behind the French Quarter made them easily accessible while keeping them comfortably outside of the city center.[176] From voodoo queen Marie Laveau to the city's first African American mayor, Ernest "Dutch" Morial, many New Orleans notables have made Iberville their final resting place.[177]

Life did not flourish in this "back of town" neighborhood until the late 1800s, when reform politicians corralled the city's prostitutes and gamblers into about nineteen blocks here. New Orleans' famed Storyville opened for business in 1898 and soon became one of the county's most notorious red-light districts. Elaborate brothels lined its Basin Street side, while low-end prostitutes rented out "cribs" at its back end.[178] One of the few and best-paying gigs for African American musicians at the time, Storyville hosted collaborations between uptown's working-class blacks and downtown's Creoles of color, who were often classically trained.[179] Louis Armstrong, Jelly Roll Morton, Joe "King" Oliver and other legends spent many late nights in Storyville, which is sometimes called the birthplace of jazz.

By memorializing Storyville as such, however, historian Emily Epstein Landau argued that it downplays the district's role in perpetuating Jim Crow inequality in New Orleans.[180] While the rest of the city enforced a strict racial caste system, Storyville famously marketed the bodies of black women—many of them "octoroons," or one-eighth black—to white men. On its surface, this seemed to defy the city's reform movement in favor of the former, looser ways of its downriver faubourgs. In actuality, though, it carried on the antebellum tradition that white men had the implicit right to

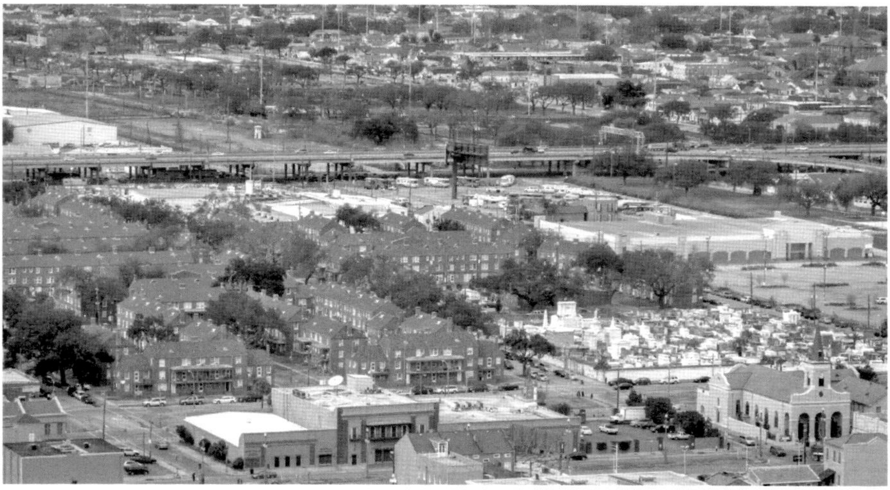

A bird's-eye view of St. Louis Cemeteries Nos. 1 and 2 and the Iberville housing project—the city's last to be torn down after Hurricane Katrina. *Photo by Bruce Cervini.*

have sex with black women. "All of the best bordellos, including those which featured women of color, barred black men," Landau wrote.[181]

At the advent of World War II, the U.S. military forced New Orleans to shut down Storyville. Even local politicians and police, who had benefited from its graft and kickbacks, mourned the vice district's closing in 1917. Then New Orleans mayor Martin Behrman is famously quoted as saying, "You can make prostitution illegal in Louisiana, but you can't make it unpopular."[182] About twenty-five years later, Iberville took its most recent identity when the all-white Iberville public housing development was erected here and military families moved in.[183]

When the projects were racially integrated in the 1960s, low-income whites living in Iberville had options in the suburbs, while their African American counterparts did not. Like all of New Orleans' projects, Iberville became home to thousands of the city's poorest African Americans over the next several decades. In 2000, 76.1 percent of households here made less than $10,000 per year.[184]

After Hurricane Katrina, the Iberville development was the last of the city's projects to be torn down. In 2011, a $30.5 million federal grant kicked off a now $660 million plan to revitalize Iberville and the neighboring Treme.[185] The development will be reinvented as a mixed-income community, with as many units as its predecessor but less public housing availability. As Iberville's "re-do" began to move forward in 2012, however, a peculiar situation held up its progress: archaeologists working on its grounds found caskets and human bones buried at least one hundred years ago underneath some of the buildings.[186] The housing project, it was discovered, sits on what is likely an extension of St. Louis Cemetery No. 1.

The Lens reported that many Iberville residents were not surprised about the bones. Living next to the cemeteries, they had grown up with ghost stories. "As the local legend goes, the apple of his eye left her purse in his car the night he took her to his school prom," Katy Reckdhal wrote. "When he brought it to her house to return it, the girl's mother said that she'd died years earlier and had been buried in the very gown he described her wearing to the prom."[187] The future of Iberville is yet to be seen, but its stories will live on, to be sure.

Festivals and Events

All Saints' Day brings many to this neighborhood's cemeteries, where they clean and repair vaults and memorialize New Orleans' departed with fresh flowers and offerings.

TREME (TREME/LAFITTE)

A Note on Identity

While the Historic District Landmarks Commission and city have different boundaries for the Treme neighborhood, many residents say that its boundaries are St. Bernard Avenue, St. Louis Street, Broad Street and North Rampart Street. The Faubourg Lafitte development borders the neighborhood's upriver end. A mixed-income community, the development replaced the Lafitte public housing project.

At the Heart of It

Recognized nationwide as the oldest African American neighborhood in the country, Treme's identity began taking shape between 1730 and 1760 in today's CONGO SQUARE. Known then as Place de Negroes, the square hosted a Sunday marketplace for slaves, where they sold crops and practiced

African drumming, singing and dancing. The opportunity for slaves to pass on African customs was unique to French Louisiana, and it influenced the evolution of New Orleans' music, including the invention of jazz.[188] Slave owners here abided by the Code Noir, which exempted slaves from forced labor on Sundays and religious holidays.[189]

The slave market at Congo Square continued through the 1840s.[190] By that time, surrounding plantation land had been subdivided into Faubourg Treme and was populated by immigrants, white Creoles and Creoles of color. Like in the French Quarter and all of New Orleans' downriver faubourgs, there was a three-tiered racial structure here. Free people of color, who were often of mixed Spanish or French descent, held a marginal status between whites and slaves.[191]

Treme's Creoles of color advocated for black rights even before Jim Crow stripped them of their distinction. In the months before the dedication of St. Augustine Church in 1842, for example, local Creoles of color bought and reserved all of the church's side-aisle pews for slaves.[192] By the late 1800s, Homer Plessy—the plaintiff in *Plessy v. Ferguson*—worshipped at St. Augustine.[193] Throughout the Jim Crow era, which commenced with the "separate but equal" ruling in Plessy's case, Treme was home to many crusaders who fought against segregation. Nevertheless, the Lafitte public housing project—one of New Orleans' "Big Four," which were built for African American residents only—was erected here in 1941.

Throughout the mid-twentieth century, civil rights champions organized in Treme. Thurgood Marshall and other national leaders met with local luminaries like Oretha Castle Haley and A.P. Tureaud in the upstairs meeting room of Dooky Chase's Restaurant (established in 1941).[194] Despite civil rights gains, the city made two "developments" here in the late 1960s that devastated the community. Its erection of the elevated I-10 highway destroyed the oak-lined North Claiborne Avenue, one of the most successful African American commercial corridors in the country.[195] Nearby, the demolition of twelve neighborhood blocks displaced almost two hundred residents and leveled two historic jazz venues for the purpose of creating a cultural center that was never completed.[196] Today, this area is home to Louis Armstrong Park.

Despite these hardships and the blight they created, Treme residents continued to build on the neighborhood's cultural traditions. In 1969, residents formed the Treme Community Improvement Association and lobbied the city to build the Treme Community Center.[197] In 1978, the Zulu Social Aid and Pleasure Club opened its headquarters on Broad Street, helping to bring Mardi Gras back to the neighborhood (it was formerly celebrated on North Claiborne Avenue).[198] Cultural growth continued leading up to

Hurricane Katrina. The famed Treme Brass Band formed in 1990, and by the end of the decade, Sylvester Francis had founded Treme's BACKSTREET CULTURAL MUSEUM, dedicated to New Orleans' black Indians, social aid and pleasure clubs, baby dolls and skull and bones gangs.[199]

When Hurricane Katrina hit, flooding in Treme ranged from two to six feet of water. Preexisting poverty made rebuilding difficult for many residents, and in 2010, the city demolished the Lafitte development here. Today, a mixed-income group of pastel-colored town homes replaces the former "bricks," and the city has launched a $660 million revitalization plan for Treme and the bordering Iberville neighborhood. Transplants and locals alike now pass through the historic district on the new LAFITTE GREENWAY bike path. They also come together at Treme's many festivals that celebrate the neighborhood's unique culture.

Festivals and Events

Each year, Treme hosts the Congo Square New Worlds Rhythms Festival, which celebrates the live music and dancing traditions of Africa, the Caribbean

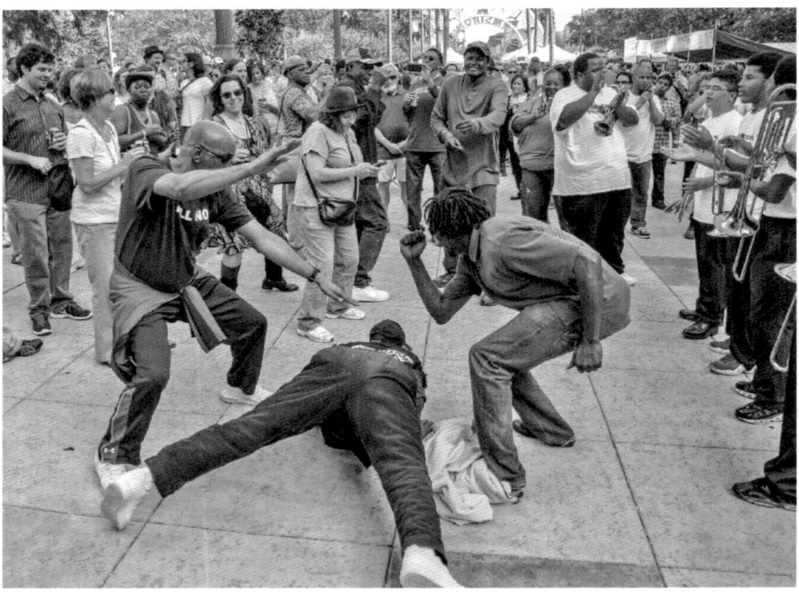

Neighbors break it down at the Treme Creole Gumbo Festival in Louis Armstrong Park. *Photo by Bruce Cervini.*

and the American Gulf South. Some of these acts return for Thursdays at the Park, a free concert held weekly at Louis Armstrong Park during the summer. Also in the park is the annual Treme Creole Gumbo Festival, which features a smorgasbord of spins on New Orleans' signature dish.

Second-lines and Mardi Gras Indian parades are regular occurrences in Treme. On Mardi Gras day, the neighborhood welcomes the Zulu Parade down Orleans Avenue.

SEVENTH WARD

A Note on Identity

The Seventh Ward neighborhood is just one neighborhood in New Orleans' actual Seventh Ward, which stretches from the Mississippi River to Lake Pontchartrain. In 1994, the New Marigny Historic District was established here. Real estate agencies now capitalize on associating the area with the gentrified Marigny neighborhood across St. Claude Avenue.

At the Heart of It

Like many downriver faubourgs, when the Seventh Ward was first subdivided in the early 1800s, it became home to a diverse group of immigrants, white Creoles and Creoles of color.[200] Over the next century, it was preserved as New Orleans' quintessential Creole neighborhood, and its Creoles of color came to define it. Before the Civil War, this group of people—often of mixed Spanish or French descent—held a marginal status between whites and slaves.[201] Many developed strengths in business, building trades and music. In the Seventh Ward, Creoles of color owned insurance companies, laundries, barbershops and funeral homes as early as the mid-1800s.[202]

Many Creoles of color claimed their mixed heritage proudly. In the 1880s, the Seventh Ward's own Becate Batiste—who was himself African American, French and Choctaw—created the Creole Wild West Indian gang, largely regarded as the first Mardi Gras Indian gang in New Orleans.[203] In doing so, Batiste celebrated diversity and the relationship between the city's African Americans and Native Americans. During slavery, Native Americans sheltered runaway slaves in large settlements called maroon camps throughout French

Louisiana. In postbellum times, white oppression and segregation continued to create shared hardships between these groups.[204]

For Creoles of color, segregation's "one drop" rule changed everything. The light-skinned community in the Seventh Ward grappled to maintain their dignity as Jim Crow stripped their status from them. "There was an expectation that you had to dress better, you had to act better, you had to be better, you had to educate yourself more to function in the segregated environment of America, not just Louisiana," A.P. Tureaud Jr. told WWNO. "A lot of the Creole families did not want their daughters to marry black men, so they didn't encourage them to visit in their homes.... I used to say, 'How can Creoles discriminate against black people when we're all black? You're doing the same thing to blacks that whites are doing to us.'"[205]

Tureaud Jr. grew up on Pauger Street as the son of the famous attorney and activist A.P. Tureaud Sr., who is honored with a main avenue and a statue in the Seventh Ward.[206] Together, their family fought righteously to knock down one civil rights barrier at a time. From 1937 to 1947, Tureaud Sr. was the only black lawyer in the entire state.[207] Throughout his long career, he won cases for black teachers demanding equal pay to white counterparts and for desegregating parks, buses and, eventually, New Orleans' public schools.[208] In the 1950s, Tureaud won three suits against Louisiana State University, forcing the institution to admit African American students.[209] His son, Tureaud Jr., became the first to attend in 1953.

Despite these gains, in the 1960s the city destroyed the Seventh Ward's oak-lined North Claiborne Avenue—then one of the most prosperous African American commercial corridors in the country—to make way for the I-10 overpass here. When whites drove to new homes in new suburbs over the new highway, the old Creole neighborhood, like many in New Orleans, suffered. Yet even in the face of harsh realities, culture in the Seventh Ward thrived. The neighborhood's Allison "Tootie" Montana—the great-nephew of Becate Batiste—became the star of Black Carnival as big chief of the Yellow Pocahontas gang. An artist and expert sewer, he created a new standard for the Indians' elaborate suits of beads and feathers.[210]

Montana evolved into a cultural leader and advocate for Mardi Gras Indians citywide, although he stayed rooted in his Seventh Ward home through the 2000s. By then, 38 percent of the neighborhood's population lived below the poverty line, and the Indians had faced repeated instances of police brutality. Just one month before Hurricane Katrina hit in 2005, Montana died at the microphone while addressing city council about the long tradition of police mistreatment of the Indians.[211]

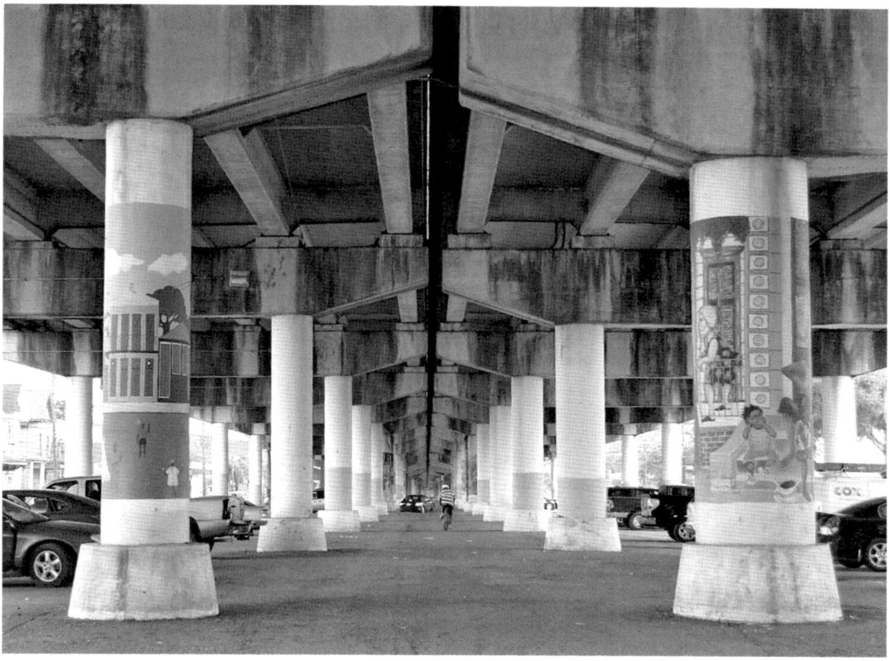

The Claiborne Avenue I-10 overpass looms above what used to be one of the most successful African American commercial corridors in the United States. *Photo by author.*

While still mourning this local leader's death, the Seventh Ward community was pummeled with between two and six feet of flooding during the storm.[212] Preexisting poverty made it difficult for many to recover, but residents worked together to keep cultural traditions alive. In the aftermath of the storm, neighbors formed The Porch 7th Ward Cultural Organization and opened a community space in a shotgun house on Pauger Street. Today, the Porch hosts a summer arts camp, a youth theater and storytelling project and bead-sewing workshops, among many other programs.[213]

Festivals and Events

The Autocrat Social and Please Club (established in 1914) hosts an annual crawfish boil each spring at its clubhouse on St. Bernard Avenue.

Second-lines are a regular occurrence in the Seventh Ward, with the Revolution Social Aid and Pleasure Club and the Original Big 7 Social Aid and Pleasure Club passing through each year.

ST. BERNARD

A Note on Identity

While the city puts St. Bernard in the Mid-City Planning District, many consider it to be in Gentilly. St. Bernard is named for the St. Bernard public housing development, which was once in the neighborhood. The mixed-income Columbia Parc development that replaced the project has rebranded the surrounding area as "the Bayou District."

At the Heart of It

In 1942, residents of the newly opened St. Bernard public housing development gathered 1,700 signatures to demand better bus lines to their neighborhood.[214] This was the beginning of a long history of community organizing in St. Bernard, where residents have notoriously expressed their grievances and joys through art, advocacy and participation in New Orleans' cultural traditions. Like the rest of the "Big Four" projects, which were built for low-income African Americans as part of the New Deal in the 1940s, St. Bernard was demolished after Hurricane Katrina. Today, 685 mixed-income town homes and apartments replace St. Bernard's almost 1,500 public housing units.[215]

A quiet neighborhood now, blaring horns once took the streets in St. Bernard. In 1970, when New Orleans' brass band tradition was considered a dying art form because of local youths' lack of interest in it, the reverend of St. Bernard's Fairview Baptist Church and local musician Danny Barker started a band for neighborhood kids. Trumpeter Leroy Jones, then just twelve years old, was one of Barker's first recruits. Jones became the leader of the Fairview Baptist Church Christian Marching Band, which practiced in his garage for the next four years.[216]

As many as thirty young musicians became part of the Fairview Baptist Band, and many of them—including clarinetist Dr. Michael White, trombonist Lucien Barbarin and Anthony "Tuba Fats" Lacen—still play.[217] Fairview Baptist inspired the city's brass band revival. The band later evolved into Leroy Jones's Hurricane Brass Band, and after Jones began pursuing a solo career, other members started the Dirty Dozen Brass Band. In turn, the Dirty Dozen inspired the formation of Rebirth Brass Band, one of the city's most popular today.[218]

At the same time that the brass band renaissance was happening in Jones's garage, local social worker and St. Bernard housing project resident

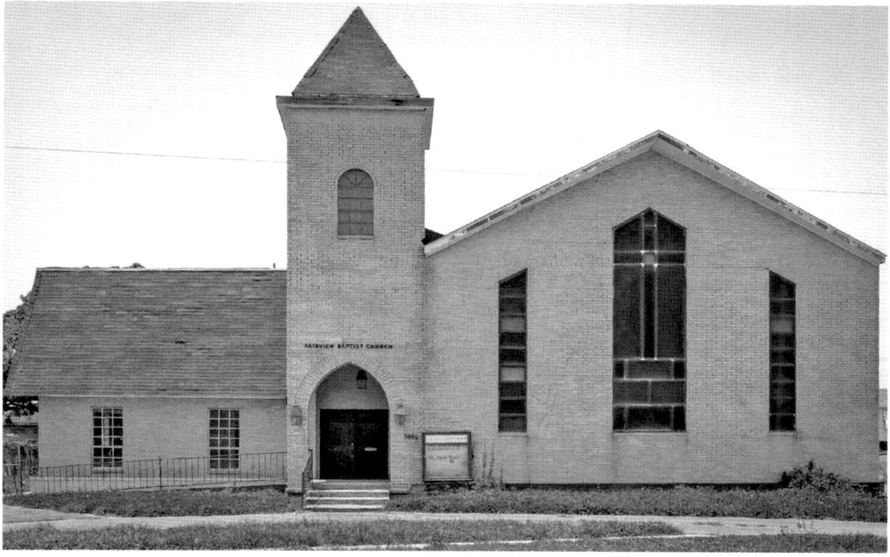

The Fairview Baptist Church, abandoned since Hurricane Katrina, is where New Orleans' brass band renaissance began. *Photo by Bruce Cervini.*

Helen Washington Lang was trumpeting the concerns of her neighbors to city council. An experienced civil rights activist, Lang became a beloved community advocate in the 1970s, pushing residents to vote, start their own businesses and pursue more education.[219] She sewed clothes and bought school supplies for children in need and even hosted a special dinner for the neighborhood's honor graduates.[220] Lang also championed the opening of the St. Bernard Community Development Center, which hosted recreational activities and meetings year-round beginning in 1980.

In the late 1990s and early 2000s, select public housing projects throughout the city began closing as part of the HOPE IV program. Despite rhetoric about "decentralizing poverty," many residents from the Desire and St. Thomas developments were relocated to St. Bernard.[221] The community became overpopulated and opportunities for economic mobility even more limited. By 2000, more than 66 percent of St. Bernard neighborhood residents lived below the poverty level.[222] When Hurricane Katrina hit, the already impoverished neighborhood took a devastating blow, as it flooded with between four and eight feet of water.[223]

Despite assessments that fixing the projects would be cheaper than leveling them after the storm, the city decided to raze public housing developments citywide and would not allow residents to return before demolition began.[224] St.

Bernard tenants staged New Orleans' first public protest addressing the issue, setting up a "survivors village" of tents in the neighborhood.[225] On April 4, 2006, the anniversary of Dr. Martin Luther King Jr.'s assassination, residents broke through police lines to get inside and gather their belongings. The media called them "terrorists" and "demagogues," and New Orleanians were encouraged to "not watch the soap opera" unfolding in the area.[226]

When the project fell in 2008, officials at HUD and HANO awarded tax credits and grants to developer Columbia Residential, a company with personal ties to then HUD secretary Alphonso Jackson. Jackson had consulted for the company and was still owed up to $500,000 when Columbia Residential was hired to redevelop St. Bernard.[227] He faced a federal investigation for alleged misconduct and resigned in April 2008.

Today, the Columbia Parc development, complete with front porches and second-story balconies, is a national model in mixed-income housing communities. It boasts an early education center, movie theater, fitness center and outdoor pool. While beautiful, this $440 million project was built at the expense of displacing thousands of public housing residents.[228] Nearby, Fairview Baptist Church has been abandoned since the storm.

Festivals and Events

Columbia Parc has a robust calendar of free activities for residents, including workforce development training, bingo and a movie night.

BAYOU ST. JOHN (BAYOU ST. JOHN AND FAIRGROUNDS)

A Note on Identity

Although the city keeps the Bayou St. John and Fairgrounds neighborhoods separate, the Faubourg St. John Neighborhood Association includes much of the Fairgrounds neighborhood in its boundaries. Likewise, many residents who live nearby the Fair Grounds Race Course call their neighborhood Bayou St. John.

At the Heart of It

In 1699, Native Americans guided French brothers Iberville and Bienville along a shortcut from Lake Pontchartrain to the Mississippi River, likely by way of Bayou St. John (the waterway) and the Esplanade Ridge (approximately along today's Esplanade Avenue).[229] This convenient path significantly reduced the time and risk it took to get from the Gulf of Mexico to the Lower Mississippi Valley.[230] Bienville was eager to test the area's suitability for settlement, and in 1708—ten years before the city was founded—a group of European colonists were granted land concessions in today's Bayou St. John neighborhood. Knowing little about the climate, their wheat crop ultimately failed, but these pioneers helped keep the city's future location on Bienville's "map."[231]

Despite this area's early beginnings, at the turn of the nineteenth century it remained mostly swamp, with scattered plantations on elevated land near the bayou. These farms were subdivided in 1809, and country homes for the city's wealthy were soon erected along the bayou's banks.[232] The incorporated city's first mayor, James Pitot, was one of the prominent New Orleanians who moved to Faubourg St. John in the early 1800s.[233] His French colonial plantation home is known as the PITOT HOUSE today and doubles as a museum and the Louisiana Landmarks Society headquarters. Farther up the bayou in 1852, the

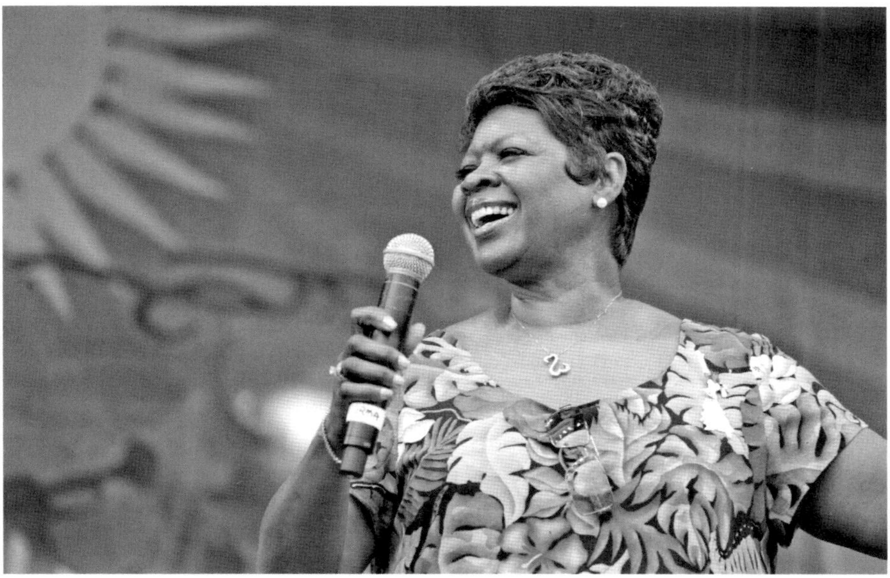

Irma Thomas at the New Orleans Jazz and Heritage Festival. *Photo by Sally Asher.*

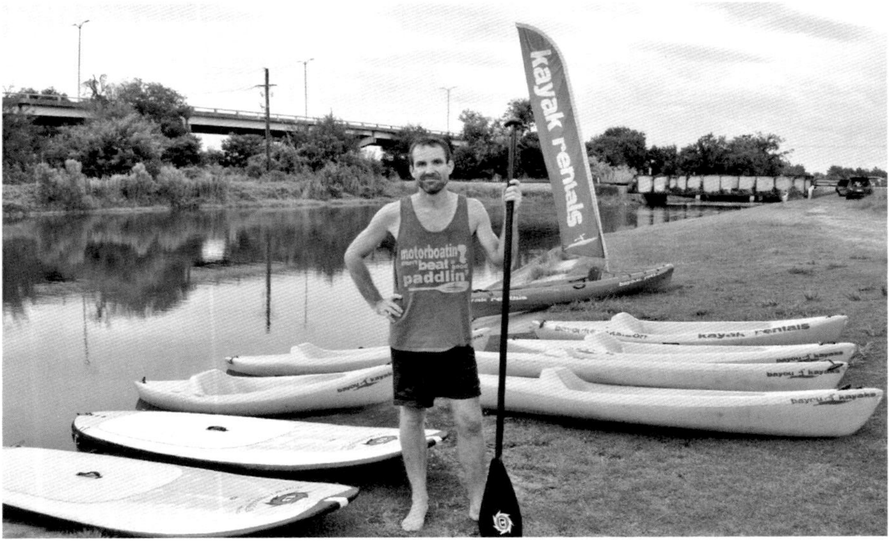

Bayou Paddlesports offers daily kayak and paddleboard rentals at Bayou St. John. *Photo by author.*

neighborhood opened a new racing course at the present-day Fair Grounds site.[234] In the 1860s, Esplanade Avenue was extended here and developed as "the grand address of the Creole upper class."[235]

Bayou St. John became more densely populated in the early 1900s, after its low-lying land was finally drained. The famed Parkway Bakery opened here in 1911 and became a go-to lunch joint for local industry workers. In 1929, the bakery added the po-boy sandwich to its menu to help feed striking streetcar workers.[236] Today, Parkway is known for having the fried oyster po-boy perfected.

Other New Orleans landmarks were built in the neighborhood in the early twentieth century, although most went unknown to tourists until the 1970s, when the New Orleans Jazz and Heritage Festival moved from Congo Square to the Fair Grounds.[237] Today, hundreds of thousands of people visit Bayou St. John every April and May. On Jazz Fest weekends, local establishments burst with out-of-towners who are excited to be exploring somewhere other than the French Quarter. Residents retreat to their porches then, where their Jazz Fest and Faubourg St. John flags fly proudly.

As for the bayou itself, after decades of neglect and unsightliness in the 1980s and '90s, Hurricane Katrina made matters worse by drowning cars and shopping carts in its murky waters.[238] Katrina flooded the neighborhood with between two and seven feet of water.[239] It was also the impetus for restoring the bayou, and many projects here have yielded impressive results. Today, Bayou St. John is busy with kayakers, runners, bikers and volleyball teams year-round.

Festivals and Events

Known as the locals' jazz fest, Bayou Boogaloo features neighborhood cuisine, vendors and three days of live music each May. The bayou also hosts an annual Fourth of July Boat Parade and the Circle of Chiefs Downtown Super Sunday—a parade of Mardi Gras Indian gangs.

Fair Grounds Race Course offers regular horse races and a variety of other events, including the New Orleans Jazz and Heritage Festival (or Jazz Fest).

MID-CITY

A Note on Identity

This neighborhood was named in 1923, when Hibernia Bank opened a branch on the corner of Canal Street and North Carrollton Avenue but did not know how to advertise its location. The bank held a company contest to determine the neighborhood's name, and the winning employee suggested "Mid-City" because it is nearly equidistant from the river and the lake.[240]

At the Heart of It

Mid-City is one of New Orleans' largest neighborhoods, both by population and landmass, giving it a robust history that varies drastically from one end to its other. During colonial times, plantation owners settled along the high-lying banks of Bayou St. John here but were mostly surrounded by swamp. In the mid-1800s, cemeteries were laid out at the neighborhood's northern corner. Among the most famous is St. Patrick No. 1, which was built for the Irish in 1841, as thousands of them died from yellow fever.[241]

Mid-City as we know it today began to take shape at the turn of the century, when its drainage system was improved. In 1901, Louis Armstrong was born on Jane Place (then Jane Alley) at the neighborhood's riverside end.[242] By the

1920s, the neighborhood was evolving, with new shotgun cottages, bungalows and Tudor- and Mission Revival–style homes. The AMERICAN CAN COMPANY and other factories incentivized working-class people to settle here.[243]

Over the next several decades, Mid-City became one of New Orleans' most diverse neighborhoods, home to whites, African Americans and, beginning in the 1960s, Latino immigrants primarily from Cuba and Honduras.[244] The neighborhood's proximity to uptown, downtown and city suburbs contributed to its diversity and integration. Still, issues that plagued most of New Orleans throughout the late twentieth century took their toll on Mid-City, too. At the height of urban renewal in 1964, for example, Armstrong's birthplace was demolished to make way for the expansion of the city's criminal justice complex.[245]

In the early 2000s, the return of streetcars to Canal Street and Carrollton Avenue helped revive the Mid-City neighborhood. Businesses were invigorated, and developer Pres Kabacoff renovated the abandoned American Can building into a mixed-use, apartment and commercial space. Just as interest in Mid-City picked up, Hurricane Katrina hit and flooded more than half of the area with five feet of water.[246] After the storm, redevelopment quickened. The neighborhood became the second-most-popular destination for transplants, next to Bywater.[247]

Despite its influx of newbies, natives still abound in Mid-City, where neighbors of all races and backgrounds gather on front porches, listen

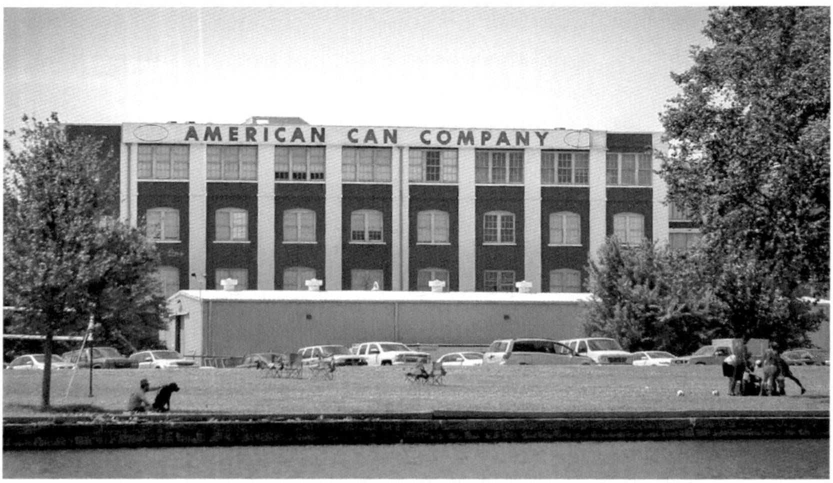

The former American Can Company, which motivated many to move to Mid-City in the early 1900s, is now a popular mixed-use building featuring shops and many apartments. *Photo by Bruce Cervini.*

to music and swat at summer flies together. At the heart of Mid-City are many smaller neighborhoods that define themselves by the lone bar on the corner, the local matriarch's house, a church, a cemetery or a thoroughfare. To help preserve the neighborhood's diversity as rents here rise, the Jane Place Neighborhood Sustainability Initiative—a community land trust—is developing housing on behalf of, and directed by, local residents. In 2015, the group committed a small Mid-City apartment building to low- and moderate-income families. The building is the first "permanently affordable" rental development owned by a community land trust in the city.[248]

Festivals and Events

Known as the locals' jazz fest, Mid-City's Bayou Boogaloo features neighborhood cuisine, vendors and three days of live music each May. Locals started the free festival in the spring after Hurricane Katrina to encourage and celebrate families rebuilding in the area.

The Mid-City Neighborhood Organization hosts an annual Mid-City Porch Crawl. Each porch on the route has a signature cocktail and dish from a local restaurant.

LOWER MID-CITY (TULANE-GRAVIER)

A Note on Identity

While trying to save part of the city's Tulane-Gravier neighborhood from demolition after Hurricane Katrina, activists made an effort to rebrand the area "Lower Mid-City."[249]

At the Heart of It

At the heart of Lower Mid-City is the spawn of New Orleans' Charity Hospital—the country's oldest medical facility before it closed after Hurricane Katrina. Located nearby in the Central Business District, Charity Hospital's roots date back to 1736, when it was established as a place of care for the city's indigent.[250] Over the next 250 years, the hospital was known citywide as a

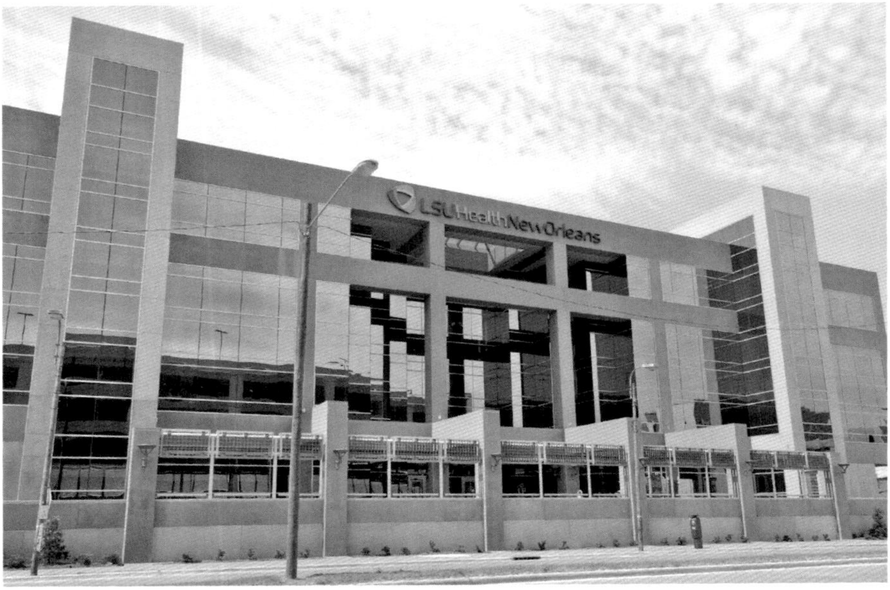

The LSU Health Sciences Center is part of Lower Mid-City's vast new medical complex. *Photo by Mitchell Mendis.*

resource where anyone could go, regardless of insurance or ability to pay. Many called it "Big Charity" or "Mama Charity," and some of New Orleans' most prominent cultural leaders are proud, self-proclaimed "Charity babies."

Across North Claiborne Avenue, however, charity has been deserted for what many see as an embodiment of disaster capitalism. In fact, the Louisiana State University's $1.1 billion MEDICAL COMPLEX, which opened in the summer of 2015, was the subject of a four-year legal battle. As the 2014 film *Big Charity* revealed, after Hurricane Katrina, LSU went through great pains to maximize its FEMA aid so that it could abandon Charity Hospital, which it owned, for a new facility. After alleged closed-door dealings, the silencing of staff members and the active ongoing sabotage of the Charity Hospital building, LSU won the case to the tune of $474.8 million.

Now defined by the medical business, Lower Mid-City has long been an industry-driven neighborhood. In the 1800s, it was bordered by competing canals, which connected to Lake Pontchartrain and facilitated the city's trade. After the turn of the century, it became known as New Orleans' beer district. While Falstaff and Jackson Breweries closed here during the beer wars of the 1970s, Dixie Brewery held on until Hurricane Katrina forced its relocation to Wisconsin.[251]

Over the last several years, developers have rushed to ready Lower Mid-City for the four thousand new jobs that the medical complex promised to create.[252] While many opposed the demolition of thirty neighborhood blocks to make way for the new hospitals and centers here, others said that the complex was just what the neighborhood—and New Orleans—needed.[253] Medical students from universities across the city and state will practice in state-of-the-art centers, and some indigent care will still be provided. Dozens of abandoned and blighted homes have been renovated in Lower Mid-City, and rents are steeply climbing. More than 86 percent of residents were renters here in 2010, and undoubtedly, many of them will not be able to afford to stay.[254]

Nevertheless, some efforts are addressing continued displacement and catering to longtime neighbors. Redmellon Restoration & Development, for example, renovates homes for people who make 60 percent of the area's median income or less.[255] On Broad Street, the REFRESH PROJECT building includes both Liberty Kitchen—a full-service café that employs at-risk youth—and Tulane's Goldring Center for Culinary Medicine Teaching Kitchen, where chefs and doctors pair up to give free community cooking classes and nutritional advice.[256] Indeed, LSU has launched Lower Mid-City's "revival," which will benefit a diverse range of New Orleanians. It also represents the state's willingness to sacrifice the care and homes of some for long-term economic development.

Festivals and Events

Tulane's Goldring Center for Culinary Medicine Teaching Kitchen hosts frequent and free community cooking classes.

GERT TOWN

A Note on Identity

Gert Town was named for German grocer Alfred Gehrke, who opened a grocery store at Colapissa Street and Carrollton Avenue in 1893 and helped develop the area with German families.[257] Resident perceptions of the neighborhood's boundaries vary. Allen Toussaint, who grew up on College Court in the city's Marlyville-Fontainebleau neighborhood, for example, proudly identifies with the Gert Town name.[258]

At the Heart of It

At the heart of Gert Town is XAVIER UNIVERSITY OF LOUISIANA, the only historically black and Catholic university in the United States. Xavier moved to the neighborhood in 1929, and its U-shaped, Gothic administration building, which is now a city landmark, was erected soon thereafter.[259] St. Katharine Drexel of Philadelphia and the Sisters of the Blessed Sacrament—a religious community dedicated to educating African Americans and Native Americans—established the school.[260]

When Gert Town welcomed Xavier, the neighborhood was home to German immigrants and African Americans. The university's arrival attracted Creoles of color here because of their Catholic heritage. It also helped spur Gert Town's light industry development. In 1941, construction began on the neighborhood's BLUE PLATE factory, which architect August Perez designed as one of New Orleans' few large-scale Art Deco–style buildings.[261] For decades, the city's favorite mayonnaise was mixed and bottled in Gert Town.

And while Xavier is at the heart of Gert Town, most agree that the leadership of Dr. Norman C. Francis has long been at the heart of Xavier. A 1952 alumnus of the university, Dr. Francis became Xavier's president in 1968. Over the course of his almost forty-year tenure, he more than doubled the university's enrollment, vastly expanded the campus and made the curriculum increasingly competitive.[262] Today, more African American students graduate with a degree in the biological and biomedical sciences, physical sciences and physics from Xavier than from any other university in the country.[263] This is just one of Xavier's many accolades and competitive rankings.

When he retired in June 2015, Dr. Francis was the longest sitting university president in the United States. He saw Xavier through the civil rights movement, Hurricane Katrina and everything in between. Hurricane Katrina flooded Gert Town with between two and six feet of water and had a severe impact on the neighborhood, where almost half of residents lived below the poverty line in 2000.[264] Dr. Francis's leadership was a beacon of hope for the broader community. He steered Xavier through budget hardships, and in 2014, the university reached three-fourths of its pre-Katrina enrollment numbers.[265]

In 2006, President George W. Bush granted Dr. Francis the nation's highest civil honor—the Presidential Medal of Freedom—for his lifetime service to civic causes. Of all his experiences, Dr. Francis told the *Times-Picayune* that the thing he'll miss the most after retirement is "shaking all those hands at the end of the year."[266] Among the almost twenty thousand

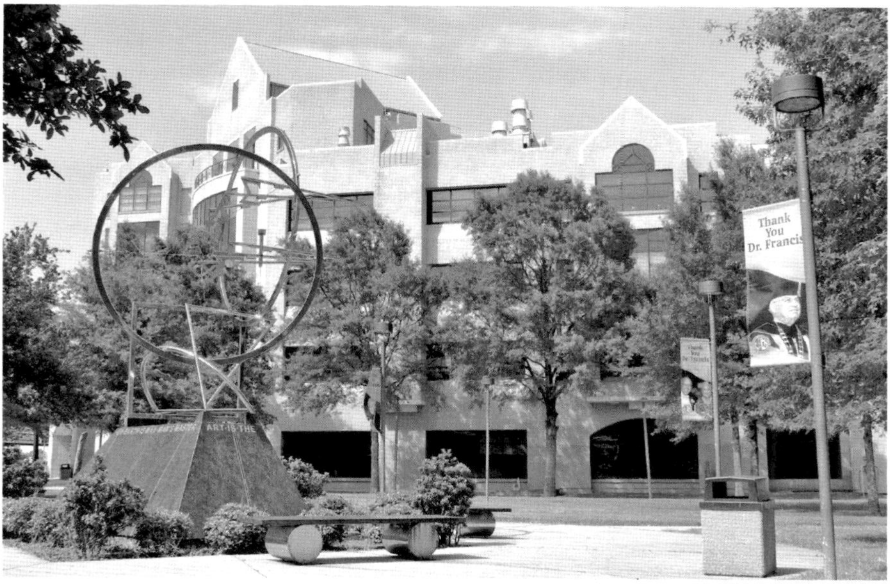

Xavier University thanks outgoing president Dr. Norman C. Francis in 2015. When Francis retired, he was the longest-serving university president in the country. *Photo by Mitchell Mendis.*

graduates he's given a diploma to in Gert Town is Alexis Herman, the first African American U.S. secretary of labor, and Dr. Regina Benjamin, whom President Barrack Obama appointed as U.S. surgeon general in 2009.[267]

As Dr. Francis walks away, he says that he is "totally confident...that the best is yet to come." The same likely is true for Gert Town, as investors are beginning to pay closer attention to the neighborhood. In 2012, developer Pres Kabacoff reopened the Blue Plate building as an artist loft complex. Complete with seventy-two units, a recording studio and gallery space, the building is part of a state cultural district, which allows those who create artwork here to sell it tax-free.[268]

Festivals and Events

Xavier's Jazz Fest is free and features concerts, clinics and workshops with world-class jazz artists.

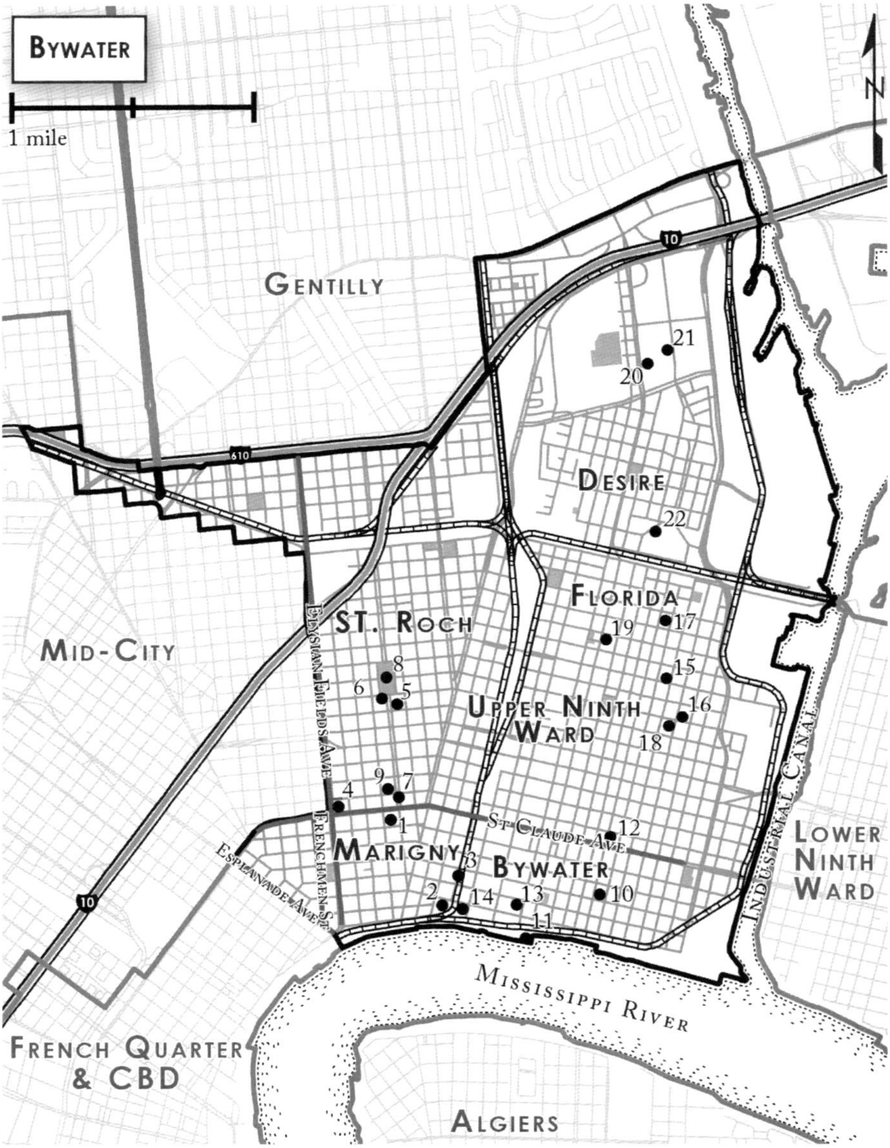

Bywater
1 mile
N
Gentilly
Desire
Mid-City
St. Roch
Florida
Upper Ninth Ward
Marigny
Bywater
Elysian Fields Ave
Frenchmen St
Esplanade Ave
St Claude Ave
Industrial Canal
Lower Ninth Ward
Mississippi River
French Quarter & CBD
Algiers
10
610
1
2
3
4
5
6
7
8
9
10
11
12
13
14
15
16
17
18
19
20
21
22

Chapter 5

Bywater

MAP KEY

MARIGNY
1. Healing Center
2. New Orleans Center for Creative Arts
3. *Plessy v. Ferguson* Plaque
4. Siberia

ST. ROCH
5. St. Roch Cemetery No. 1
6. St. Roch Community Church
7. St. Roch Market
8. St. Roch Playground
9. St. Roch Tavern

BYWATER
10. Bywater Art Lofts
11. Crescent Park
12. Dancing Grounds
13. Markey's Bar
14. Rice Mill Lofts

UPPER NINTH WARD
15. Akili Academy Charter School
16. Ellis Marsalis Center for Music
17. Florida Development
18. Musicians' Village
19. RUBARB Community Bike Shop

DESIRE
20. Delgado Community College Sidney Collier Site
21. Desire Fellowship
22. The Estates

MARIGNY

A Note on Identity

The Marigny is named for Creole aristocrat Bernard Xavier Philippe de Marigny, who owned a plantation here. The Historic District Landmarks Commission and city have different boundaries for the Marigny, but many residents say that it is bounded by St. Claude Avenue, the river, Esplanade Avenue and the Press Street train tracks. The section between Elysian Fields Avenue and Esplanade is called the "Marigny Triangle."

At the Heart of It

The Marigny's identity is inextricably tied to its adjacent neighborhoods. Wedged between the tourist-trodden French Quarter and the artist-brimming Bywater, the neighborhood hosts the confluence of these groups. Single-speed cruisers cross paths with group bike tours here. Bed-and-breakfasts weave with locally owned theaters, bars and the New Orleans Center for Creative Arts (NOCCA) to form the neighborhood streetscape. Residents enjoy the Marigny's colorful and quiet streets while being surrounded by culture and action. This ideal placement comes at an ever-increasing cost, and most who live here are wealthy and white.[269]

In that respect, today's Marigny residents differ from their historic predecessors. Faubourg Marigny—New Orleans' first downriver suburb—was home to French and Spanish Creoles, poor Irish and German immigrants and many other ethnic groups.[270] Free people of color, most of them Catholic and of mixed French or Spanish descent, outnumbered slaves here.[271] Like the French Quarter, this neighborhood had a "three-tiered Caribbean racial structure"—"a class of marginal status and frequently mixed origin was inserted between blacks and whites."[272]

After the Civil War, when segregation stripped away this marginal status, local Creole of color Homer Plessy tested the city's recently passed Separate Car Act in the Marigny.[273] In 1892, at the Royal Street train depot, Plessy was arrested and jailed for sitting in an all-white train car. Four years later, the U.S. Supreme Court ruled against him in the *Plessy v. Ferguson* case, cementing the "separate but equal" doctrine. By the end of the century, some Creoles of color had left New Orleans for Mexico, Cuba, Haiti and France as a

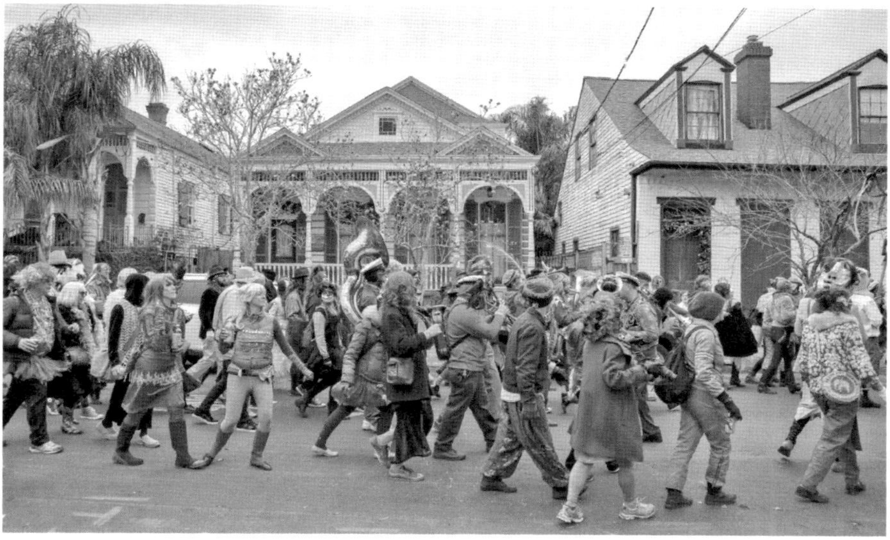

St. Anne's Parade through the Marigny neighborhood on Mardi Gras Day 2015. *Photo by Bruce Cervini.*

result of the city's new "one-drop" rule.[274] Today, Plessy is honored with a PLAQUE at the former Press Street Railroad Yards.

The Marigny was a working-class neighborhood at its founding and stayed that way through the 1970s. By that time, white flight and subsequent city neglect had taken a toll on the neighborhood's Creole cottages and shotguns dating back to the early nineteenth century. Residents formed the Faubourg Marigny Improvement Association, and in 1974, the neighborhood was listed on the National Register of Historic Places. With new attention paid to its historic significance and the neighboring French Quarter fully gentrified, the Marigny became the next frontier for middle-class newcomers.[275]

As is typically the case, bohemians and art enthusiasts paved the way. In the 1980s and '90s, artists and musicians here grew Frenchmen Street into one of the city's most popular hangouts for locals. Lined with nightclubs that featured live music seven days a week, Frenchmen became the alternative to Bourbon Street, where tourists had taken over. After Hurricane Katrina, as transplants expanded into Bywater and savvy visitors found their way to Frenchmen, the corridor reached its "hip" tipping point. Today, the saying here goes that Frenchmen Street is the new Bourbon Street and St. Claude Avenue is the new Frenchmen.

Before the storm, and even in the few years after, St. Claude Avenue was the Marigny's fringe—sought out for drag shows and punk rock but also known for its crime. Today, counterculture has nearly scorched the earth here. By night, St. Claude's bars are packed with twenty- and thirty-somethings wearing outfits they assembled at neighboring thrift stores. By day, these transplants shop for organic food at the New Orleans Food Co-op, housed in the fifty-thousand-square foot HEALING CENTER, which also offers yoga, theater and art exhibits. There is competitiveness over "who was the first pioneer and who killed the last Indian," explained Luke Allen, who co-owns St. Claude's SIBERIA bar and music venue. Many of those who claimed St. Claude early bemoan its burgeoning popularity.

Festivals and Events

The St. Claude Arts District hosts a Second Saturday Art Walk each month, which features exhibit openings at galleries on and around the corridor.

The Healing Center's annual Anba Dlo Halloween Festival features a symposium on the global importance of water, a parade and a costume

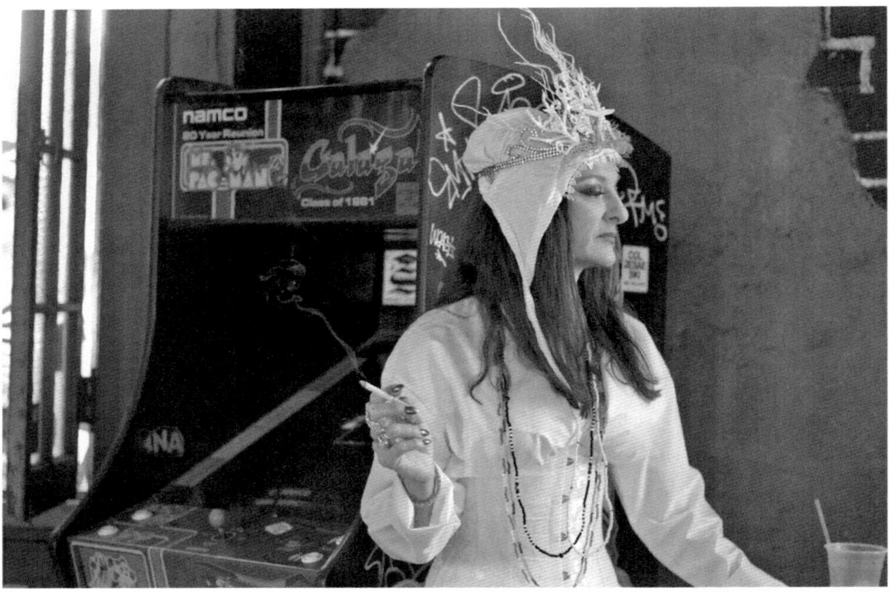

A marcher in the Anba Dlo parade takes a break at a local Marigny bar. *Photo by Lindsay Arvin.*

party. (Anba Dlo is a Haitian Creole phrase that means "beneath the waters.")

New Orleans Center for the Creative Arts puts on student productions and recitals throughout the year.

ST. ROCH

A Note on Identity

Many residents identify this neighborhood's boundaries as St. Claude Avenue, Florida Avenue, Elysian Fields Avenue and the Press Street train tracks. In 1994, the riverside section of the neighborhood was established as part of the New Marigny Historic District. Real estate agencies now capitalize on associating St. Roch with the gentrified Marigny neighborhood across St. Claude.

At the Heart of It

St. Roch was named through a bargain with God. When German priest Reverend Peter Leonard Thevis arrived in New Orleans in 1867, the terrors of the most recent yellow fever epidemic greeted him. He prayed that if no one in his parish died from the disease, he would build a chapel for the patron saint of good health in return.[276] The reverend's prayers were answered, and he fulfilled his promise here in the neighborhood. The chapel still sits inside St. Roch Cemetery No. 1 and is covered in modern-day offerings, from crosses and flowers to stone-sculpted body parts.

Residentially, St. Roch began to develop in the early 1900s. In its early days, it was made up of blacksmith shops, dairies and small farms.[277] It was a diverse neighborhood when those were the exception and home to early jazz greats, including Jelly Roll Morton.[278] By the mid-twentieth century, St. Roch burgeoned with thousands of working-class families. Almost every corner had a local business: Whitey's Sweet Shop, Mr. Otto's Pharmacy, Miss Bohannon's Grocery and Gloria's Living Room, a jazz club, were among the many. Paul Varisco grew up in St. Roch in the 1950s and '60s, and he still remembers playing in the St. Roch Playground constantly. "There were hundreds of kids, and everyone had a nickname," he said. "We'd be in that

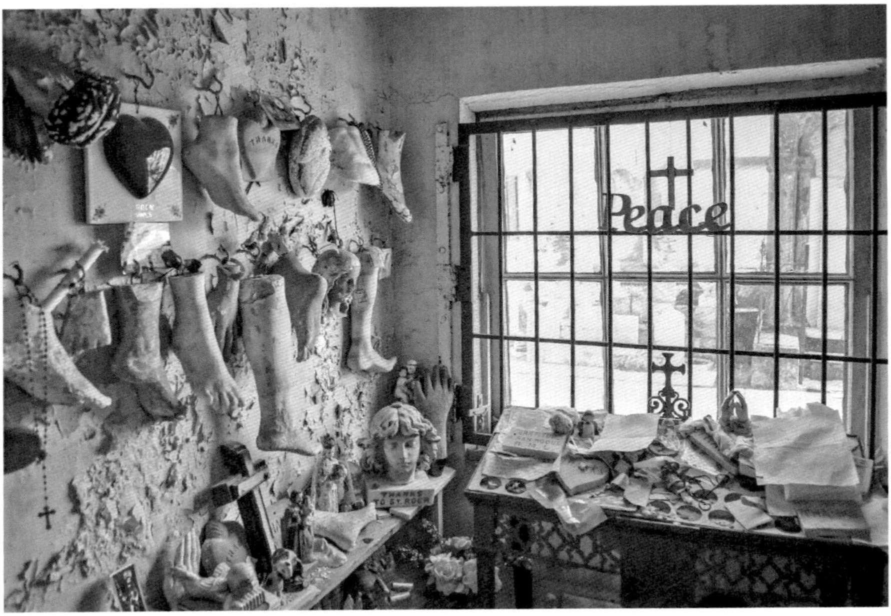

A shrine for St. Roch, the patron saint of good health, in the historic St. Roch Cemetery No. 1. *Photo by Bruce Cervini.*

playground all day, every day, playing basketball, football. We'd build carts with wheels and race them in between the cemeteries."

In the late 1960s, white flight began to take its toll on the neighborhood, and the building of the I-10 ramp here also led to St. Roch's decline.[279] Over the next several decades, drugs and violent crime became serious neighborhood issues, and by 2000, 37 percent of St. Roch residents were living below poverty.[280] When Hurricane Katrina hit, parts of St. Roch flooded with more than eight feet of water.[281] With the neighborhood completely devastated, St. Roch Community Church launched a nonprofit community development corporation to guide its recovery. Since its inception, the CDC has renovated housing and commercial space and started teaching financial literacy and job training courses.[282]

More than a decade after the storm, as St. Claude Avenue becomes one of the city's hippest hangouts, the neighborhood's riverside end is hardly recognizable. In 2015, St. Roch Market (established in 1875) reopened after a $3.7 million renovation. Lined with windows, the sleek new space features a diverse lineup of local chefs and is usually packed with young professionals, many of them transplants. Nearby, St. Roch Tavern,

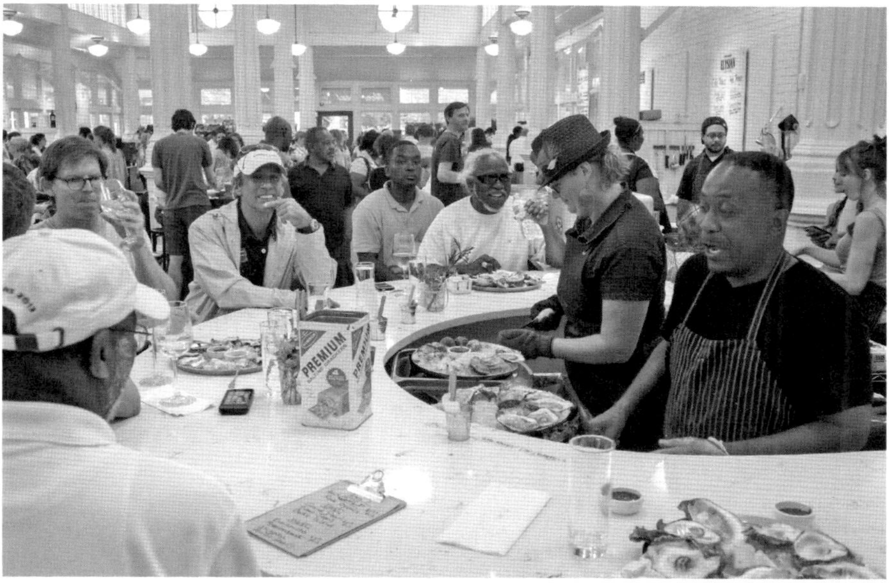

Visitors enjoy freshly shucked oysters at St. Roch Market, which dates back to 1875. *Photo by Bruce Cervini.*

which old-timers know as Caranek's, keeps its appeal to both natives and newcomers. On Sunday nights during Carnival season, Mardi Gras Indians hold practice in one corner of the bar, while punks meet up for "bike church"—a weekly social ride—in another. "It's a neighborhood bar," said manager Martha Wood. "It changes as the neighborhood does, but we've always had a mixed crowd. Even the natives who move away still come to hang out here."

Festivals and Events

St. Roch Market features a market-wide happy hour Monday through Thursday, when all of its vendors offer specials. St. Roch Tavern gets hot on Saturday nights during its weekly Bounce Party with DJ Rusty Lazer.

St. Roch Community Church hosts a community potluck every first Sunday of the month.

BYWATER

A Note on Identity

The Historic District Landmarks Commission and the city have different boundaries for the Bywater neighborhood, but many residents say it is bounded by the river, St. Claude Avenue, the Press Street train tracks and the Industrial Canal. There is a local debate over whether to call the neighborhood "Bywater" or "the Bywater." Many consider the pronoun version a representation of the neighborhood's ongoing gentrification.

At the Heart of It

At the heart of Bywater is its homegrown art scene. Visual, material and performing artists who have flocked here over the last thirty years have transformed backyards into venues and bedrooms into galleries. Many of these places have evolved into full-time art spaces. DANCING GROUNDS, for example, started as a "speakeasy studio" in a Bywater living room in 2012, and by 2015, it had reached more than eight hundred youth and one thousand adults with affordable dance classes.[283] A private developer made this possible by offering up her vacant shotgun house on St. Claude Avenue to Dancing Grounds' founders.[284]

Arrangements between artists who fuel the neighborhood's energy and others who own property here are common. Believing that Bywater's creative scene is essential to growing the neighborhood's value, developer Pres Kabacoff renovated an old garment factory here—the model for where Ignatius Reilly worked in *A Confederacy of Dunces*—into the ART LOFTS, affordable housing apartments for artists.[285] Nearer the river, graffiti on the neighborhood's old rice mill has been incorporated into its redesign as the RICE MILL LOFTS. Contrary to those in the Art Lofts, Rice Mill residents are mostly transplants or out-of-towners with the means to have a second home. The birdlike sketch in actors Cady McClain and Jon Lindstrom's living room here was a selling point for them.[286]

As more "outsiders" participate in Bywater's scene, housing and restaurants are appearing for their consumption. This trend started after Hurricane Katrina, when the high-lying Bywater was first flooded with transplants. Now, escalating property taxes and rents are pushing some bohemians out. This does not mark the neighborhood's first major transformation. In the

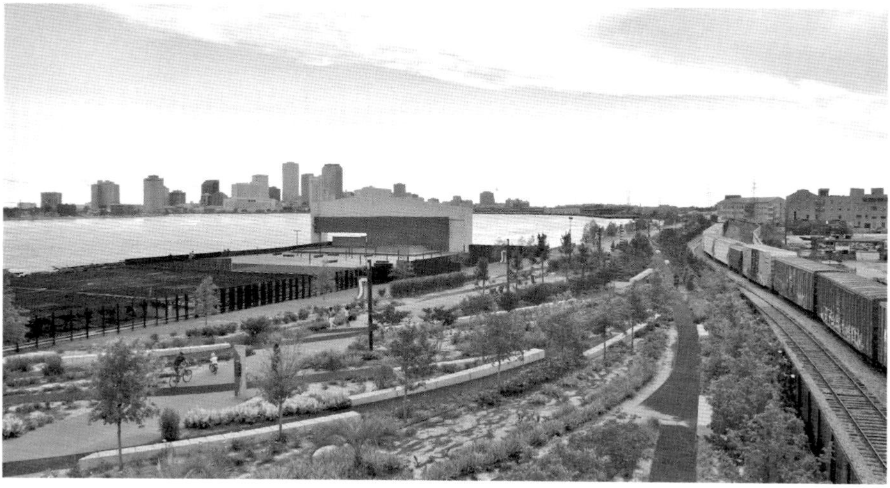

Bywater's 1.4-mile linear Crescent Park honors the riverfront's industrial history. *Photo by Mitchell Mendis.*

NPR audio documentary *Along St. Claude*, one resident summarized more than a century of Bywater's evolution like this: "It was a working class neighborhood, then it was a black neighborhood, then it was a mixed neighborhood and now it's a yuppie neighborhood."[287]

Like the neighboring Marigny, Bywater's earliest residents were also French Creoles, Creoles of color and immigrants from Germany, Italy and Ireland.[288] In the first half of the twentieth century, the neighborhood was referred to as the Ninth Ward, and it was a village unto its own. Everything residents needed was within walking distance—from pharmacies, butchers and bakeries to the post office and the bank.[289] The Piety Street Wharf was one of the neighborhood's largest employers then, and river workers fueled up at local bars, including MARKEY'S, which is still owned by the Markey family.

Today, the riverfront's CRESCENT PARK preserves the neighborhood's industrial history, while also providing gardens, walking paths and stunning views of the city skyline. Dubbed a "severe masterpiece" by *Times-Picayune* reporter Doug MacCash, the park even features a three-story, concrete remnant of the old wharf building.[290] Visitors enter the park by climbing over the high-arching Piety Street Bridge. Made up of raw, rusty steel, it's locally known as the "rusty rainbow."

As the Bywater community reconciles the past with the present, it also compromises with the future. Once called a "green banana" by developer Sean Cummings, who owns the Rice Mills Lofts, Bywater now is undeniably ripe for profit.[291] Will developers who have helped local artists in the past decide to cash in? Will bona fide gentry replace the artists, as they have done in the Marigny? "It's a neighborhood in flux," historian and geographer Richard Campanella told the *Times-Picayune* in 2013. "Is this a good or a bad thing? Well, really, change has defined most of New Orleans throughout most of its history."[292]

Festivals and Events

The St. Claude Arts District hosts a Second Saturday Art Walk each month, which features exhibit openings at galleries on and around the corridor.

Bywater's Mirliton Festival celebrates the seasonal pear-shaped green gourd. For this event, local restaurants serve mirliton-inspired dishes at pop-up tables that line the streets.

Frequently voted "Best Neighborhood Festival" by *OffBeat* magazine, Chaz Fest features local musicians and falls on the Thursday in between Jazz Fest weekends. Food and drink vendors come straight from Bywater.

UPPER NINTH WARD (ST. CLAUDE, FLORIDA AREA, FLORIDA DEVELOPMENT)

A Note on Identity

Residents in the city's St. Claude and Florida Area neighborhoods usually refer to where they live as the "Ninth Ward" or the "Upper Ninth Ward." These neighborhoods are combined here. The Florida public housing project is the predecessor to today's mixed-income FLORIDA DEVELOPMENT.

At the Heart of It

At the heart of these Upper Ninth Ward neighborhoods is the spirit of sharing ideas, skills and tools that grew out of the area's devastation during Hurricane Katrina. The Upper Ninth's patchwork of renovated and still dilapidated homes has fortifying community resources in its rough. Natives and transplants of all ages come together in places like the Ellis Marsalis Center for Music, for its low-cost music lessons and performance and recording spaces, and the RUBARB Community Bike Shop, with its free tools and bike advice.

The Upper Ninth Ward is next to the Industrial Canal, which opened in 1923 and divided the ward into upper and lower parts for the first time. During Hurricane Katrina, the canal's levees breached, flooding the area nearest Florida Avenue with up to ten feet of water.[293] Some who were not able to evacuate perished in the storm. Those who did leave faced many challenges coming back, including working with the Road Home Program, which was found to be discriminatory in a federal court in 2010.[294] The 2008 film *Trouble the Water* gives a stunning glimpse into one resilient Upper Ninth Ward family's struggle during and after the hurricane.

The Upper Ninth Ward has a long history of flooding. Poor drainage delayed its development until the 1940s and '50s, when the systems here were improved. Rural families who had come to New Orleans for work but lost their jobs after World War II settled in the Florida area, where the Florida public housing project opened in 1946.[295] Built from less durable materials than its prewar counterparts, this project immediately became known as the city's poorest.[296] While the development was for whites only, the neighborhood surrounding it was segregated by street.[297] White students

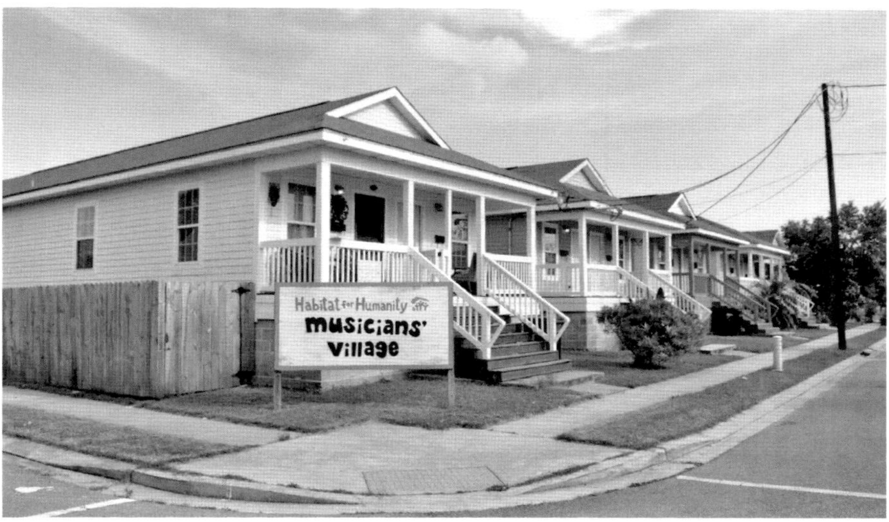

The Upper Ninth Ward's Musicians' Village was created in the aftermath of Hurricane Katrina for artists who risked being displaced. *Photo by Mitcheli Mendis.*

attended William Frantz Elementary, and African American students went to Johnson Lockett Elementary. This was the case until 1960, when a local family helped forever change learning in the neighborhood, New Orleans and the United States.

On November 14, 1960, four black elementary school students attended white schools in New Orleans for the first time. Three went to McDonogh No. 19 in the Lower Ninth Ward together, and six-year-old Ruby Bridges attended William Frantz Elementary in the Upper Ninth Ward by herself. As she drove through the mob of protestors with federal marshals and her mother, Bridges thought it was Mardi Gras because of the people shouting in the street.[298] Local whites boycotted the school as a result of Bridges's attendance, and for a full year, only she and her teacher showed up.[299] Today, William Frantz Elementary is the Akili Academy Charter School, which honors Bridges with the Ruby Bridges Room and a statue of her at its front.

Music education in the Upper Ninth Ward also honors local legends. Tuesday Night Concerts at the Ellis Marsalis Center for Music weave oral history with performance to celebrate New Orleans' early brass bands and other city traditions. The center is the focal point of the area's Musicians' Village—complete with 72 single-family homes, five duplexes for seniors and a toddler park—which was built after Hurricane Katrina for artists who risked being displaced.[300] Still, the realities of displacement have been hard to ignore here since even before Katrina's impact. Most of the old Florida project was torn down in the 1990s as part of the HOPE IV program, and 51 units replace the 734 that once stood here.[301]

Like the Musicians' Village, RUBARB Community Bike Shop was born after Katrina. It was started in 2006 by a group of Common Ground volunteers, including its current director, Liz Lichtman. "Transportation was limited at the time, and flooded bikes were all over the place, so volunteers scavenged and brought them back to life," she recalled. Lichtman added that with the neighborhood full of debris and gutted homes, youth who had returned had little to do. "They were attracted to the space, where we were doing art projects, fixing bikes and going on rides," she noted. "Over the years, RUBARB evolved into what it is today, and some of those youth are now teenagers and young adults still visiting us."

Festivals and Events

The 9th Ward Festival is a free community event with live music, beer and boiled crawfish each April. Tuesday Night Concerts at the Ellis Marsalis Center for Music are only three dollars and offer refreshments, performance and music history lectures.

DESIRE (DESIRE AREA, DESIRE DEVELOPMENT)

A Note on Identity

The Desire neighborhood is isolated from the rest of the city on all sides by I-610, train tracks and the Florida Canal. The Desire public housing project was closed in 2001 and completely torn down by 2003. Replacing the project today are THE ESTATES, a group of mixed-income communities divided into the Abundance Square, Savoy Place and Treasure Village developments.

At the Heart of It

Development of the Desire area began slowly in the mid-nineteenth century and picked up after the completion of the Industrial Canal in 1923.[302] Cut off from the rest of the New Orleans by railroads and canals, the city encouraged African American homeownership here after World War II.[303] In 1956, the Desire housing project opened in the neighborhood. Unlike its brick counterparts from the 1940s, which were built on land with higher elevation, Desire was constructed with cheap materials on what had formerly been cypress swamp.[304] It began sinking before the first tenants even moved in, "causing foundations, then pipes, to break and crumble."[305] According to Ed Arceneaux, a former Desire manager and a housing management specialist with HUD, Desire was not designed for people to live in—"it was designed, rather, to warehouse the city's poorest residents."[306]

As urban renewal projects in other parts of the city displaced poor African Americans through the 1960s, the isolated Desire warehouse expanded, even after Hurricane Betsy devastated the area with six feet of water in 1965. Eventually, Desire became the largest public housing project in the United States, complete with 1,860 units. By 1970, 10,594 residents, 75 percent of whom were under the age of twenty-one, lived here.[307] Conditions worsened as density thickened. Drugs and crime were rampant, rats infested the housing and sewage pipes leaked.

Hidden from the rest of the city, Desire's desperation was ignored and perpetuated. Resident efforts to shed light on the neighborhood's conditions were shut down. The Free Southern Theater, which moved to Desire after Hurricane Betsy, produced a play about the project called *Ghettos of Desire* in the late 1960s. When CBS decided to broadcast the play, however, the Housing Authority of New Orleans demanded its cancelation.[308] In 1970, the New Orleans Committee to Combat Fascism—a Black Panthers offshoot—moved its headquarters to the local Piety Street and took reform into its own hands. It set up free sickle cell screenings, classes on self-determination and a breakfast program that served hundreds of local children.[309] Its presence reduced crime in Desire dramatically and organized residents against police brutality.[310]

On September 15, 1970, the outing of two undercover officers at the Panthers' headquarters led to a shootout between the Panthers and police in which no one died.[311] Two months later, on November 19, 250 armed white police officers, a tank and helicopters descended on Desire in an attempt to evict the Panthers. Residents, many of them children, surrounded the Panthers' apartments to protect them until the police left.[312] A week later, on Thanksgiving, the police returned again, this time disguised as priests and postal workers, and raided the headquarters. The eighteen Panther leaders who were subsequently arrested were all acquitted.[313]

Desire is part of New Orleans' Fifth Planning District, which in the 1980s and '90s was called the "Bloody Fifth." At that time, it was a dumping ground

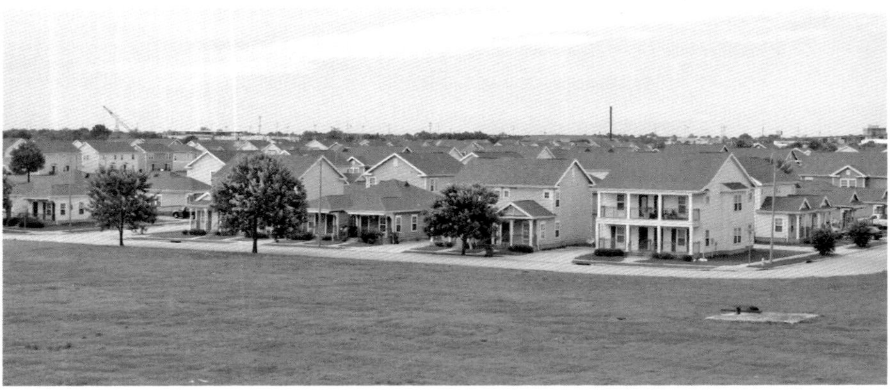

A mixed-income development called The Estates has replaced the city's Desire project. *Photo by Mitchell Mendis.*

for the city's most crooked police, many of whom had substance abuse issues and formed close relationships with the local drug dealers and criminals.[314] Together, they terrorized the neighborhood.[315] Many Desire residents found solace in religion. The Desire Community Choir, led by Alvin Bridges, was an alternative to street life for local youth and even recorded two LPs and won "Best Gospel Choir" at the 2001 Jazz Fest. From the 1990s through to when Hurricane Katrina hit, Desire Street Ministries established a church, built a junior-senior high school for local boys and partnered to provide a children's medical clinic for neighbors without adequate transportation. The ministry was an instrumental community resource as the city demolished and replaced the Desire project as part of the HOPE IV program, beginning in 1995.[316]

By the time Desire's demolition began, only 590 families lived there.[317] The rebuilding process was underway when Hurricane Katrina flooded the area with eight feet of water. Today, The Estates offer 425 pastel-colored town homes, 283 of which are public housing units.[318] Many of the former residents have moved on, and old community resources have changed. DELGADO COMMUNITY COLLEGE, for example, bought the neighborhood's Sidney Collier Technical College and reopened the campus as a satellite site. Desire Street Ministries has expanded throughout the South as a network of urban ministries and moved its headquarters to Georgia. Its neighborhood partner is now called DESIRE FELLOWSHIP.

Festivals and Events

Desire Fellowship runs summer camps, college tours and other programs for local youth.

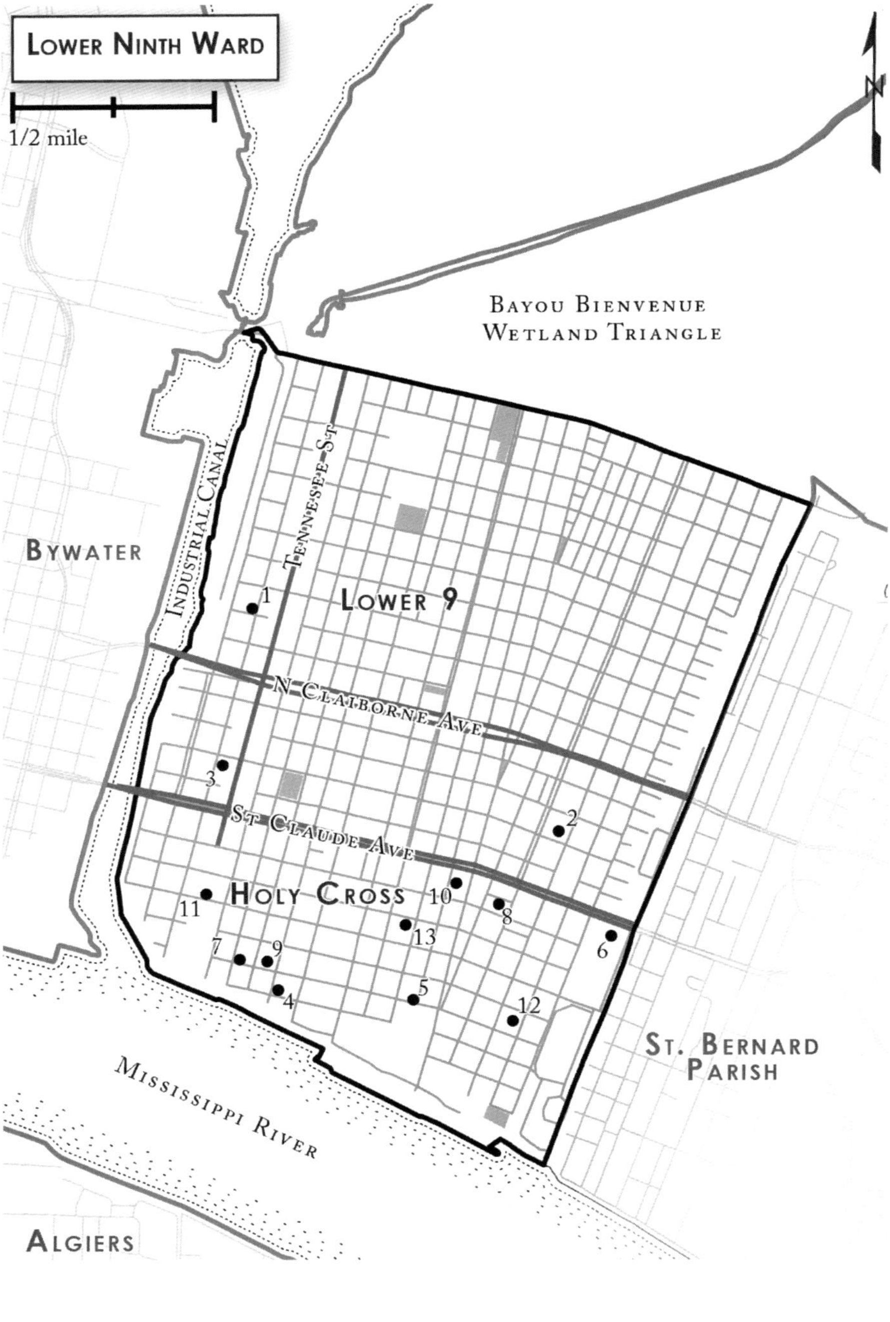
Lower Ninth Ward
1/2 mile
N
Bayou Bienvenue
Wetland Triangle
Industrial Canal
Tennessee St
Bywater
Lower 9
N Claiborne Ave
St Claude Ave
Holy Cross
St. Bernard
Parish
Mississippi River
Algiers
1
2
3
4
5
6
7
8
9
10
11
12
13

Chapter 6

Lower Ninth Ward

MAP KEY

Lower 9

1. Common Ground Relief
2. House of Dance and Feathers
3. Lower Ninth Ward Living Museum

Holy Cross

4. Doullut Steamboat Houses
5. Guerilla Garden
6. Jackson Barracks
7. Laurentine Ernst Community Garden
8. Lowernine.org
9. Lower 9th Ward Center for Sustainable Engagement & Development
10. Lower 9th Ward Village Community Center
11. Old Holy Cross High School
12. St. Maurice Church
13. Tekrema Center for Art and Culture

LOWER 9

A Note on Identity

The city's Lower Ninth Ward neighborhood is one of two neighborhoods in the Lower Ninth Ward Planning District. It is bounded by St. Claude Avenue, Bayou Bienvenue Wetland Triangle, the Industrial Canal and the parish line. The "Lower 9," as many residents call it, is distinctly separate from the Holy Cross neighborhood on the riverside of St. Claude Avenue.

The Ninth Ward was split into "Upper" and "Lower" parts in 1923, when the Industrial Canal opened.

At the Heart of It

In the 1700s and 1800s, today's Lower 9 was the backswamp of riverfront plantations in present-day Holy Cross. While Holy Cross began developing in the 1840s, the Lower 9 stayed laden with cypress and palmettos.[319] With limited options, some freed slaves moved to this mosquito-infested area before the turn of the century.[320] Drainage of this neighborhood began in preparation for building the Industrial Canal, which, when completed in 1923, was a five-mile-long, six-hundred-foot-wide shipping route connecting the Mississippi River with the lake.

While the canal created jobs and boosted port activity, it also "introduced gulf water into city limits, held back only by flimsy floodwalls and inadequate levees."[321] Likewise, it severed the newly termed "Lower Ninth Ward" from the rest of New Orleans. In the 1930s and '40s, another canal—the Intracoastal—was excavated to provide east–west navigation through the wetlands above the neighborhood. By then, the Lower 9 had expanded lakeside of North Claiborne Avenue. It was one of the few places where African Americans could buy homes after World War II, and this started a tradition of multigenerational, black homeownership here.[322]

Throughout the mid-twentieth century, Lower 9 residents made national history. Fats Domino, a lifelong community member, emerged as an R&B legend. In 1960, three African American first-graders here—Leona Tate, Tessie Prevost and Gail Etienne—led school integration citywide by attending the all-white McDonogh No. 19.[323] The Lower 9 was still rural at this time, and many found their livelihoods in farming. On the neighborhood's lakeside, Bayou Bienvenue Wetland Triangle was an "old-growth swamp filled with trees, water lilies, and freshwater wildlife such as fish, alligators, otters, birds and crawfish."[324] The swamp protected the neighborhood from floods until the completion of another nearby canal—the Mississippi River–Gulf Outlet (MR-GO)—introduced saltwater to it in 1965. Ultimately killing the cypress trees and freshwater species here, the salt turned this protective flood barrier into open water.[325]

In addition to destroying the neighborhood's wetlands, man-made canals surrounding the Lower 9 have twice been responsible for decimating homes and lives here. In September 1965, Hurricane Betsy wrought the neighborhood's first major catastrophe. Levee breaches along Intracoastal and Industrial Canals flooded the Lower 9 with between three and five feet of water near St. Claude Avenue and nine feet by Bayou Bienvenue.[326] Dozens died in the storm.[327] Forty years later, history would repeat itself—only conditions would worsen.

In the years before Hurricane Katrina, the Lower Ninth Ward was not the poorest or lowest-lying area in New Orleans.[328] In fact, it had one of the highest African American homeownership rates in the country. Next to unstable canals and long ignored, however, the neighborhood was one of the city's most vulnerable. When the storm hit in 2005, the levees of all three nearby canals breached.[329] The Lower 9 was flooded with more than ten feet of water, much of it contaminated with oil from refineries that were wiped out in the neighboring St. Bernard Parish.[330]

The great majority of people who died during Hurricane Katrina died in the Lower Ninth Ward, many while waiting to be rescued on quickly floating rooftops. Those who survived lost everything, and $15,000 settlements granted through the Road Home Program, which was later ruled discriminatory in a federal court, were not enough to help them return.[331] As a result, thousands of working-class and poor African American residents lost their security nets: homes that they owned outright and that had been passed down for generations. In June 2014, just 34 percent of Lower 9 addresses that received mail before Hurricane Katrina were again receiving mail.[332]

"Rebuilding in the Lower 9 has lagged behind that of other neighborhoods as a result of poverty, the scale of the devastation and local, state and federal government inaction," notes the website of the nonprofit Lowernine.org. "Dealing first with toxic mold, then toxic FEMA trailers and toxic Chinese sheetrock, then with unscrupulous contractors, insurance and mortgage companies, and finally struggling under a discriminatory governmental recovery program, it became clear that the Lower Ninth Ward would be much slower to recover than other areas of New Orleans and the Gulf Coast Region."[333]

Those who have helped the neighborhood's recovery include thousands of volunteers from all over the world. "In the aftermath of the storm, the volunteers believed we were worth something, and that helped us believe we were worth something," said Robert Green, a Lower 9 community leader who saw both his granddaughter and mother perish during Katrina. "Most of us who came back after the storm found our purpose—we wanted to do more, make more for the community." Today, Green acts as the cultural ambassador between his neighbors, volunteers and city officials. His time is often filled with interviews about his experience and the needs of the community going forward.

Ten years after the storm, there are a handful of organizations working to address these needs. By March 2015, Brad Pitt's Make It Right Foundation had built one hundred LEED® Platinum homes on and around Tennessee Street.[334] Lowernine.org, with its a far humbler budget, had rebuilt or renovated seventy-five throughout the Lower Ninth Ward. While these groups work on housing, COMMON GROUND RELIEF focuses on restoring the Bayou Bienvenue Wetland Triangle. The MR-GO Canal was closed after Hurricane Katrina, halting saltwater intrusion of the former swamp and giving it a chance to return to its natural state.[335]

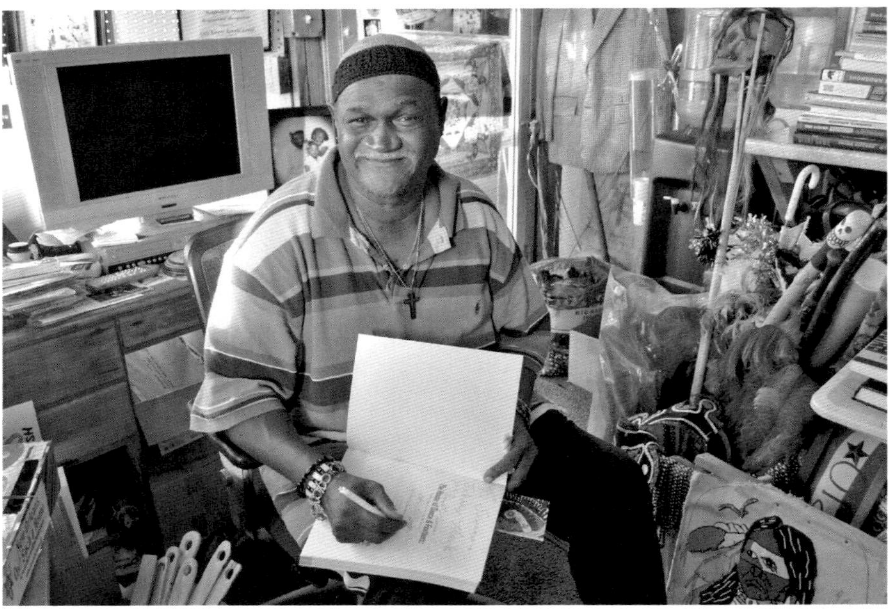

Ronald Lewis, founder of the Lower 9's House of Dance and Feathers, signs his book for visitors. *Photo by author.*

Other community efforts focus on preserving the neighborhood's culture. Lifelong resident Ronald Lewis's backyard museum, the HOUSE OF DANCE AND FEATHERS, for example, is based on his experiences participating in social aid and pleasure clubs, Mardi Gras Indian gangs and skull and bones clubs.[336] Nearby, the LOWER NINTH WARD LIVING MUSEUM is dedicated to collecting the oral histories of local residents. In 2014, the museum captured more than forty recordings. These are included in ongoing exhibits, while more oral histories are being collected.

The Lower 9's recovery varies drastically from one end to its other. Above North Claiborne Avenue, steps that once led to porches sit in front of open lots. Grass grows high around illegally dumped debris, and the streets are quiet. Along St. Claude Avenue, however, a new fire station, library and state-of-the-art community center opened in 2015, while the neighborhood's local high school was being rebuilt. "Now we have to focus on coaching young people on how to buy homes for the first time, and we have to get them to buy in the neighborhood," Green said. "If I could have one thing for the community tomorrow, it would be more people. Because the people are at the heart of it, from those of us who grew up here to everyone who helped get us through the storm."

Festivals and Events

Common Ground Relief hosts regular community events and speakers at its headquarters.

HOLY CROSS

A Note on Identity

Holy Cross is one of two neighborhoods in the Lower Ninth Ward, which was split into "Upper" and "Lower" parts in 1923, when the Industrial Canal opened. The neighborhood is named for its historic HOLY CROSS SCHOOL (established in 1871).[337] The city and the Historic District Landmarks Commission have different borders for Holy Cross, but most agree that it is bounded by the river, the Industrial Canal, St. Claude Avenue and JACKSON BARRACKS.

At the Heart of It

Today's Holy Cross neighborhood dates back to the early 1730s, when plantations first lined the riverfront here.[338] It stayed plantation land until the 1840s and '50s, when many farms were subdivided into faubourgs. By that point, New Orleans Barracks (today's Jackson Barracks) sat at the neighborhood's downriver border and served as a cautious greeting both to incoming ships and local immigrants and Creoles, whom the new American government did not trust.[339] In 1857, ST. MAURICE CHURCH was erected to serve the growing population here, and in 1871, the Brothers of the Holy Cross established a school that would eventually inspire the neighborhood's name.[340]

By the turn of the century, Holy Cross had become a small village of cottages and open fields.[341] In 1905, steamboat captain Paul Doullut built the first of two identical Japanese-inspired mansions (known today as the DOULLUT STEAMBOAT HOUSES) along the Mississippi River here.[342] Near these ornate architectural masterpieces, however, were railroads, a cotton press, a livestock landing and slaughterhouse—infrastructure that the government preferred to keep out of the city center for a number of reasons.[343] "This would become a familiar theme for the future Lower Ninth Ward: first on

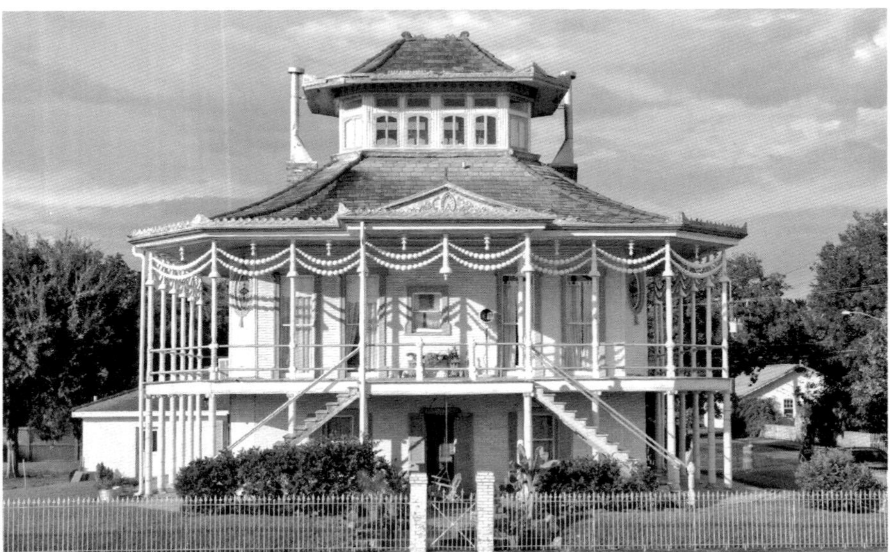

Captain Doullut's Steamboat Houses have pagoda-style roofing, inspired by the Japanese exhibit at the 1904 World Fair. *Photo by author.*

the list for urban nuisances, last in line for amenities," wrote historian and geographer Richard Campanella.[344]

Holy Cross's isolation was exacerbated with the building of the Industrial Canal, which opened in 1923 and severed the newly termed "Lower Ninth Ward" from the rest of New Orleans. Still, the neighborhood fared better than its lakeside counterpart, the Lower 9. While land above St. Claude Avenue was low-lying and its residents predominantly African American and either poor or working class, Holy Cross had historical significance and racial diversity, both of which were tied to its proximity to the river and resulting elevation. Diversity wouldn't last, however. In 1960, when the desegregation of New Orleans' schools began in the Ninth Ward, whites in Holy Cross started crossing the border into St. Bernard Parish.[345]

Five years later, Hurricane Betsy hit, and the Industrial and Intracoastal Canals' levees breached. While surrounding areas—the Lower 9 and St. Bernard Parish—lost property and lives, Holy Cross came out of the storm intact. Still, Betsy further perpetuated white flight, and by 2000, more than 87 percent of Holy Cross residents were African American.[346]

When Katrina's storm surge again burst open and overtopped canal levees meant to protect the Lower Ninth Ward, water in Holy Cross ranged from eight feet of flooding along St. Claude Avenue to two feet near the river.[347] On the other side of St. Claude, much of the Lower 9 was decimated by more than ten feet of flooding.[348] While residents nearest the river dealt with moderate damage, many died and lost everything throughout the rest of the Lower Ninth Ward.

After the storm, as a debate over the devastated Lower 9's fate played out, the high-lying Holy Cross was instead designated an "immediate opportunity area."[349] In June 2006, the community published a detailed rebuilding plan for the entire Lower Ninth Ward. Today, many of the greater area's main relief organizations are headquartered in Holy Cross. The LOWER 9TH WARD CENTER FOR SUSTAINABLE ENGAGEMENT AND DEVELOPMENT (CSED), for example, is focused on creating access to Bayou Bienvenue Wetland Triangle and tracking the ownership and use of every land parcel between the river and the bayou to help inform city planning, as well as coordinating volunteers on hundreds of neighborhood projects.[350] In 2013, the CSED was donated a one-hundred-year-old barge house to use as an office space and educational center.[351]

While private donors have made the success of many Lower Ninth Ward organizations possible, some have complicated matters with unfulfilled promises. In 2012, for example, the DEWeezy marketing campaign—a joint venture involving Lil Wayne, Mountain Dew and the Glu Agency strategy group—turned the LOWER 9TH WARD VILLAGE COMMUNITY CENTER into a skate park for local kids. With the exception of a few sporadic weeks of operation, the park was scarcely open, and it soon closed indefinitely because of funding shortages.[352]

"Never in my wildest dreams did I think things would have turned out the way they did," Village founder Ward "Mack" McClendon told the *Times-Picayune* in 2014.[353] McClendon, a community leader who passed away in February 2015, bought and opened the ten-thousand-square-foot former auto-body shop as the "Village" in 2007. It soon became an all-purpose gathering space, complete with a computer lab, library, food co-op and community garden. The Village hosted people and programs essential to the Lower Ninth Ward's slow recovery, from Saturday morning neighborhood meetings to volunteers who slept on cots in its spare room. With the failed DEWeezy project rocking the Village's financial stability and McClendon gone, its future is uncertain.

LOWERNINE.ORG executive director Laura Paul said that funding is her organization's biggest challenge. With an annual operating budget of just $149,000, this group has helped rebuild seventy-five homes for people who lived in the Lower Ninth Ward before Hurricane Katrina. Paul, who bought a house in Holy Cross in 2011, said that gentrification of Holy Cross is another one of her frustrations. "It's part of the riverfront development citywide: more people who look like me, who are white and middle class, are moving to these raised, historic, Holy Cross homes and driving prices up," she said. "I believe—and this is what Lowernine.org is all about—that the people who lived here before should have right of first return, and every possible resource should be offered to help them come back. Is that realistic? No. But we are fighting for it anyway."

President of the Holy Cross Neighborhood Association Sarah Debacher empathizes. Debacher, who is white and identifies as middle class, said that she and her husband bought a home in Holy Cross in 2007 because "it is important to us that we learn from people of different racial and socioeconomic backgrounds and that our children do too." Now that gentrification is in full swing, Debacher said that she regrets her passive role in propelling it forward. "The real estate agent told me he uses me to sell houses here," she noted. "He says, 'Look, she's a UNO professor, she's the president of the neighborhood association and she lives right here.'"

Still, as president of the neighborhood association, Debacher said that she is committed to looking back as the community moves forward. She is a leading voice in the neighborhood's battle against Perez Architects, which in 2013 released its plan to redevelop the historic Holy Cross High School into a 180-unit riverfront apartment building—one that is sure to attract people in a higher-income bracket than the neighborhood's average.

Festivals and Events

Committed to preserving local culture, TEKREMA CENTER FOR ART AND CULTURE offers dance classes and organizes performing and visual art shows with a pan-African focus.

The Backyard Gardeners Network organizes hands-on gardening workshops, art activities, storytelling, food preparation demos, African-centered history lessons and community food celebrations at the local GUERILLA GARDEN and LAURENTINE ERNST COMMUNITY GARDEN.

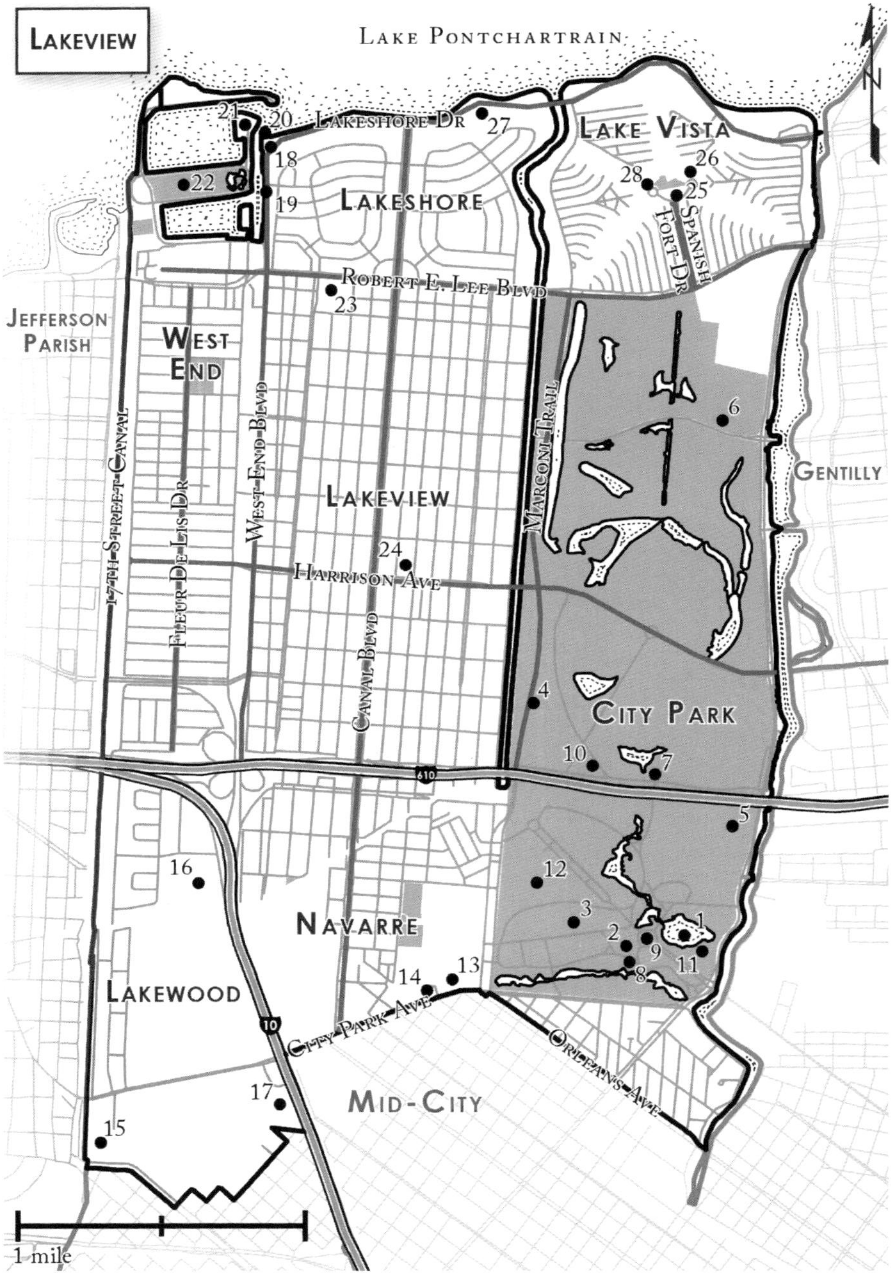

Lakeview
Lake Pontchartrain
N
Lakeshore Dr
Lake Vista
Lakeshore
Spanish Fort Dr
Robert E. Lee Blvd
Jefferson Parish
West End
West End Blvd
17th Street Canal
Fleur De Lis Dr
Lakeview
Marconi Trail
Gentilly
Harrison Ave
Canal Blvd
City Park
610
Navarre
Lakewood
10
City Park Ave
Orleans Ave
Mid-City
1 mile
1
2
3
4
5
6
7
8
9
10
11
12
13
14
15
16
17
18
19
20
21
22
23
24
25
26
27
28

Chapter 7

Lakeview

MAP KEY

City Park
1. Big Lake
2. Besthoff Sculpture Garden
3. Carousel Gardens Amusement Park
4. City Park/Pepsi Tennis Center
5. Festival Grounds
6. Golf Complex
7. Grow Dat Youth Farm
8. Morning Call
9. New Orleans Museum of Art
10. NOLA City Bark
11. Singing Oak
12. Tad Gormley Stadium

Navarre
13. Delgado Community College
14. Holt Cemetery

Lakewood
15. Longue Vue House and Gardens
16. Metairie Cemetery
17. New Orleans Country Club

West End
18. The Blue Crab/Landry's
19. Brisbi's
20. New Canal Lighthouse Museum
21. Southern Yacht Club
22. West End Park

Lakeview
23. Mount Carmel Academy
24. St. Dominic Church and School

Lakeshore/Lake Vista
25. Lake Vista Community Center
26. Lake Vista United Methodist Church
27. Mardi Gras Fountain
28. St. Pius X Church and School

CITY PARK

A Note on Identity

The City Park neighborhood is made up of the park itself, as well as the residential area immediately south of the park. This essay focuses on the park itself.

At the Heart of It

City Park is New Orleans' largest public space. Within its 1,300 acres, the park features everything from manicured fields flanked with benches to playgrounds, a GOLF COMPLEX, FESTIVAL GROUNDS and an arboretum accessed by hiking paths and bayous. At the heart of City Park are its trees. It is home to the biggest collection of live oaks in the world, and nearly every tree found in Louisiana is represented here.[354]

Now the sixth-largest urban park in the country, City Park did not begin as such an expanse. Instead, it started as a one-hundred-acre plain on the high-lying Metairie Ridge, near City Park Avenue. The ridge was created thousands of years earlier when a channel of the Mississippi River came through the area and made a natural levee here out of sediment. In the 1700s and early 1800s, plantation owners profited from this elevated, fertile ground. At the famed Dueling Oaks here (one of which still survives), men settled disputes over women, politics and everything in between by drawing their swords, pistols and sabers.[355]

New Orleans acquired this old plantation land and pronounced it a public space in the 1850s, although the park was not really developed until the 1890s, when the City Park Improvement Association also formed.[356] The park's carousel and miniature train at its CAROUSEL GARDENS AMUSEMENT PARK date back to this time. Today, the carousel is recognized on the National Register of Historic Places, and its hand-carved wooden horses are still in use. Likewise, the updated train continues to weave through the park's canopy of oaks, delighting kids and adults alike for just a few dollars per ride.

On the heels of those early attractions came a deepened investment in the park. By 1917, it boasted a golf course, peristyle, bandstand and refreshment stand.[357] Bridges were built across its lagoon, and sugar broker Isaac Delgado created an art museum here in his name—now the NEW ORLEANS MUSEUM OF ART (NOMA).[358] All of these structures are well preserved today. The peristyle hosts weddings on many weekends in the spring and fall, and MORNING CALL serves fresh beignets and café au lait in the old refreshment building. NOMA

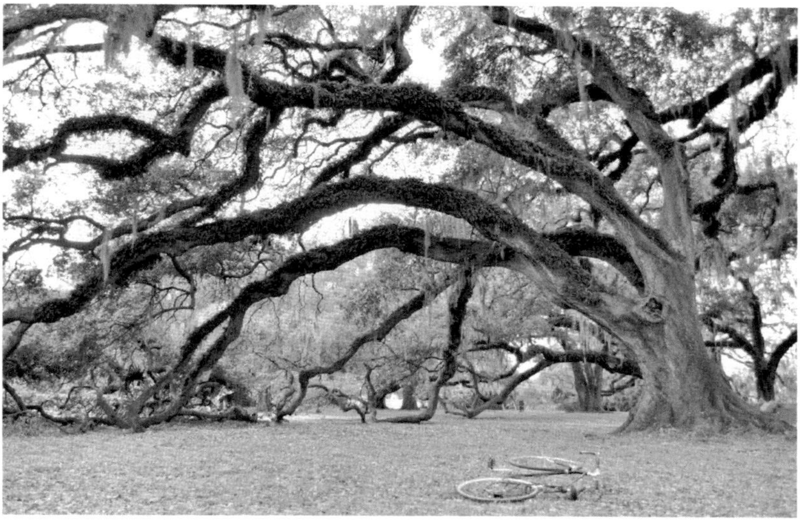

A live oak in City Park, home to the oldest grove of mature live oaks in the world. *Photo by Mitchell Mendis.*

now even includes the outdoor BESTHOFF SCULPTURE GARDEN, complete with more than sixty sculptures made by artists from around the world.

After the city drained New Orleans' backswamp in the early twentieth century, City Park was extended all the way to Lake Pontchartrain.[359] The WPA pursued many projects here during the Great Depression, and in 1937, President Franklin Delano Roosevelt visited to dedicate the Roosevelt Mall and City Park Stadium (renamed TAD GORMLEY STADIUM in 1965).[360] Two decades later, in 1958, the park was desegregated. The stadium hosted the Beatles, Sam Cooke and James Brown through the '60s, while the park's golf complex was expanded to include four eighteen-hole courses.[361]

At the turn of the century, City Park's stakeholders began drafting its next chapter. Regional surveys and public meetings led to the completion of the park's 2018 master plan, which called for making the golf complex smaller but stronger, as well as creating recreational paths and more space for festivals and cultural activities, among other initiatives.[362] When Hurricane Katrina hit, it submerged parts of City Park in up to ten feet of water and caused $43 million in damage to the beloved space.[363] The plan was adjusted with community input, but not drastically changed, and parts of it were put on hold until FEMA funding came in.[364]

In the meantime, park officials let much of the destroyed golf course grow wild. Community members became accustomed to the area's natural beauty,

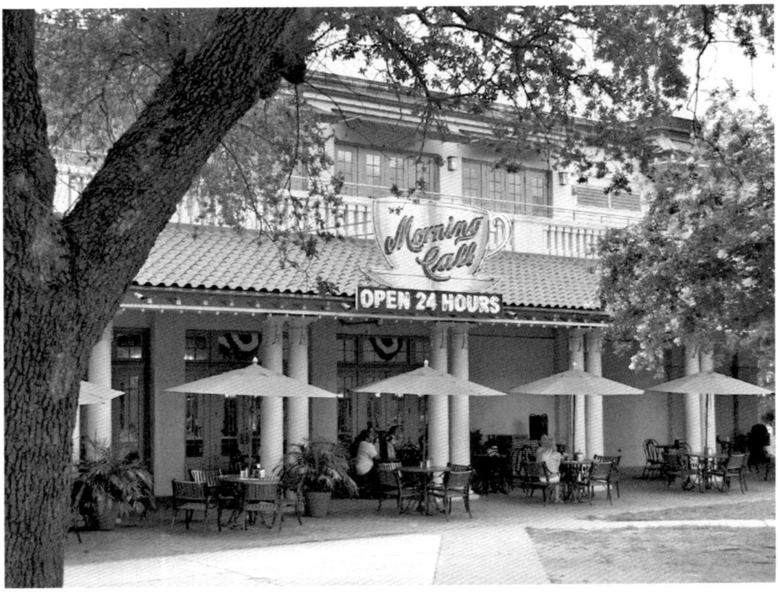

Morning Call in City Park serves fresh beignets twenty-four hours a day. *Photo by author.*

and neighbor Roland Le Blanc even began cutting walking paths through the space as a volunteer. When the plan to redevelop the golf complex finally took effect in 2015, newly erected gates around the area were met with public outcry. Le Blanc said that while he loves the open space, he understands the park's need to generate revenue from the golf course and to get its FEMA funding, which was dependent on rehabilitating the space to how it was used before the storm.

"This plan has been on the books for more than a decade, and the community had many years after the storm to organize and propose other, revenue-generating uses for it," he said. "Believe me, I'd love for it to be kept wild, but I think the park officials are being unfairly scrutinized for this. They really care about the space, but they have an operating budget and they need to meet it." Le Blanc added that while people are unhappy with the new golf complex, the park administration has reduced the golf footprint here, as outlined in the master plan, and created almost 150 more acres of open space than existed before Katrina.

Taking up part of this land now is the Big Lake, a body of water that is modeled after Lake Pontchartrain and offers kayak, canoe and paddleboat rentals. Surrounding the lake are paths and special surprises like the Singing Oak, which is draped in different-sized chimes that are tuned to the pentatonic scale. On a breezy day, the oak sings song after song, and no one of them is ever the same. Other new additions to the park after Hurricane Katrina include the CITY PARK/PEPSI TENNIS CENTER, the NOLA CITY BARK dog park and the GROW DAT YOUTH FARM, a seven-acre campus for sustainable farming where high school students from around New Orleans grow about ten thousand pounds of produce each year.[365]

Festivals and Events

City Park hosts tons of programs—including games and matches, concerts and learning opportunities—each year, but three events are particularly popular. VooDoo Fest is an annual three-day music and arts "experience" featuring local talent, as well as internationally known bands.

Hogs for the Cause pits more than eighty teams against one another in a culinary competition that raises money for families coping with pediatric brain cancer. Attendees donate in exchange for sampling foods, and music plays throughout the two-day event. The winning team is named Louisiana's pork champion.

Celebration in the Oaks features light displays throughout twenty-five acres of the park during the holiday season.

NAVARRE

A Note on Identity

The city bounds the Navarre neighborhood by City Park Avenue, I-10, I-610 and Orleans Avenue. Many here identify with the Lakeview name instead.

At the Heart of It

At the heart of the Navarre neighborhood is DELGADO COMMUNITY COLLEGE, the city's largest higher-education institution and Louisiana's oldest and largest community college.[366] Named for its benefactor, Isaac Delgado, a businessman and sugar planter who emigrated from Jamaica, the college was founded as a trade school for boys in 1921.[367] When it opened next to the lush City Park, it had 1,300 male students, and the surrounding neighborhood was just beginning to develop residentially.[368]

In the previous century, today's Navarre neighborhood was mostly swampland, although its riverside end does sit on the Metairie Ridge. Taking advantage of this limited elevation, Dr. Joseph Holt, a New Orleans Board of Health official, established Holt Cemetery for the indigent here in 1879.[369] Today, the cemetery is known for its underground tombs and unmarked graves. Buddy Bolden, often credited as the "inventor of jazz," is buried here. Although no one knows which tombstone is his, a monument was erected here for him in 1996 and dedicated with a proper jazz funeral, organized by Delgado's jazz studies program.[370]

The New Orleans Land Company drained Navarre's swamp in 1905, following an assessment of the area's potential for development.[371] After Delgado opened here, its first few decades were marked by a series of booms and busts. After thriving in the 1920s, the vocational school suffered during the Great Depression.[372] Delgado was revived during World War II, when the city needed technically skilled workers in aircraft construction, metalwork and woodwork, but after the war—even as the surrounding area prospered—its future again fell into question. Tulane University surveyed the trade school and recommended that it expand as a technical institute at the junior college level.[373] Delgado's board and the New Orleans City Council accepted this recommendation and successfully restructured.

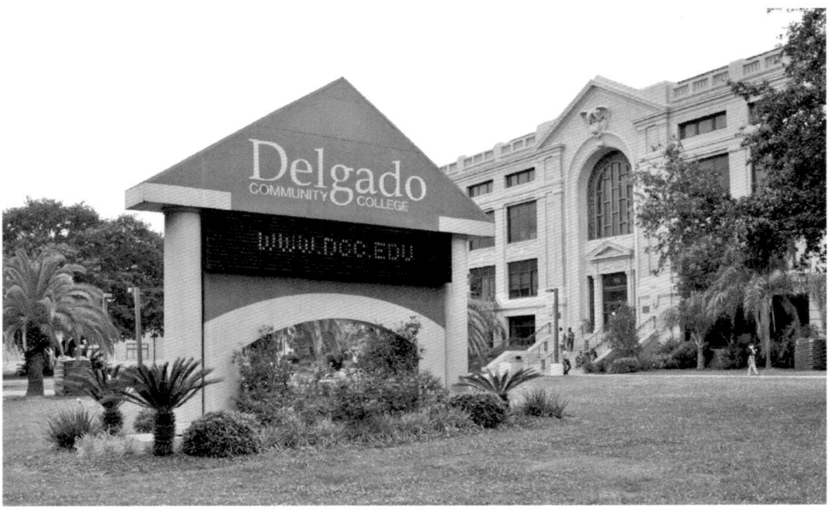

Delgado Community College is New Orleans' largest higher-education institution. *Photo by Mitchell Mendis.*

Today, Delgado has satellite sites throughout the Greater New Orleans area, although its City Park campus remains its largest.

Hurricane Katrina created new challenges for the community college, as flooding and wind during the storm damaged about 70 percent of its City Park facilities. Despite this devastation and recent state funding cuts, Delgado has surpassed its pre-Katrina enrollment numbers with a roster of more than eighteen thousand students at its nine campuses in recent years.[374] Two-thirds of Delgado students are in career-based programs, while the rest are preparing to transfer to four-year institutions.[375] Among the college's most popular tracks are business and management, accounting, criminal justice, culinary arts and programs in the automotive, welding and electrician trades.[376]

Festivals and Events

Each year, Delgado's City Park Campus hosts hundreds of high school students and community members at its Discover Delgado Day, where visitors meet faculty, current students and industry partners, as well as tour the campus.

LAKEWOOD

A Note on Identity

Lakewood is split into north and south parts, which are divided by I-610. Residents who live directly adjacent to METAIRIE CEMETERY and the NEW ORLEANS COUNTRY CLUB historically identify with the "Country Club Gardens" neighborhood name.[377]

At the Heart of It

At the heart of Lakewood is the Metairie Ridge, a quarter-mile-wide, elevated stretch of land that runs through the neighborhood's center. The Metairie Ridge formed thousands of years ago, when a Mississippi River distributary came through the area and created a natural levee here out of sediment.[378] Surrounded by swamp, this sturdy ground offered many development opportunities in the 1700s and 1800s. First passed through the hands of various plantation owners, today's Lakewood eventually became home to attractions and resources that were too big to put in the city center.[379]

In 1838, for example, a racecourse was created just north of where Metairie Road is today. Not long after the track's founding, a Louisiana State Lottery Company official, Charles T. Howard, tried to become part of its Metairie Jockey Club. Howard was rejected because he'd made his fortune in the gambling business; legend has it that as revenge, he vowed to make a cemetery out of the track.[380] When the racecourse closed after the Civil War, Howard lived up to his promise. Metairie Cemetery's design incorporates the old 1$^{1}/_{16}$-mile track and is the final resting place of more than nine thousand people. Nine Louisiana governors, seven New Orleans mayors and three Confederate generals—one of whom is Richard "Dick" Taylor, son of United States president Zachary Taylor—are buried here.[381]

Lakewood's modern development began in 1918 with the construction of the West End Country Club here.[382] The Country Club Gardens, advertised as "aristocratic homes" that could "please those hard to please," were soon built nearby.[383] The country club eventually closed because of financial difficulties—it was succeeded by the New Orleans Country Club—but nevertheless, the surrounding neighborhood boomed residentially from the 1940s through the 1960s.[384] It became home to some of city's wealthiest families, including Edgar and Edith Stern. Edgar was a New Orleans cotton broker and his wife an heiress to the Sears Roebuck fortune. They were well-known philanthropists and beneficiaries of Dillard University.

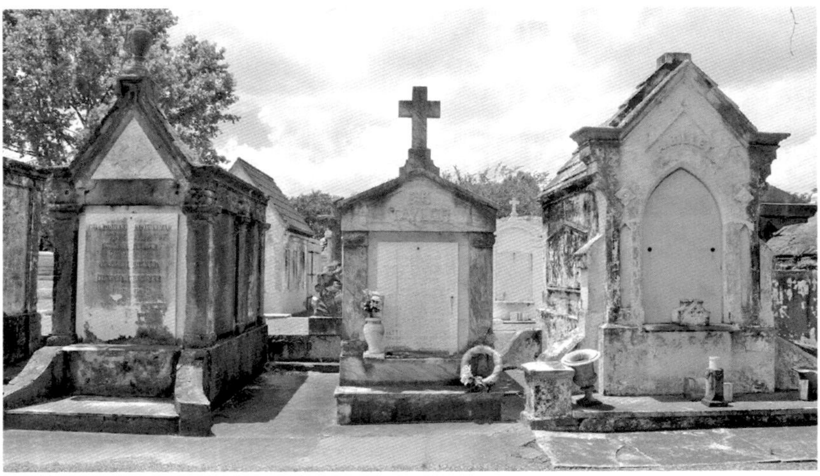

Confederate general Richard Taylor's tomb (center) in Metairie Cemetery. General Taylor was the son of United States president Zachary Taylor. *Photo by author.*

The Sterns named their Lakewood mansion Longue Vue after the teahouse on the Hudson River where they had gotten engaged.[385] After hiring famed landscape architect Ellen Biddle Shipman to design their gardens, Edith Stern was disappointed that her home had limited views of the grounds. She had the house lifted and a new one constructed in the center of the colorful oasis. Today, the LONGUE VUE HOUSE AND GARDENS are open for public tours. Among the many rooms visitors can admire are the Blue Room, the Art Gallery and the Drawing Room, which once hosted Eleanor Roosevelt and John and Robert Kennedy, among many other cultural and political icons.[386]

Festivals and Events

In addition to its regular tours, Longue Vue has several annual fundraising events, including the Essence of Style Design Symposium, which features speakers in the fields of interior design, horticulture and art. Longue Vue also organizes educational field trips, garden-based activities in its Discovery Garden for children and rotating art exhibits.

WEST END

A Note on Identity

When New Orleans' lakefront first developed, West End was called "New Lake End" to distinguish it from "Old Lake End" (which was also known as "Milneburg").[387] Some refer to this area as "West Lakeview."

At the Heart of It

At the heart of this neighborhood are its marinas, restaurants and yacht clubs. Clad in bathing suits and beachwear, boaters retreat in West End after long days in the sun. The neighborhood has a history of revelry and as a port. It was established in the 1830s after the excavation of the New Basin Canal, which ran along today's West End Boulevard. Guided by the New Canal Lighthouse, schooners loaded with lumber, fruit and bricks reached the canal from Lake Pontchartrain and used it to carry goods to the city's new American Sector (today's Central Business District).[388]

In the neighborhood's early days, only canal workers, rowers and yachters—including members of the Southern Yacht Club, which began practicing on Lake Pontchartrain in 1857—visited the West End.[389] After the city built a one-hundred-foot-wide wooden boardwalk here, however, it grew into a bustling resort that competed with counterparts at the Spanish Fort and in Milneburg.[390] During its heyday, from the 1880s to the 1920s, West End boasted a hotel, gardens, restaurant, confectionery shop and boardwalk rides. Visitors rode the Ferris wheel and danced to the music of New Orleans' early jazz greats at the pavilion here.[391] Joe "King" Oliver wrote his "West End Blues" about the neighborhood.[392]

In 1921, as part of the Lakefront Reclamation Project, the city removed West End's boardwalk, constructed a seawall five hundred feet into the lake and filled in the space to create West End Park.[393] Lined with oaks and rose arbors, the park featured walking paths, a bandstand and a fountain where children swam.[394] Residential development around the park began soon after it was completed in the 1920s, while the rest of the neighborhood stayed rural—home mostly to fishermen and trappers. West End's southern side boomed in the 1960s and '70s, after the New Basin Canal—which had isolated the neighborhood from the rest of Lakeview—was filled in.[395]

While the West End neighborhood grew, however, its shoreline became polluted as the city dredged up shells in the lake, and oil and gas companies began drilling here. In 1979, "No swimming" advisories were posted along the lake's former beaches. A decade later, frustrated locals organized and formed the Lake Pontchartrain Basin Foundation (LPBF), dedicated to restoring the lake's health.[396] The LPBF lobbied quickly, and in 1990, shell dredging was banned here. An oil and gas moratorium on new drilling followed in 1991.[397]

Hurricane Katrina created new challenges for the West End community in 2005. The storm decimated much of the neighborhood with more than ten feet of water, and even though the man-made lakefront was elevated, winds slanted the historic lighthouse to one side and a fire destroyed the historic Southern Yacht Club clubhouse here.[398] LPBF surfaced from the storm with a broadened sense of purpose. In 2006, it signed a lease to restore the lighthouse as a museum and education center. That same year, Lake Pontchartrain was removed from the Department of Environmental Quality's Impaired Waterbodies list.[399]

Today, the Southern Yacht Club has a new clubhouse, and the New Canal Lighthouse Museum welcomes visitors on guided tours that reveal the history of West End, the New Basin Canal and Lake Pontchartrain. LPBF is now working on saving Louisiana's wetlands, as well as continuing to advocate for the lake's wellness. Out on the water,

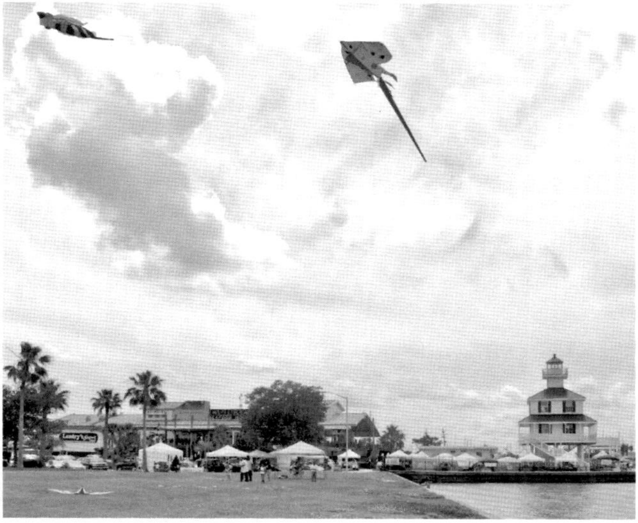

The New Canal Lighthouse Museum preserves the history and protects the future of the West End neighborhood and Lake Pontchartrain. *Photo by author.*

people sail, fish and do sports before relaxing over food and drinks at LANDRY'S, THE BLUE CRAB and BRISBI'S.

Festivals and Events

The LPBF hosts annual Spring Sweep and Fall Beach Sweep events, during which volunteers help clean up areas that drain into the lake. It also coordinates the Save Our Lake and Coast Fishing Rodeo, as well as an annual Arts and Crafts Fair that features local artwork and décor.

The Southern Yacht Club organizes more than ten regattas on Lake Pontchartrain each year and a series of club events, including Twilight Racing on Fridays.

LAKEVIEW

A Note on Identity

Many refer to Lakeview as the area of the city that is bounded by Robert E. Lee Boulevard, Orleans Avenue, City Park Avenue and West End Boulevard. This encompasses the city's Navarre and Lakeview neighborhoods.

At the Heart of It

Families have been at the heart of Lakeview since it first developed in the 1900s. Before that, the neighborhood was low-lying swampland, avoided until the 1830s, when the New Basin Canal was excavated along present-day West End Boulevard. Schooners coming in from Lake Pontchartrain used the canal to bring goods like lumber, fruit and bricks to the city's new American Sector (today's Central Business District). Land surrounding the canal was drained after the turn of the century, and slowly, people began moving here.[400] In the 1920s, ST. DOMINIC CHURCH AND SCHOOL and MOUNT CARMEL ACADEMY opened to serve the neighborhood's growing population.[401]

In its early neighborhood days, Lakeview was still very rural and the canal still in use. Jill Varisco, a second-generation Lakeview resident, still remembers her father's stories about jumping into the New Basin behind boats stacked high with watermelons and shimmying off some of the fruit for himself. Decades later, when Varisco was growing up in Lakeview in the 1950s and '60s, she said that she had snakes in her yard and that her neighbor raised chickens. Her best friend lived on the other side of the bushes then, and her parents would call her in from riding her bike with a whistle.

In those years, Lakeview's brick, ranch-style homes became increasingly popular among the city's suburb-seeking whites.[402] Young families flocked to the neighborhood, and its Harrison Avenue became the center of town, boasting theaters, restaurants and St. Dominic's famed school dances. Racist deed covenants barred African Americans from Lakeview, and even as the city became majority-black in the 1970s, the neighborhood remained racially homogenous.[403] Many of the children who grew up here either stayed or came back to raise their own families. Because of its low elevation and proximity to the Seventeenth Street Canal levees, which breached during Hurricane Katrina, Lakeview was one of the few historically white and upper-middle-class neighborhoods to significantly flood during the storm.

When Katrina hit in 2005, Lakeview homes—including Varisco's and her father's—were pummeled with more than ten feet of water.[404] Many lost everything. "I cried for months about the photos and about losing my grandmother's furniture that I wanted to pass on to my children," Varisco said. "Until finally my daughter said, 'Mom, you've got to stop crying because none of us wanted that furniture anyway.'" The Variscos were displaced for two years, first coming home on the day their daughter Michel married Saints player Steve Gleason. "She wanted to get dressed in the

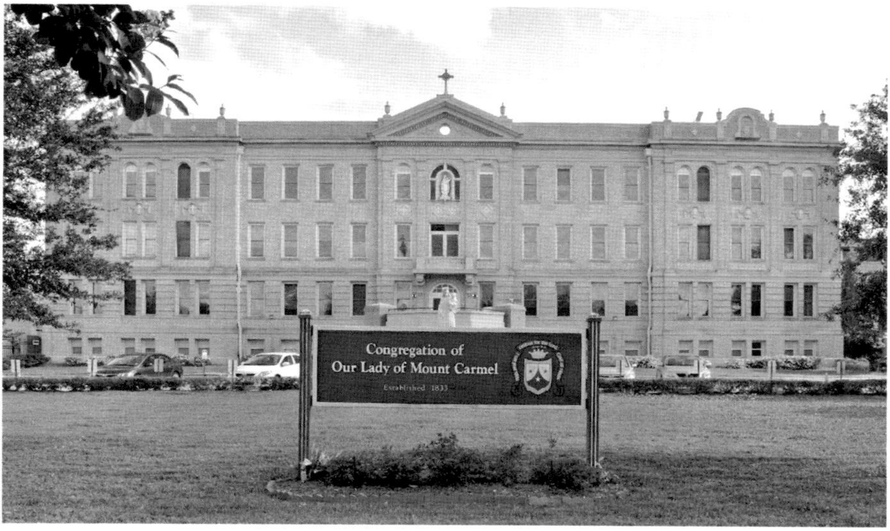

Mount Carmel moved to the Lakeview neighborhood from Treme in the 1920s. *Photo by Mitchell Mendis.*

house," Varisco said. "It was totally empty, but we got a couple picnic tables and chairs, put them in the living room and made it happen."

While some Lakeview families never returned after Hurricane Katrina, those who did had resources. As a result, Lakeview bounced back faster than most of the other neighborhoods that the storm crushed. On many streets, new grandiose homes have replaced brick ranches that had to be demolished. Today, Lakeview again thrives as a sought-out community among the city's young families. Home to many schools, it was in the top ten most-searched zip codes nationwide on Realtor.com in 2014.[405]

Festivals and Events

On the second Wednesday of the months March through June, generations of neighbors reconnect at the outdoor Harrison Avenue Marketplace, a family event with live music and more than seventy-five local vendors.

Each year, the Lakeview Civic Improvement Association hosts Taste at the Lake, a celebration of food, music, wine and community that also raises funds for local projects.

LAKESHORE/LAKE VISTA

A Note on Identity

Lakeshore and Lake Vista are the names of subdivisions located between Robert E. Lee Boulevard, Lakeshore Drive and Bayou St. John. Lakeshore is split into east and west parts.

At the Heart of It

From New Orleans' founding through the 1820s, explorers, settlers and tradesmen came to city by way of the Gulf, Lake Pontchartrain and Bayou St. John.[406] Lake Vista is adjacent to where the lake and bayou meet, and during Spanish rule, it was viewed as a point of access to the city that needed to be defended.[407] A brick fort was built here in 1770, although it saw little action until the War of 1812, when New Orleans' new American government used it to prevent a British attack.[408]

In the 1820s, the government sold the old Spanish Fort to an investor, who built a hotel here. Within half a century, the area blossomed into a lakefront haven, complete with a casino, restaurants, cabarets and a theater famous for its operas.[409] The resort competed with those at Milneburg and West End, and like its counterparts, it hosted some of New Orleans' earliest jazz legends.[410] In the 1930s, Spanish Fort was turned into a park during the Lakefront Reclamation Project. The Orleans Levee Board deepened the lakefront coast with seawalls and used new man-made land for recreational and residential development.[411]

The Lake Vista subdivision was among the first of those residential developments to open, and when it did in 1938, it was unlike any other neighborhood in New Orleans.[412] It is still completely unique today. Shaped like a wagon wheel, Lake Vista's roads all lead inward to the neighborhood's center, which boasts a park, Lake Vista United Methodist Church, St. Pius X Church and School, the Lake Vista Community Center and small businesses. Streets are named after birds—Crane, Dove, Egret, Flamingo—and are laid out behind each row of homes, while landscaped "lanes" connect front yards. As a result, children in Lake Vista can play outside and visit one another's homes without crossing a single street.

After World War II, while families settled into their new Lake Vista homes, two military hospitals operated where today's Lakeshore developments stand.[413] When a new veterans hospital opened downtown in 1952, the

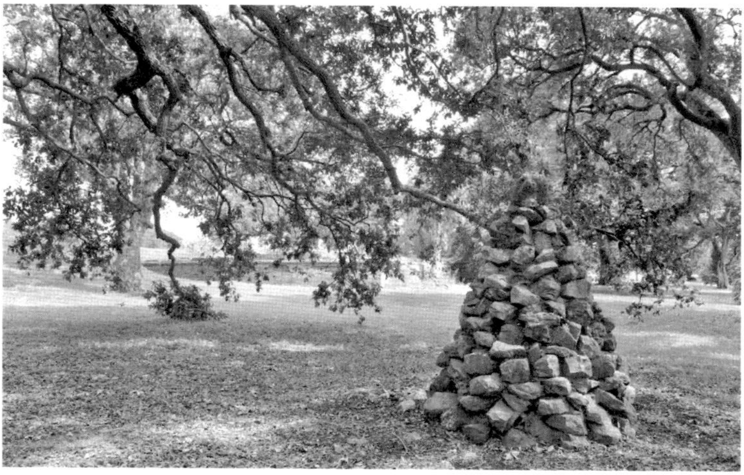

Traces of the Old Spanish Fort's days as a resort. *Photo by Mitchell Mendis.*

Lakeshore area was subdivided and its streets named for jewels.[414] Mardi Gras innovator and float builder Blaine Kern visited Europe around that time and came back inspired by the many fountains he'd seen on his travels.[415] He convinced the levee board president of the value of having a MARDI GRAS FOUNTAIN on the new lakefront, and in 1962, the project was dedicated in the Lakeshore neighborhood.[416]

Today, East and West Lakeshore and Lake Vista are some of the city's wealthiest and most private subdivisions.[417] These neighborhoods are on elevated, man-made land, and flooding here during Hurricane Katrina ranged from less than one foot to six feet, with the worst of the damage being along Robert E. Lee Boulevard.[418] While the storm brought challenges to this community, residents were able to rebuild much faster than the surrounding Lakeview District neighborhoods. Almost 90 percent of homes receiving mail before the storm were again receiving mail in June 2008.[419] In 2014, the Orleans Levee Board and Kern Studios finished restoring the Mardi Gras Fountain, which now features ninety-eight ceramic tile plaques displaying the crests of the city's Carnival krewes. On spring and summer days, families picnic and cast lines from the benches along the lake's coast, while people sail and do watersports down below.

Festivals and Events

The Lake Vista Garden Club hosts an annual spring barbecue and Easter Egg Hunt, as well as a Halloween Party.

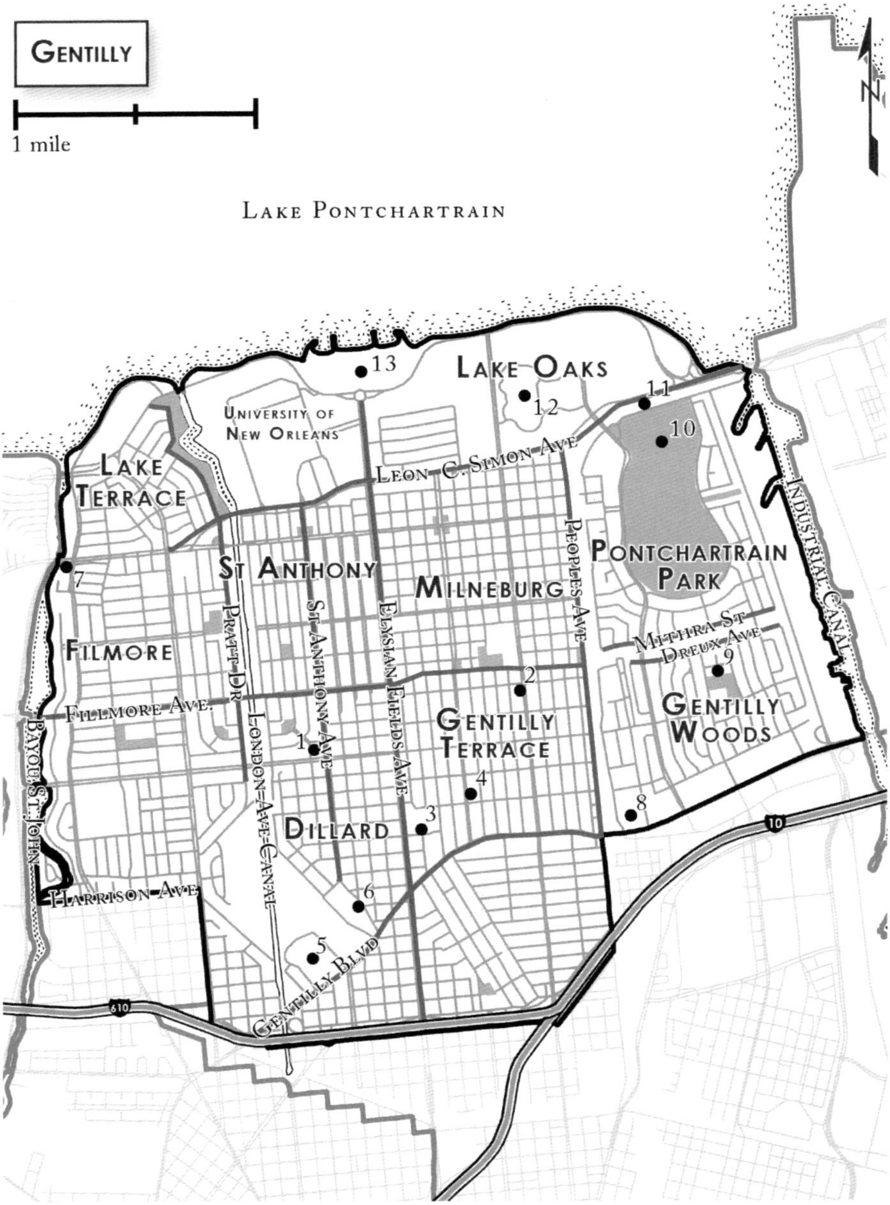

Gentilly
1 mile
Lake Pontchartrain
Lake Oaks
University of New Orleans
Lake Terrace
Leon C. Simon Ave
St Anthony
Milneburg
Pontchartrain Park
Industrial Canal
Peoples Ave
Pratt Dr
St Anthony Ave
Elysian Fields Ave
Filmore
Mithra St
Dreux Ave
Fillmore Ave
Gentilly Terrace
Gentilly Woods
Bayou St John
London Ave Canal
Dillard
Harrison Ave
Gentilly Blvd
610
10
1
2
3
4
5
6
7
8
9
10
11
12
13

Chapter 8

Gentilly

MAP KEY

Milneburg
1. Beacon Light International Baptist Church
2. Old Milne Boys Home/NORD

Gentilly Terrace
3. Brother Martin High School
4. Old Gentilly Terrace Company House

Dillard
5. Dillard University
6. Mount Olivet Cemetery

Filmore
7. Holy Trinity Greek Orthodox Cathedral

Gentilly Woods
8. New Orleans Baptist Theological Seminary
9. St. Gabriel the Archangel Roman Catholic Church

Pontchartrain Park
10. Joseph M. Bartholomew Golf Course
11. Southern University of New Orleans

Lake Terrace/Lake Oaks
12. UNO Lakefront Arena
13. UNO Research and Technology Park

MILNEBURG (ST. ANTHONY AND MILNEBURG)

A Note on Identity

The historic Milneburg community along New Orleans' lakeshore encompassed both the present-day St. Anthony and Milneburg neighborhoods. It was known colloquially as "Old Lake End."

At the Heart of It

At the heart of these neighborhoods is their shared, rich history as New Orleans' first lakefront suburb. Until the 1920s and '30s, when the city extended the coast here by a half mile into the water, present-day Leon C. Simon Boulevard marked the shoreline.[420] In the early 1800s, trade ships from Biloxi, Mobile and Pensacola could much more easily navigate to Lake Pontchartrain through the Rigolets than they could steer against the tide of the long and winding Mississippi River. As a result, the lakeshore became an important early harbor for New Orleans. The hardest part of the journey for arriving ships was taking Bayou St. John and the Carondelet Canal from the lake to the city proper's "back door."[421]

In the 1820s, New Orleans businessmen proposed the construction of Pontchartrain Railroad along Elysian Fields Avenue as a solution.[422] In a few short years, the men secured a charter for the railroad, bought out five plantation owners along the proposed route and started construction.[423] Alexander Milne, a Scottish immigrant and plantation owner who had dreams of developing the shoreline, eagerly obliged to selling this portion of his large lakefront plot.[424] The area was founded as "Milneburg" in 1831. That same year, the Pontchartrain Railroad was completed, and an official port opened at the lake.[425]

From 1831 through the 1850s, thousands of people who came to New Orleans by boat took the Pontchartrain Railroad from the lake to the city proper.[426] Many stayed at Milneburg's Washington Hotel, which became the community's social epicenter.[427] Whitewashed, raised camps were built along the water, and restaurants and saloons opened on both sides of the tracks.[428] The Pontchartrain Railroad's locomotives were powered by steam and soon earned the nickname "Smoky Mary."[429]

When other railroads started connecting eastern cities with New Orleans' riverside in the 1850s, Smoky Mary lost its historic significance.

Instead of carrying visitors and cargo arriving to New Orleans by ship, it took locals and tourists from the Marigny to Milneburg, which began developing as a resort town. By the 1880s, it had evolved into a sought-out entertainment district where many early jazz greats played. Jelly Roll Morton, Leon Roppolo and Paul Mare even wrote their famous "Milneburg Joys" about the cultural metropolis.

Milneburg's resort days came to an end in the late 1930s, when the city's Lakefront Reclamation Plan was put into action. The Orleans Levee Board deepened the coast and used new land for recreational and residential development, as well as to build seawalls and strengthen the city's levee system.[430] Old camps and bathhouses were demolished, and Smoky Mary's service ended in 1932. The post–World War II ranch-style homes subsequently erected here left no trace of the city's oldest lakeside town.[431]

At the same time that Milne's namesake suburb was reinvented, his estate opened the MILNE BOYS HOME here, a residential facility for troubled youth.[432] Over the next several decades, hundreds of children ages eight to sixteen benefited from its programs. Meanwhile, beginning in the 1970s, descendants of New Orleans' Creoles of color moved from riverfront neighborhoods of the Seventh, Eighth and Ninth Wards to lakeside neighborhoods in these

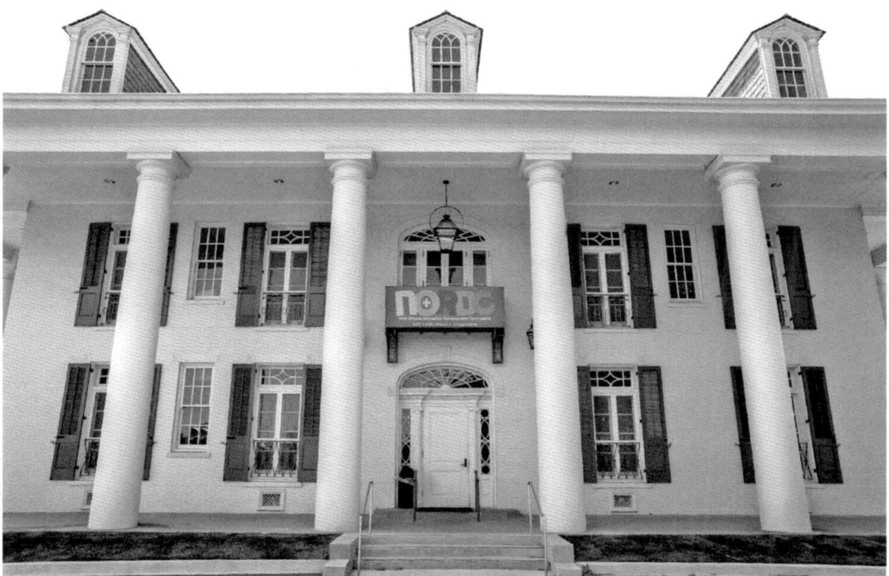

The New Orleans Recreation Development Commission headquarters is on the grounds of the former Milne Boys Home. *Photo by Bruce Cervini.*

same jurisdictions, including St. Anthony and Milneburg. In 2000, St. Anthony was one of New Orleans' most racially integrated neighborhoods.[433] Milneburg was predominantly African American and had a 71 percent homeownership rate (the city's average was 46.5 percent).[434] At the core of the community was the Beacon Light International Baptist Church, which had a congregation of nine thousand members by 2004.[435]

When Hurricane Katrina hit, St. Anthony and Milneburg experienced some of the worst flooding in the city. Breaches in the Industrial Canal and London Avenue Canal levees, along with the swelling of Lake Pontchartrain, devastated the majority of land here with more than ten feet of water.[436] Today, homeownership rates have dropped dramatically, and many have not returned.[437] Rebuilding is still in progress, but in 2014, a "beacon" of hope finally emerged: after nine years and seven bank loan denials, the Beacon Light International Baptist again opened its doors in the neighborhood.[438]

After the storm, the seven antebellum-style buildings on the Milne Boys Home campus were left abandoned, with easy access for squatters.[439] Addicts and homeless people took refuge here until 2012, when FEMA allotted millions in state and city funds to repair the campus.[440] In 2014, the New Orleans Recreation Development Commission consolidated its three offices into one headquarters on the former Boys Home grounds. The facility also supports the city's NOLA for LIFE murder reduction initiative.

Festivals and Events

Beacon Light International Baptist offers the Financial Peace University program, a biblically based curriculum that coaches participants on how to get out of debt and invest in the future. The church also hosts Family Night and Bible study regularly.

GENTILLY TERRACE

A Note on Identity

The city and the Historic District Landmarks Commission have different boundaries for Gentilly Terrace, which got its name from the Gentilly

Terrace Company, which developed the land here. This essay focuses on the area between Fillmore Avenue, I-610, Elysian Fields Avenue and Peoples Avenue.

At the Heart of It

At the heart of Gentilly Terrace is the historic Gentilly Ridge—a quarter-mile-wide, elevated stretch of land that runs through the neighborhood's center along present-day Gentilly Boulevard.[441] The Gentilly Ridge formed thousands of years ago, when a Mississippi River distributary went through the area and created a natural levee here out of sediment.[442] When European settlers first explored the Mississippi Gulf Coast, this ridge formed a convenient west–east passageway through the swamps.[443]

Beginning in 1727, plantations were developed along the Gentilly Ridge.[444] When the Pontchartrain Railroad's Smoky Mary began running down Elysian Fields Avenue through the future Gentilly Terrace in the 1830s, the ridge hosted one of its three stops. The old plantation house here was converted into a bunkhouse for railroad employees, and a small community formed near the tracks.[445] In 1862, the Confederate army even built a fort near where BROTHER MARTIN HIGH SCHOOL stands today to prevent Union

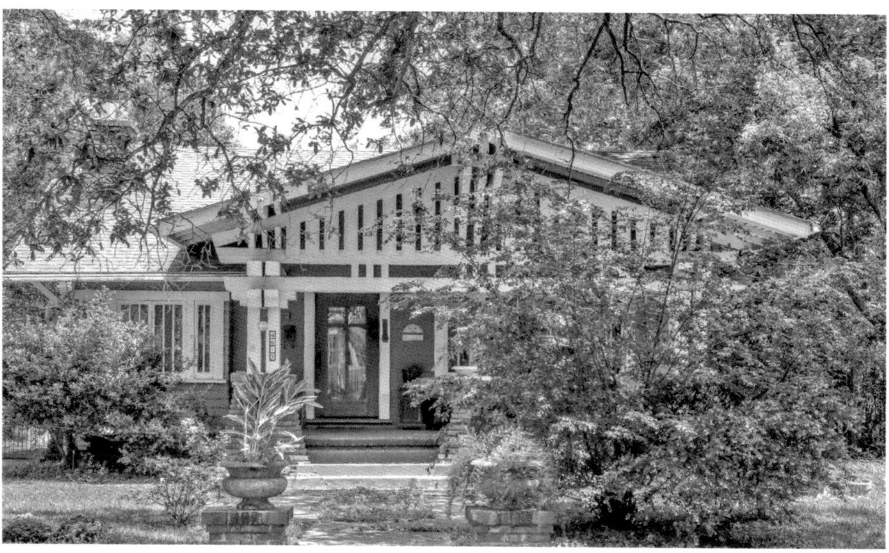

Built as the GENTILLY TERRACE COMPANY HOUSE in 1912, this bungalow on St. Roch Avenue is widely regarded as the finest Craftsman home in Louisiana. *Photo by Bruce Cervini.*

Soldiers from entering New Orleans via the railroad. No trace of this early neighborhood history remains.[446]

In the early 1900s, while much of today's Gentilly District was still poorly drained, developers turned this section of the ridge into the Gentilly Terrace neighborhood. Homes here were advertised as being "built on hills," and some even sat on man-made mounds on top of the already elevated ridge.[447] By the 1930s, the neighborhood boasted the largest collection of California Craftsman–style bungalows in the state—a status it still holds today—as well as English cottages and Spanish Mediterranean Revival–style raised houses, all with front yards.[448] In its early years, Gentilly Terrace was an all-white neighborhood, and residents protested the opening of the neighboring Dillard University in 1935.[449]

While middle-class African Americans had already settled in the Dillard, Sugar Hill and Pontchartrain Park neighborhoods in the 1940s and 1960s, it wasn't until the 1970s that members of this community began moving to the Gentilly District in droves.[450] Gentilly Terrace became an integrated neighborhood in the decades before Hurricane Katrina. And when the storm hit and decimated most of the surrounding areas, Gentilly Terrace's elevation, while ever so slight, saved much of the neighborhood from destruction.

Festivals and Events

Gentilly Terrace and Gardens Improvement Association hosts an annual ice cream party in July and a holiday potluck in December.

DILLARD

A Note on Identity

The city's Dillard neighborhood is named for Dillard University, which has been located here since 1935. The area between Gentilly Boulevard, Florida Avenue, Elysian Fields Avenue and A.P. Tureaud Avenue (some of which is in the city's St. Roch) is known as "Sugar Hill."

At the Heart of It

At the heart of the Dillard neighborhood is DILLARD UNIVERSITY, a historically black private college chartered in 1930. This oak-lined campus, complete with brick, Classic Revival–style architecture, opened in Gentilly at a time when there was only one public high school for African Americans in New Orleans.[451] Throughout the Deep South, many black youth were still learning in one-room wooden schools.[452]

When classes commenced in Gentilly, Dillard had an immediate impact on the neighborhood and the broader African American community in New Orleans. While many other institutions nationwide focused on providing African Americans with an industrial education—a model that some whites preferred because it would keep African Americans as part of the working class—Dillard University had a liberal arts curriculum with an emphasis on music and drama.[453] Within its first decade, Dillard began hosting a major arts festival where local and national artists could "enjoy and debate the nature of African American art—past, present and future."[454]

In the 1940s, black businessmen, pharmacists, doctors and Dillard professors settled south of Gentilly Boulevard in what came to be known as Sugar Hill.[455] Sugar Hill was on the Gentilly Ridge, elevated land that was built up thousands of years earlier, when a Mississippi River distributary created a natural levee here.[456] The migration of black professionals to Sugar Hill attracted other middle-class African Americans to Gentilly over the next half century.[457] Albert W. Dent was president of the university for much of

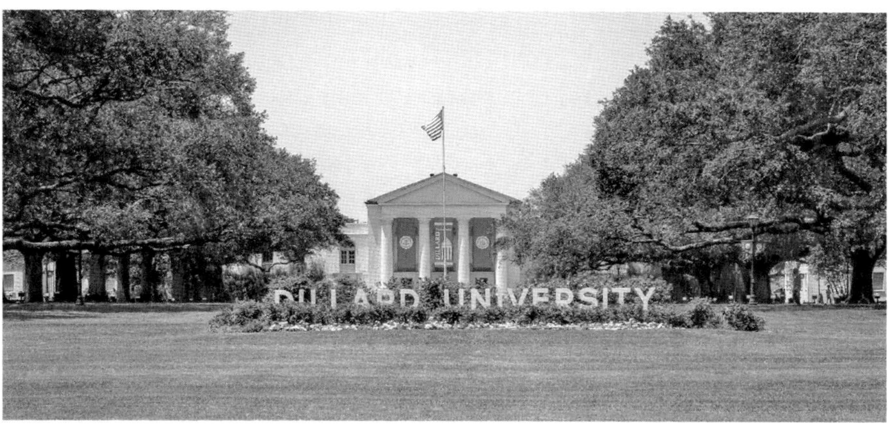

When the historically black Dillard University was chartered in 1930, there was only one public high school for African Americans in New Orleans. *Photo by Bruce Cervini.*

that time and led the community through "the challenging decades of World War II, the Civil Rights Movement and the Black Power movement."[458] In the 1970s, the city destroyed homes and divided Sugar Hill when it erected the I-610 overpass through the neighborhood.[459]

Despite this disruption, Dillard University continued to thrive. In the last few decades, its National Center for Black-Jewish Relations and International Center for Economic Freedom have earned worldwide recognition.[460] As Dillard made recent history, African American community stalwarts were laid to rest at the nearby MOUNT OLIVET CEMETERY (established in 1920). Two among many were R&B legend Henry Roeland Byrd (known as Professor Longhair) in 1980 and Louis Westerfield, the first African American law school dean at Ole Miss, in 1996.[461]

In the month before Hurricane Katrina, Dillard University named its first female president, Dr. Marvalene Hughes. When the storm hit, flooding reached seven to eight feet in the northern and southern parts of the Dillard neighborhood, while the elevated area near Gentilly Boulevard—including much of Sugar Hill—was spared.[462] Between damage and business interruption, Dillard University suffered a loss of $400 million.[463] Yet compared to many other areas in Gentilly, which were devastated by Lake Pontchartrain's swell and levee breaches in the London Avenue Canal, the university and the neighborhood came out of the crisis in a much better position to rebuild.[464]

And so they did. Dillard's ridge of elevated land became an island of hope in the vastly devastated Gentilly District. At the university, President Hughes launched an aggressive fundraising campaign and succeeded in opening a new Professional Schools and Sciences Building and Student Union–Recreation Center, both of which are LEED® registered.[465] Dillard continues to promote "cultural enlightenment and participation" among Gentilly residents and all New Orleanians with regular festivals, lectures and art exhibits.[466]

Festivals and Events

The Dillard University President's Lecture Series, called "Brain Food," is a tradition that dates back to Dillard's founding (although the name has changed). Speakers have included Eleanor Roosevelt, Thurgood Marshall, Mary McLeod Bethune, Martin Luther King Jr. and Jackie Robinson. The campus also hosts an annual International Arts & Music Festival complete with entertainment, art and cuisine from countries around the world.

FILMORE

A Note on Identity

The city's Filmore neighborhood is bounded by Bayou St. John, Robert E. Lee Boulevard, the London Avenue Canal and Harrison Avenue. Many who live here simply say they live in Gentilly.

At the Heart of It

For more than a century after New Orleans' founding, settlers, traders and adventurers used Bayou St. John to access the city's "back door."[467] An alternative route to the long and winding Mississippi River, the bayou provided access from Lake Pontchartrain to the Esplanade Ridge (and eventually the Carondelet Canal), which led to the rear of the French Quarter.[468] Every one of these travelers passed by the present-day Filmore neighborhood, which despite this nearby traffic was low-lying and had little opportunity for growth.

In the 1860s and '70s, the London Avenue Canal was dredged along the Filmore's eastern border, but this did not effectively drain the area.[469] In fact, Filmore did not become a neighborhood until the mid-1900s, after drainage here was improved.[470] Beginning in the 1940s, residential subdivisions of California bungalows and Craftsman cottages were built here. Filmore was fully developed within twenty years, and in the 1950s it welcomed its iconic HOLY TRINITY CATHEDRAL.[471] Holy Trinity traces its roots to the first Greek Orthodox congregation in the Americas, first established in Treme in 1867.[472]

From the 1970s through the turn of the century, as descendants of New Orleans' Creoles of color moved from riverfront neighborhoods of the Seventh, Eighth and Ninth Wards to lakeside neighborhoods in these same jurisdictions, Filmore became one of the city's most integrated neighborhoods.[473] When Katrina hit, it was also one of New Orleans' most stable, with an average household income far exceeding the city's average and a homeownership rate of more than 85 percent.[474] Directly next to the breached levees of the London Avenue Canal, however, Filmore experienced some of the worst flooding in the city. The neighborhood's one-story bungalows and cottages were decimated with more than ten feet of water.[475]

While the most recent homeownership rates and income levels are still high in Filmore compared to the city's average, many Filmore residents have

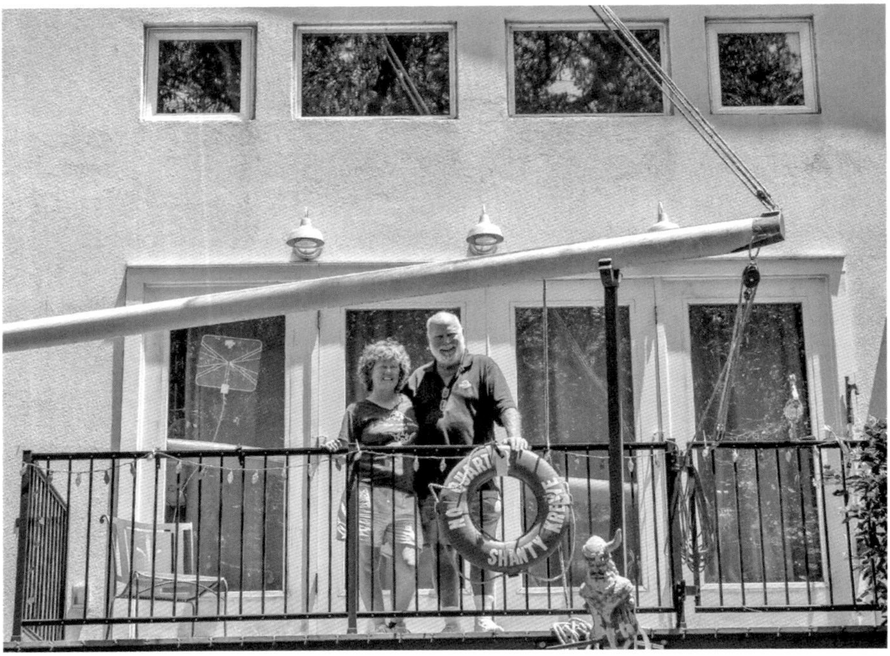

K.C. and Kathleen King, who lost their Filmore home during Hurricane Katrina, modeled their new house to look like a boat. *Photo by Bruce Cervini.*

not come back, and some are still rebuilding today.[476] K.C. and Kathleen King, who started from scratch on their devastated lot on Pratt Drive, have made a statement with their new home. Its aquatic theme is complete with a three-story sail mast and a submarine control room mural; its first level starts at nine feet, just above the artistically labeled Katrina flood line. K.C. is a vocal advocate of creating a shared neighborhood safety vision. He is known to invite awestruck passersby inside to hear his story.

Festivals and Events

Each Memorial Day weekend, the Holy Trinity Cathedral hosts the New Orleans Greek Fest, complete with traditional Greek food and drinks, performances by the Hellenic Dancers, tours of the cathedral and live music.

GENTILLY WOODS

A Note on Identity

Gentilly Woods is bounded by Peoples Avenue, the Industrial Canal, Dreux Avenue and Gentilly Boulevard. Many who live here simply say they live in Gentilly.

At the Heart of It

In the early 1800s, Scottish brick manufacturer Alexander Milne owned a huge lakeside plot that he hoped to develop and which included present-day Gentilly Woods.[477] The neighborhood was swampland then, and although much of the land to its west developed over the next century, Gentilly Woods did not see growth until after the Industrial Canal was completed at its east end in 1923. Higgins Industries opened a shipbuilding plant here during World War II, where it produced boats for the D-Day invasion.[478] Workers lived in plywood homes called "Higgins Huts," which veterans were able to rent out immediately following the war.[479]

Beginning in 1950, however, the Higgins Huts were torn down and a new housing development created to attract former GIs.[480] Just three years later, the New Orleans Baptist Theological Seminary moved to the neighborhood from the Garden District.[481] Over the next two decades, the seminary's Georgian Colonial–style campus expanded to more than one hundred buildings, most of them built with stately red brick.[482] As the seminary grew, so did the neighborhood. White, middle-class families moved to Gentilly Woods throughout the 1950s and '60s, and the Gentilly Woods Shopping Center, a thirteen-acre mall with an "ultramodern Sears" and ample parking space, opened to accommodate the new suburb. Nearby, St. Gabriel the Archangel Roman Catholic Church became the neighborhood's main parish.

While middle-class African Americans had already settled in the Pontchartrain Park neighborhood just north of Gentilly Woods, it wasn't until the 1970s that members of this community—many of them descendants of New Orleans' Creoles of color—began moving to the Gentilly District in droves.[483] Gentilly Woods became an integrated neighborhood in the decades before Hurricane Katrina, closely reflecting the city's racial demographics.[484] When the storm hit, the neighborhood was flooded from all sides. Levee breaches in the Industrial and London Avenue Canals, along

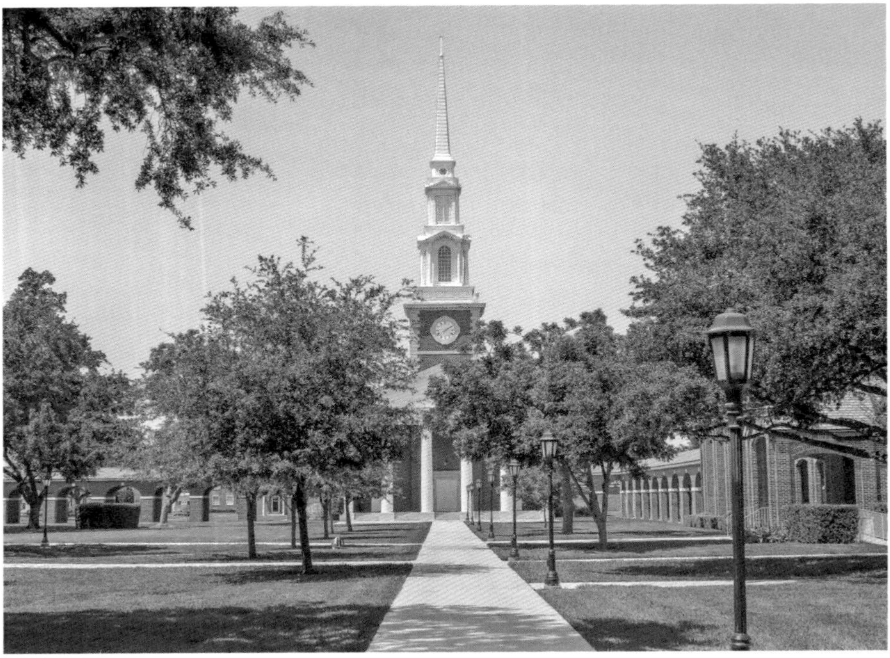

Leavell Chapel at New Orleans Baptist Theological Seminary. *Photo by Bruce Cervini.*

with the swelling of Lake Pontchartrain, devastated Gentilly Woods with more than ten feet of water.[485]

Rebuilding in Gentilly Woods has been a decade-long challenge. While the neighboring Gentilly Terrace boasts a 92.5 percent recovery rate, based on the number of addresses receiving mail there in June 2005 and June 2014, Gentilly Woods is behind at 77.1 percent.[486] A patchwork of abandoned and rebuilt properties, the neighborhood welcomed the 2014 opening of a Walmart where the Gentilly Woods Shopping Center once stood. Before Walmart's opening, this was one of the largest blighted properties in post-Katrina New Orleans.[487] Throughout the rebuilding process, St. Gabriel has been committed to helping its parishioners return by organizing volunteers and supplying insulation and sheetrock.[488]

Festivals and Events

The New Orleans Baptist Theological Seminary hosts an annual Fun Fest, complete with a 5K run through campus, lunch and carnival games.

PONTCHARTRAIN PARK

A Note on Identity

Pontchartrain Park is bounded by Peoples Avenue, Leon C. Simon Boulevard, the Industrial Canal and Mithra Street.

At the Heart of It

When it opened in Gentilly in 1955, Pontchartrain Park was the first subdivision in New Orleans designed for African Americans. An island in a sea of white Gentilly suburbs, the development represented a reversal of historic trends.[489] Before Pontchartrain Park's opening, the city relegated African Americans to areas that were undesirable to whites and excluded them from those that were.[490] Instead, Pontchartrain Park was created for the city's growing middle-class African American community, much to the discontent of many whites in the neighboring Gentilly Woods.[491]

When Pontchartrain Park opened in 1955, many of the city's African Americans lived in the projects or in modest shotgun houses without air conditioning or indoor plumbing. The development made the country's new suburban dream accessible to black New Orleanians for the first time.[492] Like Gentilly Woods, it featured two- and three-bedroom, ranch-style homes that boasted modern kitchens, fenced-in yards and driveways.[493] In 1956, the eighteen-hole Lake Pontchartrain Golf Course opened as the neighborhood's centerpiece.[494] Designed by African American golf pro Joseph M. Bartholomew Sr., who also designed the golf courses in Metairie and City Park, it was the only course on which he and other African Americans could play.[495] Today, it is named the JOSEPH M. BARTHOLOMEW GOLF COURSE.

In 1959, SOUTHERN UNIVERSITY OF NEW ORLEANS (SUNO) opened on seventeen acres next to the golf course. In its first year, 15 dedicated faculty members taught 158 African American freshmen in just one building here.[496] By then, doctors, postal employees, contractors, ministers and veterans with loans from the GI Bill had moved to Pontchartrain Park.[497] Neighbors knew one another by name and prided themselves on sharing the same community and family-based values.[498]

Over the next several decades, African Americans—many of them descendants of New Orleans' Creoles of color—integrated Gentilly's

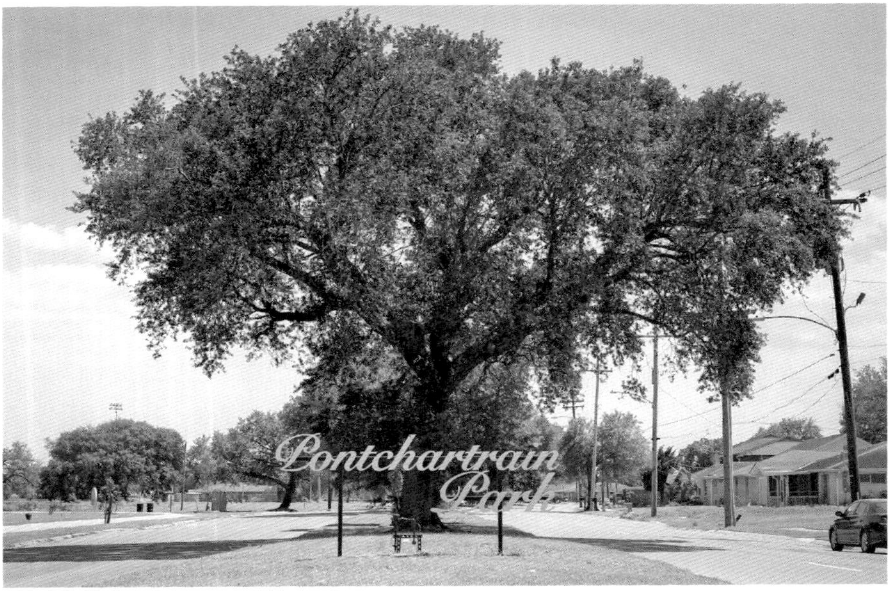

The Pontchartrain Park neighborhood was developed in the 1950s for New Orleans' growing middle-class African American community. *Photo by Bruce Cervini.*

historically white subdivisions. Pontchartrain Park "took on almost a mythical status as the wellspring of prominent New Orleanians, a local Strivers Row."[499] It was home to the fist African American mayor of New Orleans, Ernest "Dutch" Morial, and his son, Marc Morial, who also became mayor and is the president of the National Urban League. The head of the U.S. Environmental Protection Agency, Lisa Jackson, grew up here, as did the city's first African American district attorney, Eddie Jordan Jr. Among many other prominent African Americans, Pontchartrain Park was also home to Grammy Award–winning jazz musician Terence Blanchard and Wendell Pierce, star of HBO's *The Wire* and *Treme*.[500] Both Blanchard and Pierce have been integral to the neighborhood's recovery after Hurricane Katrina.

When Hurricane Katrina hit in 2005, flooding reached the rooftops of homes in Pontchartrain Park throughout the neighborhood. Lake Pontchartrain's swollen waters, combined with levee breaches in the Industrial and London Avenue Canals, left the residential community and SUNO completely devastated.[501] Three years later, while other middle- and upper-class communities were bouncing back, more than 60 percent of Pontchartrain Park's lots stayed vacant.[502] The Road Home Program, which was later ruled discriminatory in a federal court, had bought 110 properties here, many from families who had owned their homes outright but could not justify rebuilding with the insufficient recovery money allocated to them.[503]

Determined to save their old neighborhood, Pierce and Blanchard created the Pontchartrain Park Community Development Corporation and announced that it would buy back all of the vacant Road Home lots with the help of developers, nonprofits and residents.[504] Bureaucratic red tape has made the process difficult, but the CDC has had success. Due partially to Pierce's and Blanchard's efforts, 90 percent of the neighborhood households receiving mail before Katrina were again receiving mail in June 2014.[505] Likewise, SUNO has topped its pre-Katrina enrollment numbers.[506] "We're exercising our right to self-determination," Pierce told the *Times-Picayune*.[507] It's what Pontchartrain Park residents have historically done, after all.

Festivals and Events

Pontchartrain Park is home to Gentilly Festival, an annual three-day festival with live music and local food and art vendors.

LAKE TERRACE/LAKE OAKS

A Note on Identity

Lake Terrace and Lake Oaks are two subdivisions in this broader lakefront area, which is bounded by Lake Pontchartrain, Leon C. Simon Boulevard and Bayou St. John.

At the Heart of It

Today's Lake Terrace and Lake Oaks neighborhoods did not exist until the early twentieth century. Before the city's Lakefront Reclamation Project, present-day Leon C. Simon Boulevard marked New Orleans' shoreline. Seeing an opportunity to create residential and recreational space while also improving flood protection, the Orleans Levee Board deepened the coast here by a half mile in the 1930s.[508] By 1939, Pontchartrain Beach Amusement Park had opened on this new land with its signature ride, a

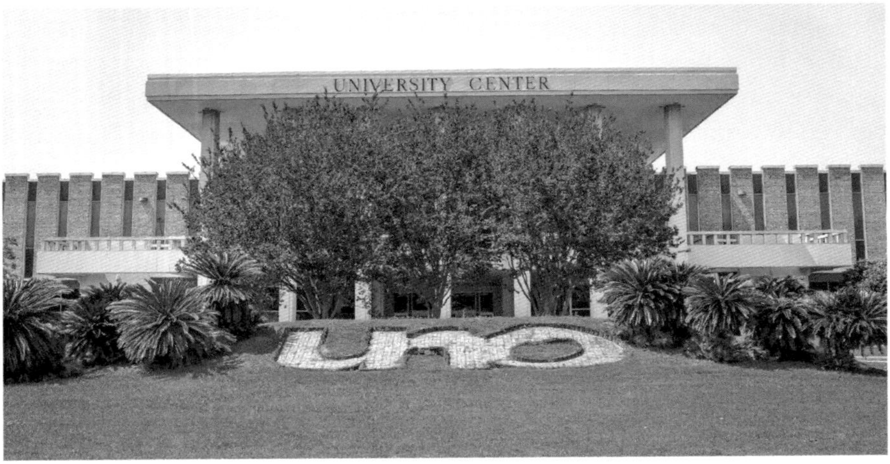

The University of New Orleans' student center. *Photo by Bruce Cervini.*

wooden roller coaster named the Zephyr. That year's Miss New Orleans, Irene Schoenberger, brought a bottle of champagne with her when she christened its tracks at the park's inaugural event.[509]

By the 1960s, the levee board had realized its dream. Lake Terrace and Lake Oaks subdivisions had opened on the new lakefront, and Pontchartrain Beach was a favorite weekend hangout for New Orleanians citywide.[510] From the top of the Zephyr, just before its big drop, thrill-seekers could look over the Louisiana State University of New Orleans. Known today as the University of New Orleans, when it opened on a former U.S. Navy air training facility here in 1958, it was the first racially integrated public university in the South.[511] The university's first class of freshmen reached 1,460 students, doubling the founders' anticipated number.[512]

Unable to keep up with larger amusement parks sprouting up throughout the South, Pontchartrain Beach had its last hurrah in 1983. That year, sixteen thousand students attended the University of New Orleans, which had expanded its campus and academic offerings to include five senior colleges, a junior division and a graduate school.[513] Today, the university's tagline says it is "the heartbeat of the Crescent City." Indeed, many UNO graduates apply what they learn here to better the broader city and state. More than half of the university's seventy thousand alumni live in the Greater New Orleans area.[514] In 2001, UNO expanded its campus along the lakefront. Today its Research and Technology Park stands where Pontchartrain Beach once thrived.[515]

When Hurricane Katrina hit in 2005, Gentilly was one of the city's most devastated districts. Built on man-made, elevated land, much of the lakefront was spared high flooding, but Lake Pontchartrain's swollen waters did rush through and damage the area.[516] While Tulane and Loyola Universities stayed closed throughout the fall 2005 semester, University of New Orleans resumed classes within six weeks.[517] Still, it would face many challenges ahead. Funding cuts and budget deficits after the storm led to layoffs and slashes to academic and recreational programs.[518] Enrollment likewise has dropped significantly; the school reached just more than half of its pre-Katrina student numbers in 2015.[519] Still, the Privateer spirit here remains strong. UNO faculty, staff and students are committed to using the resources available to them to continue benefitting New Orleans and Louisiana.[520]

FESTIVALS AND EVENTS

UNO's LAKEFRONT ARENA hosts tons of festivals and concerts throughout the year, and it is also home to the Privateers men's and women's basketball teams.

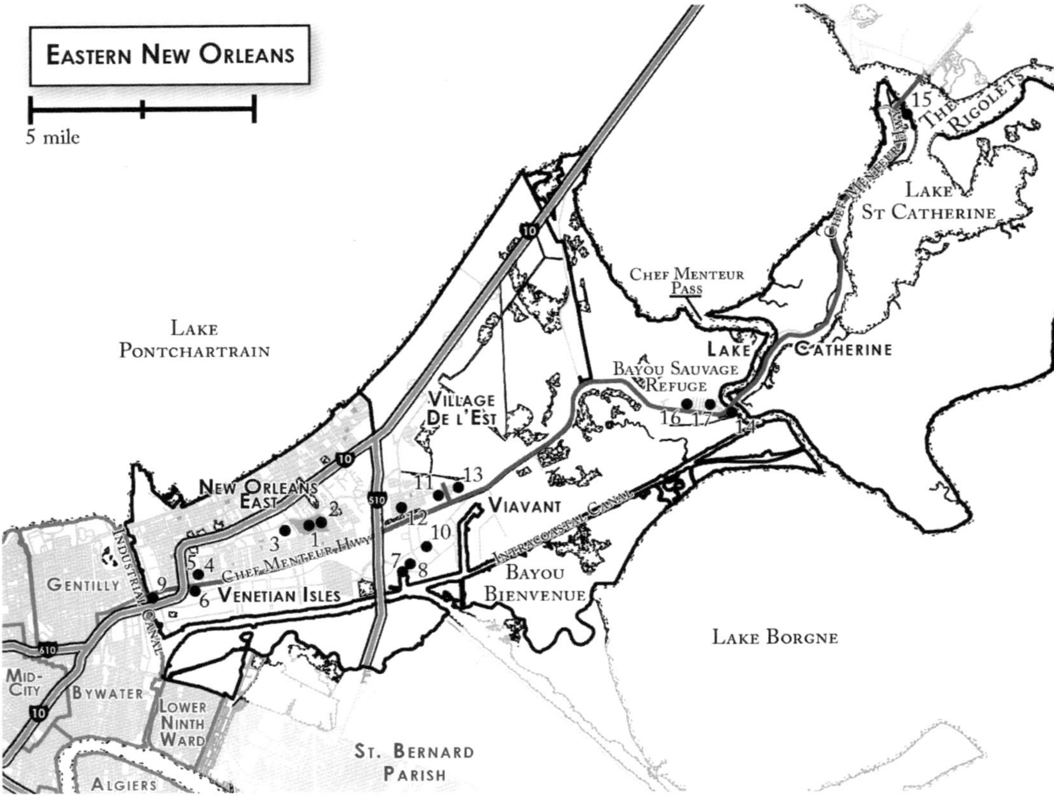

Eastern New Orleans
5 mile
Lake Pontchartrain
New Orleans East
Village De l'Est
Viavant
Venetian Isles
Gentilly
Mid-City
Bywater
Lower Ninth Ward
Algiers
St. Bernard Parish
Bayou Bienvenue
Lake Borgne
Bayou Sauvage Refuge
Chef Menteur Pass
Lake Catherine
Lake St Catherine
The Rigolets
Chef Menteur Hwy
Industrial Canal
Intracoastal Canal
1
2
3
4
5
6
7
8
9
10
11
12
13
14
15
16
17

Chapter 9

Eastern New Orleans

MAP KEY

New Orleans East
1. Joe Brown Memorial Park
2. Louisiana Nature Center
3. New Orleans East Hospital
4. Sisters of the Holy Family
5. St. Mary's Academy
6. St. Paul the Apostle Church and School

Viavant/Venetian Isles
7. Coast Guard Base Support Unit
8. Delgado Maritime, Fire and Industrial Training Facility
9. Folgers Coffee Company
10. NASA Michoud Assembly Facility

Village de l'Est
11. Mary Queen of Vietnam Church
12. Vietnamese American Young Leaders Association of New Orleans
13. Vietnamese Farmers' Market

Lake Catherine
14. Fort Macomb
15. Fort Pike
16. Fort Pike Volunteer Fire House
17. Venetian Isles Development

New Orleans East (Pines Village, Little Woods, West Lake Forest, Plum Orchard, Read Boulevard West and Read Boulevard East)

A Note on Identity

New Orleans East got its name from a land development company called New Orleans East Inc. Before the company cancelled its extensive development plans here after the 1980s oil market crash, it erected a concrete sign bearing its name on Chef Menteur Highway.[521] After that, New Orleans East, or simply "the East," became the moniker for most of Eastern New Orleans. This essay focuses on the neighborhoods between Chef Menteur Highway, Lake Pontchartrain, the Industrial Canal and I-510.

At the Heart of It

In the 1800s, before subdivisions burgeoned throughout these New Orleans East neighborhoods, the area was made up of marshland to the north and a narrow ridge of land along today's Chef Menteur Highway. This ridge had formed thousands of years earlier, when a Mississippi River distributary created a natural levee here out of sediment.[522] Until the 1870s, when railroads started providing access to the city's eastern marshes, this levee was the only way in. With no drained, centralized land on which people could settle, development began along this access route, a pattern that continued throughout the next century.[523]

As historian and geographer Richard Campanella put it, instead of growing "outwardly from an original core" like historic New Orleans, New Orleans East grew "inwardly from a peripheral framework of transportation arteries."[524] The Industrial Canal was one of them. When completed in 1923, it boosted port activity and created jobs at the area's upriver boundary. Meanwhile, clubs and hotels opened to support a new "weekend economy" along the lakefront.[525] Lined with raised, wooden hunting and fishing camps, the lakeshore evolved into a retreat destination.[526] In 1939, a quarter-mile stretch of beach here was reserved as an African American swimming area.[527] By the 1950s, "Lincoln Beach" had grown into a vacation destination for black New Orleanian families. It had an amusement park and featured regular performances by local legends like Fats Domino and the Ink Spots.[528]

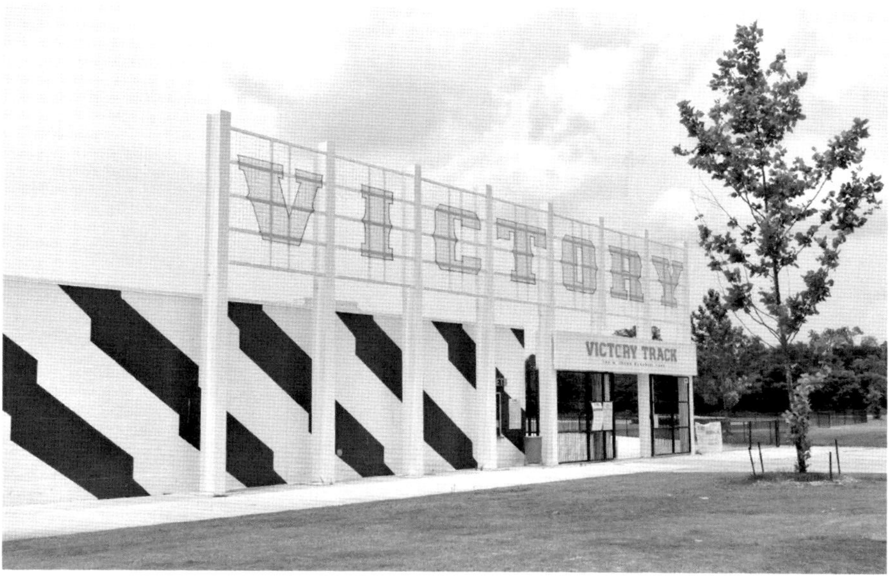

With the support of Nike, Allstate Sugar Bowl and the Brees Dream Foundation, the city dedicated Joe Brown Park's Victory Track and Field in 2012. *Photo by Mitchell Mendis.*

It wasn't until the 1960s, however, that development in New Orleans East really boomed. Instead of hindering growth, Hurricane Betsy helped propel it in 1965 by convincing the city to install hurricane-protection levees here.[529] By this time, NASA had already created hundreds of jobs in the area when it took over the Michoud plant south of Chef Menteur Highway. Brick, ranch-style subdivisions sprouted from the former marsh and were designed with scenic canals and man-made lakes that helped drain the area. Suburb-seeking whites flocked here over the newly built I-10 High Rise bridge and settled.[530]

"It was mostly newlyweds buying these houses, so everyone on the block was having kids at the same time," said Natalie Hooks, who was born in the local Methodist Hospital and grew up in the East in the 1970s and '80s. "There were probably fifteen kids on my block, with no two of us more than seven years apart," she recalled. Hooks still remembers weekends at camps along the lake, when the kids would fish and the parents played cards late into the night. She went on field trips to JOE BROWN MEMORIAL PARK, complete with a recreation center and nature trails, and hung out at the Lake Forest Plaza ice skating rink on the weekends.

At that time, the dreams of developers in Eastern New Orleans stretched all the way to the far end of today's Bayou Sauvage. After the fall of the oil industry in 1985 and '86, however, grand plans came to a screeching halt. As New Orleans became a majority African American city with an African American government, whites who had sought out this "suburb within a city" left Orleans Parish altogether.[531] The oil market crash accelerated their departure, and within one generation, the East went from an almost exclusively white area to an almost exclusively African American area.[532]

Many of the African Americans who first settled here were middle class and Catholic—likely the descendants of New Orleans' Creoles of color.[533] Their faith is evident along Chef Menteur Highway, which is lined by the Sisters of the Holy Family campus, St. Paul the Apostle Church and School and St. Mary's Academy. On the heels of this community came working-class African Americans. In 1990, the Section 8 housing program was established, and many landlords in New Orleans East were approved to provide government-subsidized low-income housing.[534] Residents from the Desire, Florida and St. Thomas housing projects moved to the East when their developments started closing as part of the HOPE IV program.[535]

When Hurricane Katrina hit, New Orleans East was the first area to significantly flood. Rising water in the Industrial Canal leaked through damaged gates on both sides of the I-10 High Rise, and soon levee breaches at the Intracoastal Canal—which runs south of Chef Menteur Highway—let a deluge through.[536] To the north, water from Lake Pontchartrain overtopped a one-mile stretch of floodwall.[537] Much of the East flooded with more than ten feet of water.[538]

A decade after the storm, the East's return rates are low, and rebuilding is still in progress.[539] New homes, playgrounds and schools are couched between blighted properties and abandoned lots. New Orleans East Hospital, formerly Methodist, reopened in 2014, after years of delays and resident pleas.[540] Likewise, the Audubon Institute nearly lost its funding to rehabilitate its Louisiana Nature Center here, after waiting too long to restore the property, which it finally began doing in 2014.[541] Despite its slow recovery, neighbors in New Orleans East know one another by name, and kids again play together in front lawns. New Orleans East's arteries remain strong, and many believe that its pulse will beat loudly once again.

Festivals and Events

Each year, Joe Brown Park hosts the Nola East Friends Fest, which celebrates diversity in the community with food, music and free health screenings. The park also hosts an Easter Eggstravaganza—complete with an egg hunt, face painting and a visit from the Easter Bunny—and a Holiday Celebration in December. Its Back to Nature Heart Walk has become popular among neighbors, as has its annual basketball competition between local church teams, called the Men of Valor Basketball Throwdown.

VIAVANT/VENETIAN ISLES

A Note on Identity

The city calls the area west of Paris Road "Viavant," after the Viavant family, who were major landowners in the area. It refers to the area east of Paris Road as "Venetian Isles"—not to be confused with the development of the same name in the Lake Catherine area. Many New Orleanians just refer to this area as New Orleans East, south of Chef Menteur Highway.

At the Heart of It

At the heart of Viavant/Venetian Isles is industry, from concrete and construction to cold storage and coffee. Cut through by the Intracoastal Canal, which provides east–west access for ships to the Industrial Canal, this neighborhood is lined by port activity. Driving down its few main thoroughfares, one will find wrecking yards, dumping grounds and buildings for storing, packaging and transporting international deliveries. FOLGERS COFFEE COMPANY has had a presence in the neighborhood for decades, and in 2010, it began investing $70 million to expand its operation here while closing sites in Texas and Missouri.[542] One of the largest coffee roasting plants in the world, Folgers makes "the best part of waking up" easy to smell throughout much of Eastern New Orleans.

Undoubtedly, however, the most impressive and influential facility in Viavant/Venetian Isles belongs to NASA. For more than fifty years, staff at the MICHOUD ASSEMBLY FACILITY have designed and assembled large space vehicle parts here, including rockets for the Apollo missions in the 1960s and external tanks for the NASA Space Shuttle Program. The plant itself, which measures more than forty acres under one roof, was dedicated in 1943 as the Michoud Aircraft Plant.[543] Originally, it was where Higgins Shipbuilding

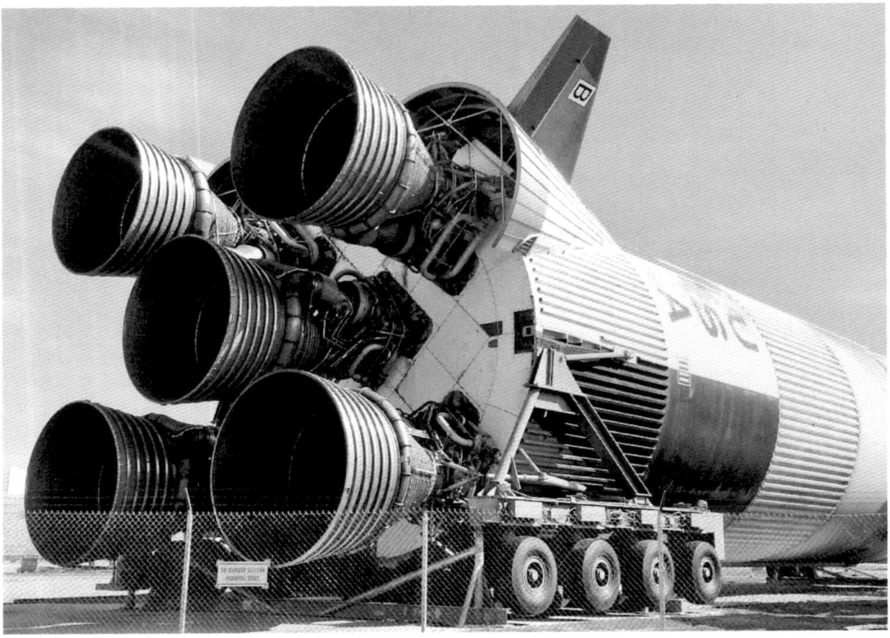

The first stage of a Saturn V Moon Rocket, which was assembled at NASA's Michoud Facility and pushed Apollo astronauts to the moon. *Photo by Mitchell Mendis.*

Company built planes during World War II.[544] While Higgins and the canals boosted activity in the city's eastern marshes in the early half of the twentieth century, it was not until NASA took over the plant in 1961 that widespread residential settlement of the surrounding area began.[545]

The Michoud plant's name dates back to this area's early history, when the son of Napoleon's administrator of domains, Antoine Michoud, operated a sugar cane plantation and refinery where the assembly plant stands today.[546] Surrounded by swamp to the north and an extension of Bayou Sauvage to the south, Michoud's plantation was on a naturally elevated ridge of land, formed by a Mississippi River distributary thousands of years earlier.[547] Despite this area's slight elevation, when Hurricane Katrina breached the nearby Intracoastal Canal levees in 2005, it did not stand a chance against the twenty-foot flood.[548] A team of thirty-seven employees stayed behind at the Michoud Assembly Facility to keep its generators and water pumps operating. Against all odds, it succeeded in protecting the NASA equipment inside the plant.[549] The team members were awarded NASA's Exceptional Bravery Medal after the storm.[550]

In 2006, the United States Coast Guard moved its BASE SUPPORT UNIT (BSU) from the Upper Ninth Ward to the Michoud Assembly Facility. The base supports more than nine hundred local personnel with financial and housing assistance, among other services. The construction of the $90 million Administrative and Berthing Building here represents the largest single facility contract in U.S. Coast Guard history.[551] Nearby, the DELGADO MARITIME, FIRE AND INDUSTRIAL TRAINING FACILITY has an international reputation for providing high-quality, affordable, U.S. Coast Guard–approved training.[552]

Now that the space shuttle program has ended, scientists and engineers at Michoud are gearing up to be part of a new project: the Space Launch System. Through at least 2021, staff here will be building the main components of NASA's most powerful rocket to date—a rocket designed to send astronauts to the moon, asteroids and, eventually, Mars.[553] About $250 million has been invested in readying the Michoud Facility for the task, and while robots have replaced some employees, those who've stayed are more technically skilled than ever before, representatives say.[554] Indeed, Viavant/Venetian Isles will continue to affect New Orleans, the world and beyond.

Festivals and Events

Each year, the NASA Michoud Assembly Facility hosts the Bayou Regional First Robotics Competition, which challenges students to fundraise, brand their teams and build and program robots with limited time and resources. The facility also hosts an annual community health fair and events for National Engineers Week, including student tours and demonstrations.

VILLAGE DE L'EST

A Note on Identity

This neighborhood got its name from the Village de l'Est development here, which opened in the 1960s. Some call the area "Versailles," after the Versailles Gardens subdivision and the former Versailles Arms Apartments here.

At the Heart of It

At the heart of Village de l'Est is New Orleans' largest enclave of Vietnamese and Vietnamese-Americans. This community took root here in 1975, after the communist siege of Saigon. Many refugees from communist Vietnam were Catholic, and after meeting priests in refugee camps across the United States, New Orleans' archbishop invited them to settle in Orleans Parish.[555] The Associated Catholic Charities of New Orleans found public housing for one thousand emigrants at the Versailles Arms Apartments.[556] Most who settled here came from the vicinity of Vung Tau city or the village of Phuc Tinh. These are coastal areas about seventy-five miles southeast of Saigon.[557]

In 1976, about two thousand more Vietnamese refugees moved into the Versailles Arms. Some of these people had been traveling together since 1954, when communists took hold of North Vietnam and caused Catholics and others to flee to the south.[558] Close-knit and experienced at rebuilding, when these refugees arrived in New Orleans, they took to gardening and farming right away.[559] Soon, people from across the city began seeking out the Saturday morning VIETNAMESE FARMERS' MARKET and shops on Alcee Fortier Boulevard, which became stocked with Vietnamese imported foodstuffs and products.

Starting in the 1980s, Vietnamese community members began moving out of the Arms and into the nearby Village de l'Est and Versailles Gardens subdivisions. By 1986, the group had founded its own ethnic parish, MARY QUEEN OF VIETNAM CHURCH.[560] Still, poverty was a challenge for many, and there was tension between the Vietnamese community and the local African American community as they sought out the same limited resources.[561] In 1990, the neighborhood was almost equally divided between Vietnamese and African Americans, and more than 30 percent of both communities lived below the poverty line.[562]

When Hurricane Katrina hit in 2005, Eastern New Orleans was the first area to significantly flood. Rising water in the Industrial Canal leaked through damaged gates on both sides of the I-10 High Rise, and soon the Intracoastal Canal's levees breached, letting a deluge through. To the north, water from Lake Pontchartrain overtopped a one-mile stretch of floodwall. With protective wetlands to its northeast, Village de l'Est was not the worst hit neighborhood in the East, but it did flood up to eight feet in some areas and suffered considerable damage.[563]

Just after the city was deemed safe for return in early October 2005, Vietnamese-American community members returned in droves to rebuild.

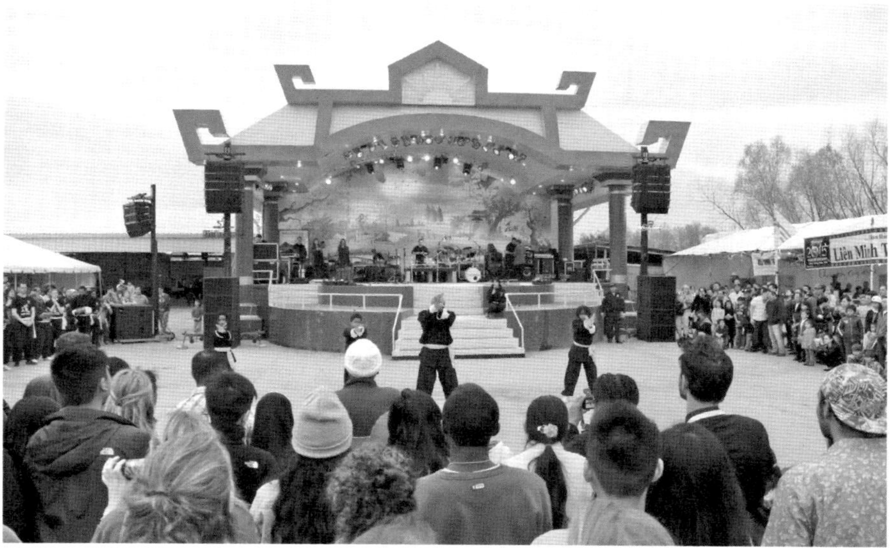

A martial arts demonstration at Mary Queen of Vietnam's Tet Festival. *Photo by Bruce Cervini.*

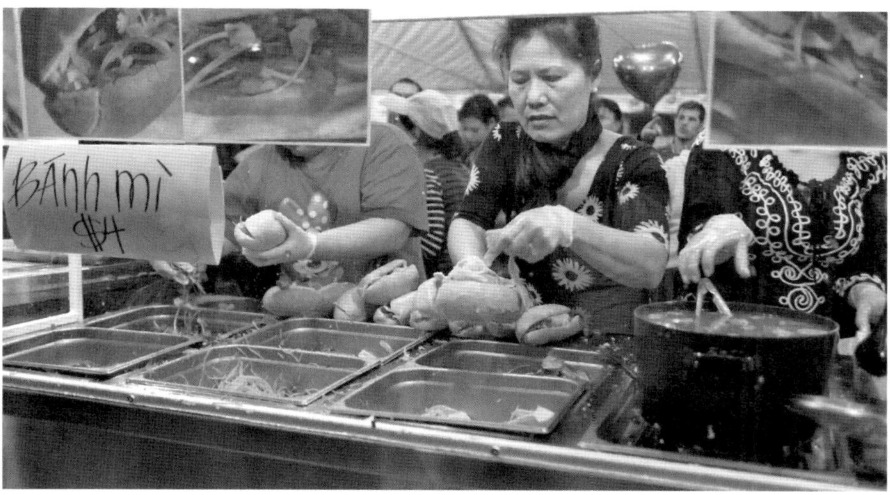

Tet Festival offers traditional Vietnamese favorites like banh mi, egg rolls and pho, as well as delicacies for more adventurous eaters. *Photo by Bruce Cervini.*

They signed a petition to restore power to the neighborhood and forced the city to provide them with dumpsters.[564] By December, church leaders estimated that about six hundred had come back.[565] The number steadily grew. African Americans were returning, too, but at a slower pace. Nearly

40 percent of the African American community here lived in just three apartment complexes before Katrina, and the unavailability of affordable rental housing after the storm was a major barrier to them returning home.[566]

As the country watched the "Versailles Vietnamese" rebuild, the national media and others reinforced the old "model minority" narrative. The touting of these Asian Americans as hardworking and self-sufficient again prompted assumptions that, in contrast, African Americans were not.[567] But instead of accepting these stereotypes, the Vietnamese Americans and African Americans in Versailles defied them. Media-savvy Father Vien Nguyen of Mary Queen of Vietnam Church made sure that when he interviewed with news channels, he disassembled their false constructions.[568] He and his community members were the first to admit that the reason they were so good at rebuilding was because they had done it before—many of them twice—as refugees.

And so it went that these two communities, who had interacted very little before Katrina, made a decided effort at solidarity. When Mary Queen of Vietnam Church held its first mass after the storm, Father Vien reached out to the African American community—whose church suffered worse damage and had not yet been rebuilt—and invited them to attend.[569] He visited neighborhood meetings throughout Eastern New Orleans and offered help in rebuilding. Likewise, in February 2006, when Mayor Ray Nagin opened a dump site just two miles from Village de l'Est, African American political leaders cautioned Father Vien against accepting the deal.[570]

"They said, 'They're telling you [the landfill] is not toxic, they're telling you it's lined, but we in the African American community have a long history of dealing with environmental racism, and you need to be sure the city is shooting straight,'" Dr. Eric Tang explained in an interview on the VietNOLA podcast. A community organizer, activist and scholar, Tang worked in Eastern New Orleans after Katrina and has written extensively about race relations here after the storm. "So Father Vien took that to heart...and his African American colleagues were right: there were toxins in the landfill, it wasn't as safe as the mayor and the State Environmental Protection Agency were saying."[571] After many public protests, the city closed the dump.

While it took Hurricane Katrina to bring these neighboring communities together, local youth are carrying on the spirit of inclusiveness, collaboration and advocacy work in the neighborhood. The Vietnamese American Young Leaders Association of New Orleans (VAYLA), for example, brands itself as a "progressive multi-racial community-based organization."[572] Born out of the landfill crisis, the organization has since grown tremendously and offers programs focused on everything from language access and citizenship assistance—which many Latino community members have taken advantage of—to youth leadership and academic support.

Festivals and Events

Mary Queen of Vietnam Church draws thousands to its Vietnamese New Year celebration, the Tet Festival, which promises a weekend full of authentic Vietnamese cuisine, dragon dances and fireworks.

VAYLA's headquarters on Chef Menteur Highway hosts weekly dance classes, community meetings, leadership training classes and financial planning workshops.

LAKE CATHERINE

A Note on Identity

The city's Lake Catherine includes a great portion of Bayou Sauvage, the strip of land on either side of Chef Menteur Highway between Lake St. Catherine and Lake Pontchartrain and the wetlands between Lake Borgne and Lake St. Catherine.

At the Heart of It

When French brothers Iberville and Bienville explored the Mississippi Gulf Coast in 1699, the Rigolets and Chef Menteur Pass proved welcome shortcuts to the long journey up the Mississippi River. These channels, which connected the Gulf with Lake Pontchartrain, influenced Bienville when he chose the city's location.[573] They also isolated—and still do—the land area called Lake Catherine today.

A mosquito-infested wetland where few white men ventured, Lake Catherine was home to a maroon camp, or a large settlement of runaway slaves, in the 1700s. Led by a man named Juan San Malo, the runaways here stole food from plantations and killed livestock, and even people, to survive.[574] The Spanish governor ordered their capture, and in 1784, more

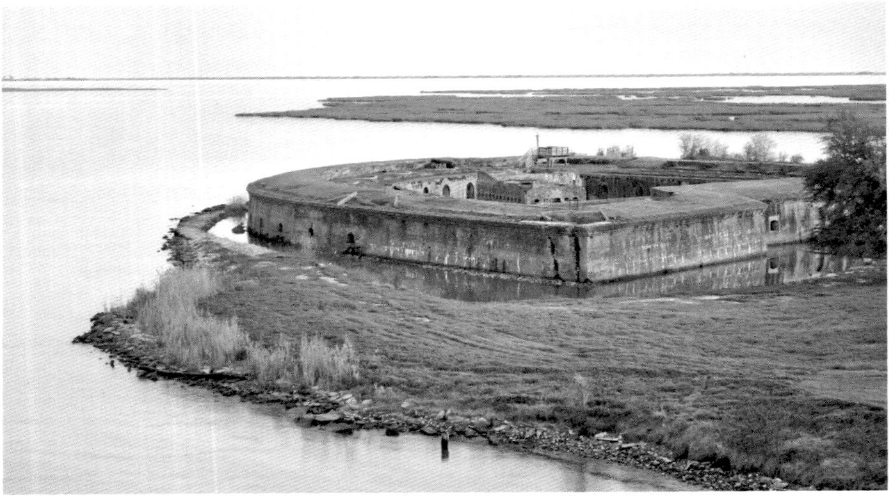

Fort Pike was built to guard the Rigolets, an entranceway to Lake Pontchartrain from the Gulf of Mexico. *Photo by author.*

than sixty runaways were caught in Lake Catherine. Most were punished with three hundred lashes, while San Malo and three others were hanged in today's Jackson Square.[575]

During the War of 1812, the city made an effort to secure its eastern marshes by building Fort Petite Coquilles on the Lake Pontchartrain side of today's Chef Menteur Highway. After American gunboats were captured in Lake Borgne in 1814, Andrew Jackson criticized the fort's one-sided placement as being "of little service in protection of the pass."[576] To make up for its poor placement, FORT MACOMB was erected at Chef Menteur Pass in 1815 and FORT PIKE along the Rigolets in 1822, although neither was ever used for offensive purposes.[577]

Across Lake Saint Catherine from today's Chef Menteur Highway, the Louisville and Nashville Railroad began running through the area's wetlands in the 1880s.[578] A small community of railroad workers, trappers, hunters and fishermen formed where the maroons had previously put down stakes.[579] They lived in small wooden homes built on stilts and, like the maroons before them, caught most of what they ate.[580] A hurricane devastated the "Town of Lake Catherine" in 1915 and again in 1947, but its real demise came when passenger railroad service here was cut in the mid-1900s.[581] With no access route in or out of town, many residents relocated along Chef Menteur Highway.

In the 1960s, as suburb-seeking whites flocked to Eastern New Orleans, development expanded along the lakeshore. The Venetian Isles development—with rear boat access—opened, and raised camps popped up on either side of Chef Menteur Highway's nine-mile stretch into the lakes. Investment in the area all but stopped, however, when the oil market crashed in the mid-1980s. As a result, the federal government received a vast span of land here and designated it as Bayou Sauvage National Wildlife Refuge.[582] A twenty-four-thousand-acre oasis of fresh and brackish marshes and coastal hardwood forests, Bayou Sauvage is the nation's largest urban wildlife refuge.[583]

When Hurricane Katrina hit in 2005, it decimated Lake Catherine with more than twenty feet of water. Bayou Sauvage and the historic forts were badly damaged, while camps were washed away. Although most evacuated before the storm, Arthur Ginart, who served as priest of Lake Catherine's Saint Nicholas of Myra Church for thirty years, refused to leave. The rebuilt Fort Pike Volunteer Fire House is named for him, "Father Red," who perished in the storm.[584]

The month before Katrina hit, there were 733 households receiving mail in Lake Catherine. In June 2014, there were 506.[585] The neighborhood is being rebuilt slowly, and restoration of Bayou Sauvage is likewise ongoing. Fort Pike is again open to tourists. And while the park system has abandoned Fort Macomb, its appearance in the first season of *True Detective* has made it a popular (and illegal) pilgrimage for youth.

Festivals and Events

Fort Pike offers tours Monday through Friday.

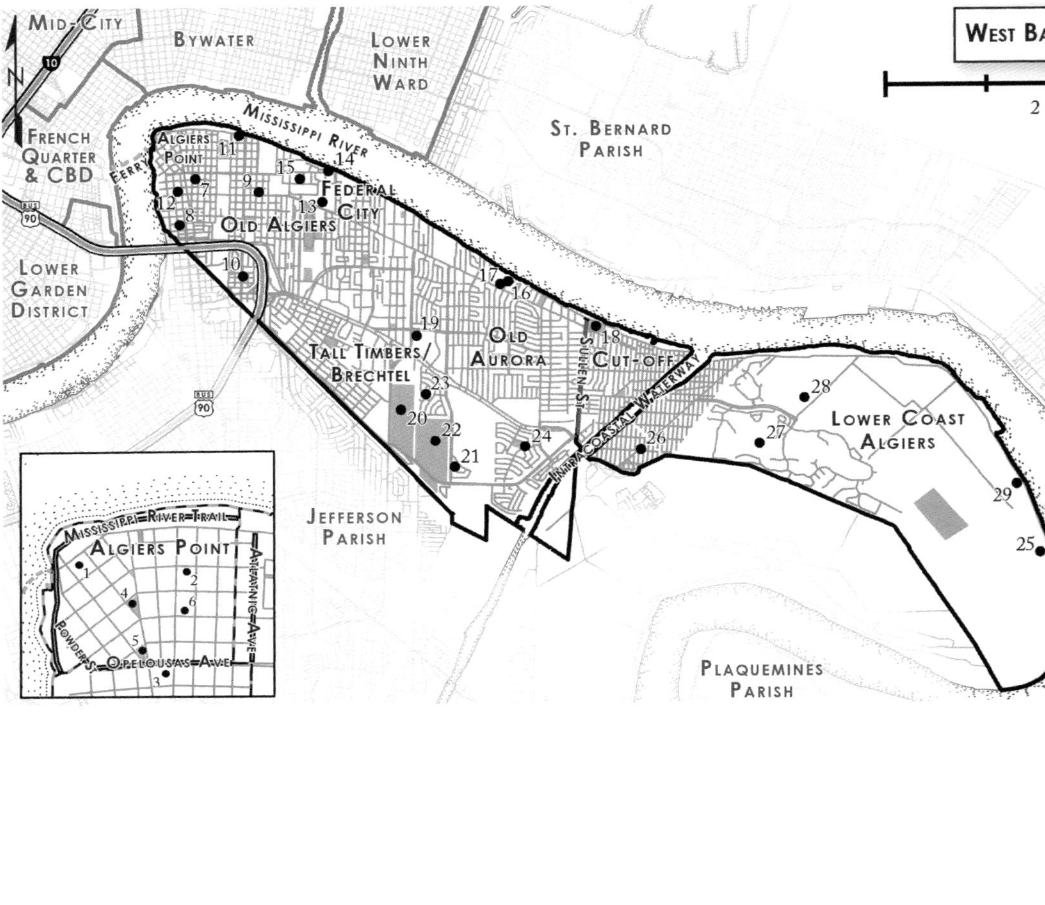
West Ba
Mid-City
Bywater
Lower Ninth Ward
St. Bernard Parish
French Quarter & CBD
Ferry
Algiers Point
Mississippi River
Federal City
Old Algiers
Lower Garden District
Tall Timbers/ Brechtel
Old Aurora
Sullen St
Cut-off
Intracoastal Waterway
Lower Coast Algiers
Jefferson Parish
Plaquemines Parish
Mississippi River Trail
Algiers Point
Powder St
Opelousas Ave
Atlantic Ave

Chapter 10

West Bank

MAP KEY

ALGIERS POINT
1. Algiers Courthouse
2. Algiers Point Public Library
3. Algiers United Methodist Church
4. Confetti Playground
5. Delcazel Playground
6. Trinity Lutheran Church

OLD ALGIERS
7. BlackStar Books and Caffé
8. Common Ground Health Clinic
9. Craige Cultural Center
10. Fischer Apartments
11. Folk Art Zone and Blues Museum
12. Pride of Algiers Masonic Lodge

FEDERAL CITY
13. Delgado Community College Student Life Center
14. LeBeuf-Ott Country Retreat
15. YMCA Fitness Center

OLD AURORA/CUT-OFF
16. Aurora Gardens
17. Aurora Swim and Tennis Club
18. Cut-Off Recreation Center
19. Village Aurora Shopping Center

TALL TIMBERS/BRECHTEL
20. Brechtel Memorial Park and Golf Course
21. Lakewood Development
22. Lakewood Golf Club
23. Park Timbers Development
24. Tall Timbers Development

LOWER COAST ALGIERS
25. A Studio in the Woods
26. Chua Bo De Buddhist Temple
27. English Turn Development and Golf Course
28. Wat Wimuttayaram Buddhist Meditation Center
29. Wilderness Park

ALGIERS POINT

A Note on Identity

The city and the Historic District Landmarks Commission have different boundaries for Algiers Point. Gentrifiers who have flocked to the neighborhood in the twenty-first century have generally settled between Opelousas Avenue, Atlantic Avenue and the river. The Algiers Point Association popularized the "Algiers Point" moniker in the 1970s.[586] Old-timers usually just call it "Algiers."[587]

At the Heart of It

At the heart of Algiers Point are creative couples who have steered away from suburban humdrum and the chaos of city living. Instead, these mimosa-drinking bohemians are using their talents to nourish a vibrant, family-oriented community with a small-town feel. Musician Kathryn Hobgood, for example, directs a local children's choir—the Confetti Park Players—and is a board member of Confetti Kids Inc., which organizes kid-focused programming for the neighborhood.

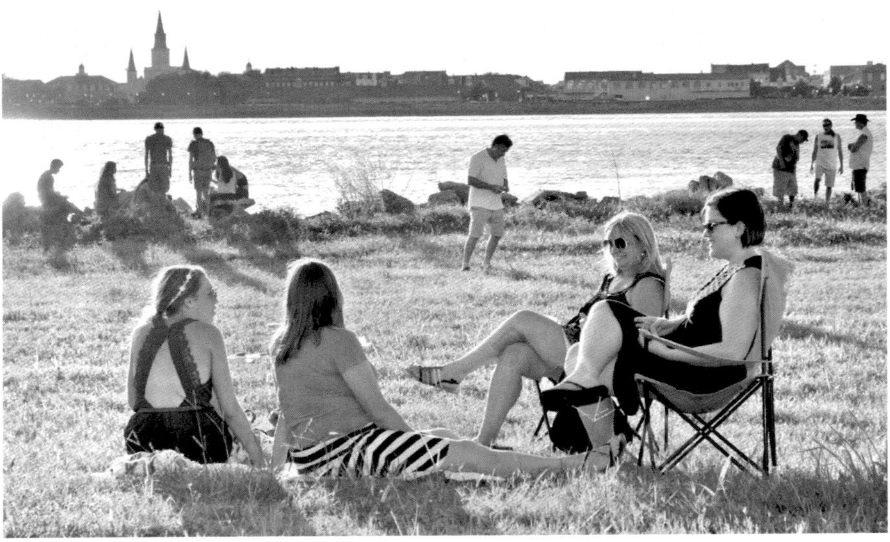

Neighbors relax on Algiers Point on a summer afternoon. *Photo by author.*

Among the group's events are weekly play-dates at the CONFETTI and DELCAZEL PLAYGROUNDS.

The Point, however, is hardly homogenous. Alongside new families are veteran "Algerines" who keep tradition and oral history here strong. Some trace their lineage to the Irish, German and Italian immigrants who settled here in the 1800s and relish in opportunities to talk about life in Algiers back when.[588] Called New Orleans' second-oldest neighborhood (established in 1719), Algiers Point was founded as the French Quarter's support side. Originally, it was plantation land, as well as the location of the city's slaughterhouse and slave corral, where thousands of Africans were brought on slave ships.[589] By the mid-1800s, shipyards, sawmills and lumberyards lined the levee, and many of the town's residents found their livelihoods in shipbuilding.[590]

While locals celebrate historic neighborhood industries, gentrification has quieted the Point's role as a slave port, which, to the contrary, is often talked about across Opelousas Avenue, where residents are creating a "Little Afraka." In 2005, local artist Cathy Smith aimed to spread awareness about the slave port's history by leasing a grassy field on the riverside of the Algiers Point levee and opening the Village at Algiers Point—a cultural marketplace that re-created the lifestyles of Algiers's African slaves.[591] The city drowned the land seven years later, justifying the flooding as a means to protect the integrity of the levee, although many blame the Village's demise on gentrification.[592] Nevertheless, Hobgood said that when she thinks of her neighborhood, she thinks far beyond Opelousas Avenue. She is partnering with leaders throughout Old Algiers to broaden Confetti Park Players' reach and create a new park outside the Point's borders. "It's important to me and many of the community members here that we bridge this gap," she said.

Other aspects of Algiers Point's history stay standing tall: the Romanesque-style ALGIERS COURTHOUSE (1896), the ALGIERS POINT PUBLIC LIBRARY (1907) and the neighborhood's late eighteenth- and early nineteenth-century churches. Powder Street dates back to the powder magazine housed here soon after the neighborhood's founding, and along the levee's Mississippi River Trail there are plaques recalling almost three centuries of the Point's evolution. Many Algiers musicians played in the city's earliest brass bands, and the Algiers Historical Society website offers two self-guided tours through the neighborhood's musical streets.[593]

From the Mississippi River Trail, Algerines can hear the calliope music of the *Steamboat Natchez*, overlook the clamor and excitement of New Orleans' French Quarter and Central Business District and even board the Algiers

Ferry to join the ruckus if they so please. If not, they can stay quietly insulated, mingle with neighbors and friends and enjoy what is arguably the best view of the city skyline.

Festivals and Events

The Algiers Irish Rebel & Friendship Club celebrates Friendship Day each March, complete with green beer, live music and a parade. For the Germans, Trinity Lutheran Church serves up bratwurst, beer and potato salad in celebration of Oktoberfest each year. Along the river, Wednesdays at the Point concerts feature musicians and vendors throughout the summer. In December, residents second-line to the same grassy field for the Algiers Holiday Bonfire and Concert.

OLD ALGIERS (MCDONOGH, WHITNEY, BEHRMAN AND FISCHER DEVELOPMENT)

A Note on Identity

Many residents do not identify with the McDonogh, Whitney or Behrman neighborhood names and instead say that they live in "Algiers" or "Old Algiers." The Fischer public housing project, which was razed and redeveloped as the mixed-income Fischer Apartments beginning in 2004, is also included in this essay.

At the Heart of It

The descendants of New Orleans' enslaved Africans have deep roots in Old Algiers. For almost 150 years, Algiers Point was home to the city's slave corral, where thousands were brought from Africa and kept in pens before being auctioned off across the river.[594] In the 1830s, as slave owners grappled with what the future might hold for them, the American Colonization Society sent freed slaves to Africa as an alternative to emancipation in the United

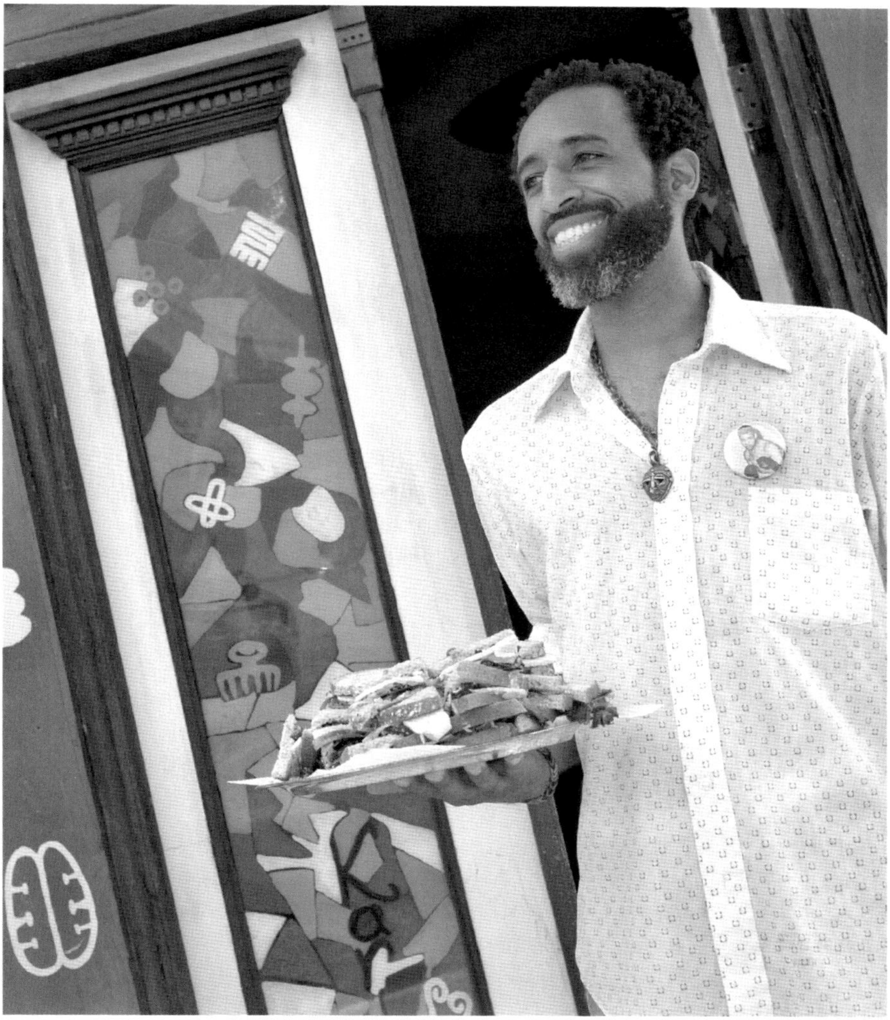

Owner Baakir Tyehimba serves up his famous "san'miches" at BlackStar Books and Caffé. *Photo by Hilary Bronwyn Gayle.*

States.[595] Local plantation owner and advocate of the colonization movement John McDonogh created "Freetown" in Algiers—a place for his freed slaves to prepare for colonizing what would eventually become Liberia.[596] After the Civil War, many newly emancipated slaves settled in Freetown, keeping the area closely tied to its African heritage.[597]

At the heart of Old Algiers today, then, is an effort to create a "Little Afraka" here—a cultural and economic district for people who trace their lineage to Africa. Algerine Baakir Tyehimba's BlackStar Books and Caffé offers a robust library of pan-African literature and nonfiction, as well as African-influenced healthy cuisine. Todd and Vince Craige, whose late father was the first African American chiropractor in New Orleans and a beloved champion of the Algiers people, own the Craige Cultural Center. Maintaining their parents' legacy of serving the community, the Craiges host everything from Conscious Movie Nights and neighborhood meetings to the CompTIA A+ certification program, which empowers locals to start careers in IT. Vince also runs his Algiers Design screen-printing business here, through which he has served like-minded groups citywide, from the Congo Square Preservation Society in Treme to the Ashé Cultural Arts Center in Central City.

With African rhythms and harmonies influencing nearly all American music, it is no wonder that New Orleans—once the busiest slave market in the South—has been so important to the country's creative evolution.[598] As the place where slaves arrived, and where many of them lived their entire lives, Algiers has an especially rich artistic history. The Algiers Historical Society website offers self-guided tours to the homes of many of the city's original brass band performers, including cornet player Henry Allen, trumpeter and violinist Peter Bocage and trumpeter "Kid" Thomas Valentine.[599]

Algerines celebrate and continue the neighborhood's tradition of creativity today. Local artist Charles Gillam, for example, runs the Folk Art Zone and Blues Museum out of his home and hosts a festival each year that honors the neighborhood's influence on these early art forms. In 2014, the South's largest street art exhibit took over a vacant Algiers apartment complex for a few months. The five-story, block-long collaborative art project, titled ExhibitBe, featured murals of civil rights activists, musicians and local victims of violence. It engaged the community in "necessary conversations on housing, blight and accountability."[600]

In Algiers, these conversations have long been necessary. The Fischer public housing project, the last of New Orleans' conventional projects to be erected, was also one of the first to be razed, months before Hurricane Katrina. Hundreds from around the city gathered to see Fischer's thirteen-floor unit fall in half-second delays.[601] The HOPE IV program replaced its more than one thousand public housing units with about half as many mixed-income apartments, displacing hundreds of families.[602]

While the West Bank avoided flooding during Katrina, the storm did provide an opportunity to call attention to, and serve, many in the community who had been ignored during the decades before it hit. Local leaders formed the Common Ground Collective, which continues to runs the area's Common Ground Health Clinic today. In 2013, the clinic launched the Old Algiers Harvest Fresh Market in collaboration with several partnering organizations. The market, which brings nutritious foods and health education to the former food desert, is located in the Pride of Algiers Masonic Lodge—one of the oldest African American masonic lodges in the nation, dating back to 1952.[603]

Festivals and Events

BlackStar Books and Caffé hosts Liberation Lounge each Sunday, an open mic for singers, rappers, poets, spoken-word artists and musicians from across the city.

The Mohawk Hunters—the only Mardi Gras Indian gang on the West Bank—and the Westbank Steppers Social Aid and Pleasure Club parade each spring during West Fest.

The Algiers Folk Art Festival features local blues legends, a bicycle secondline, activities for children and refreshments.

FEDERAL CITY (U.S. NAVAL SUPPORT AREA)

A Note on Identity

The former U.S. Naval Support Area—a military base—is now a public-private development called "Federal City."

At the Heart of It

Algiers's Federal City has a 110-year history as a military base. Built on former plantation land during the Spanish-American War,[604] it grew tremendously during World War II, when thousands of sailors met their ships here before being deployed.[605] For many years, the base was Algiers's largest employer.[606] During the nationwide Base Realignment and Closure process in 2005, it was decided that locally stationed troops would move to Tennessee, Virginia and the nearby Belle Chasse, Louisiana.[607] Sailors lowered the flag here for the last time in 2011, and civilians could at once drive through.

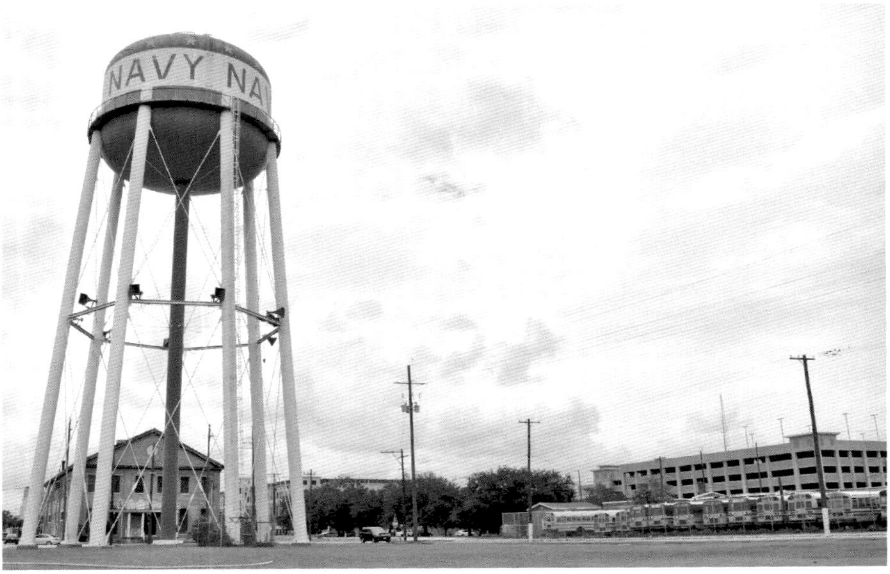

The U.S. Navy water tower still stands in Federal City, commemorating the area's history as a base. *Photo by author.*

Today, $150 million in government money is being funneled into making Federal City a mixed-use development of federal agencies, private businesses and residences.[608] The U.S. Marine Corps, U.S. Coast Guard and New Orleans Police Department have impressive facilities here, but most base structures have been repurposed to serve the broader Algiers community.[609] The former U.S. Navy gym is the West Bank's YMCA FITNESS CENTER, and its chapel is being developed as one of DELGADO COMMUNITY COLLEGE'S STUDENT LIFE CENTERS.[610] The college bought two and a half acres of land here in 2014 to create a West Bank campus.[611] When fully developed, Federal City is expected to create an estimated ten thousand jobs.[612]

The property's transition from private to public, however, has been complex. Resident military families have had to adjust to a lessened sense of security, while new businesses are not yet receiving the traffic they had hoped for.[613] West Bank YMCA membership director Terrion Jones is partnering with the New Orleans Recreation Development Commission, local churches and nonprofits to spread the word about the Y's robust programming. Because the grounds were closed to civilians for so long, locals are not yet in the habit of passing through Federal City, she noted.

Likewise, much of the public is not privy to the outstanding historical architecture on the grounds. The oldest property on the former base is a French Creole cottage that dates back to the 1840s.[614] First a plantation home, the LEBEUF-OTT COUNTRY RETREAT (which the military calls "Quarters A") was home to a series of the base's senior-ranking officers from 1943 until it closed. Carrying on this tradition today, it is now home to the senior officer at the area's Marine Corps facility.[615] This was originally President Theodore Roosevelt's idea. At the navy's dry dock dedication ceremony in 1901, he was so impressed with the villa that he suggested its use as such.[616]

Festivals and Events

The Federal City YMCA hosts clinics on everything from diabetes prevention to healthcare enrollment, regular fitness classes and a biweekly Youth Leaders Club. It also organizes special seasonal events like a Thanksgiving potluck and Breakfast with Santa.

OLD AURORA/CUT-OFF

A Note on Identity

Old Aurora is named for the Aurora Plantation, which once made up much of the land here. Many Algerines refer to the section of land between Sullen Street and the Intracoastal Waterway as the "Cut-Off."

At the Heart of It

In 1940, when the AURORA GARDENS development first opened, it advertised such "features for gracious living" as air conditioning, kitchen cabinets and terraced lots.[617] Today, Aurora Gardens is just one of many developments in the Aurora neighborhood, where most homes are California Cottages, which were popular in the mid-twentieth century. Indeed, the neighborhood feels more like a suburb of New Orleans—with the VILLAGE AURORA SHOPPING CENTER, the AURORA SWIM AND TENNIS CLUB, healthcare facilities and schools—than part of the city's Fifteenth Ward.

Yet Old Aurora's history is closely woven with that of the greater city. Across the river from the Chalmette Battlefield, the front yard of the Aurora Plantation home served as a fort location during the 1815 Battle of New Orleans.[618] As other plantations were sold and subdivided, Aurora continued to produce hundreds of pounds of sugar until as late as 1906.[619] In the early 1900s, before the neighborhood's housing developments were erected, "open fields, snake hunts and wilderness" surrounded the farm.[620] Young Algerine boys ventured here for overnight hiking and camping trips.[621]

With New Orleans' slave corral being located on Algiers Point and agriculture driving much of the area's early economy, the descendants of New Orleans' African slaves have deep roots on the city's West Bank. Oral history in the Cut-Off has it that in the 1700s, the area was home to a maroon camp, or a large settlement of runaway slaves. French Louisiana hosted some of the largest maroon settlements in the South, as local Native Americans often adopted runaways into their communities and lived together with them.[622] Many say that New Orleans' Mardi Gras Indian tradition has its roots in these camps.

Today, the Cut-Off maintains its own identity and is home to a predominantly African American community. The CUT-OFF RECREATION CENTER is one of the neighborhood's busiest meeting places. It offers free

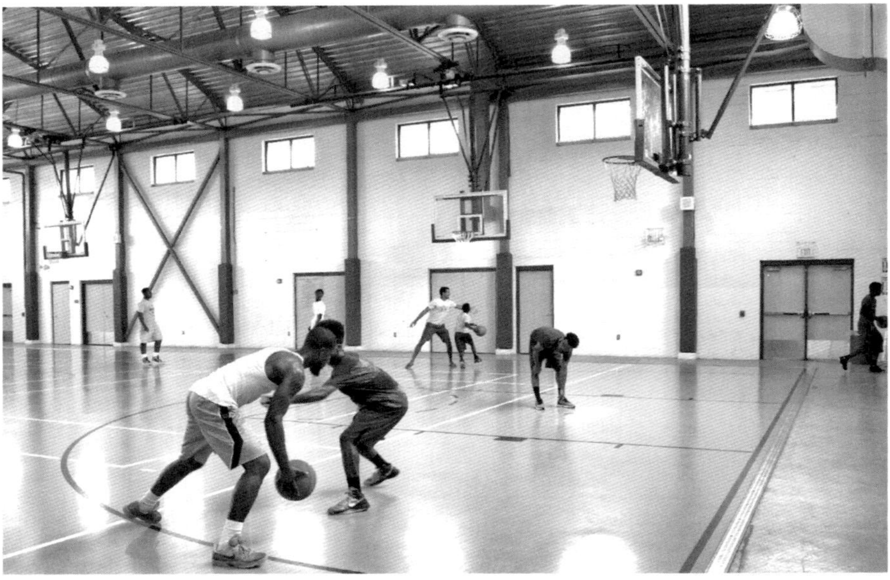

Saturday morning free-play at the Cut-Off Recreation Center. *Photo by author.*

piano and ballet lessons, basketball camps and after-school programs. On spring and fall days, it's not unusual to see kids playing football nearby on the neutral ground of General Meyer Avenue.

Festivals and Events

The Cut-Off Recreation Center has a robust calendar of rotating special events.

TALL TIMBERS/BRECHTEL

A Note on Identity

Tall Timbers is the name of just one housing development in the city's Tall Timbers neighborhood. Others are named Park Timbers and Lakewood. The rest of this neighborhood is usually referred to as "Brechtel." It is named for John P. Brechtel, the Algerine who started New Orleans Recreation Department.

At the Heart of It

This area's development began in the mid-twentieth century, as the newly completed Greater New Orleans Bridge (today's Crescent City Connection) accelerated the West Bank's growth.[623] Today, the neighborhood is made up of housing developments, Brechtel Memorial Park and Golf Course and the private Lakewood Golf Club. Of all the recreational resources here, Brechtel Park is the most popular. A 120-acre expanse, it is full of treasures undiscovered by much of the Greater New Orleans community.

Complete with camping and picnic grounds, two of the city's tallest hills, forests and a lagoon, Brechtel Park is included in one of America's Wetland Birding Trails.[624] It is also part of the Trail of Whispering Giants—a collection of twenty- to forty-foot sculptures of Native Americans that spans all fifty states, Europe and Canada.[625] Hand-carved from trees stumps and large logs by artist Peter Toth, the Whispering Giants are meant to chronicle the "epic struggle of all men facing injustices, inhumanity and tyranny."[626] Standing at Brechtel Park's

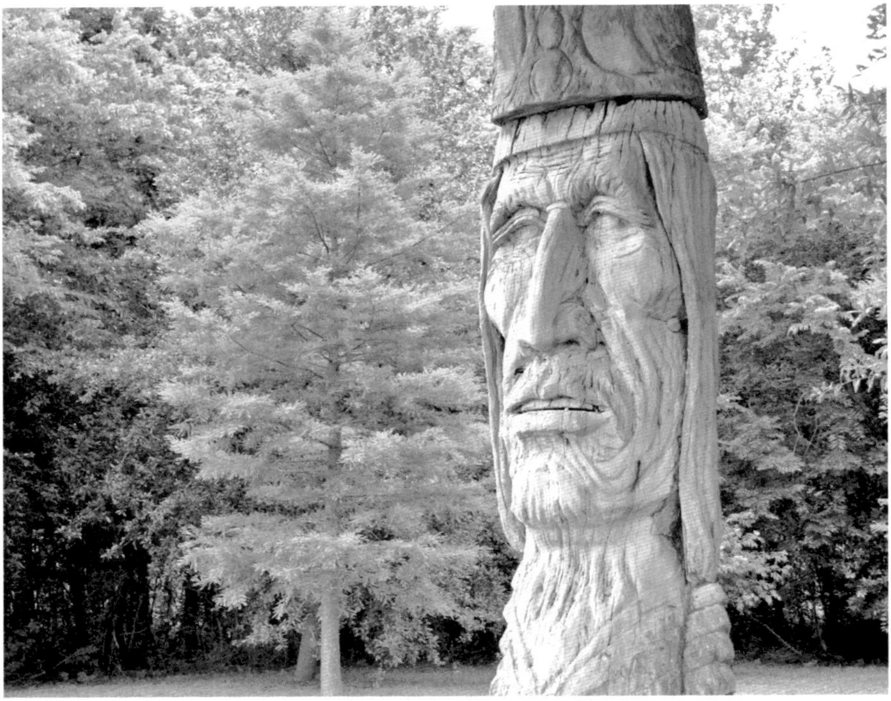

Brechtel Park's Whispering Giant is a hand-carved representation of all people who face injustice. *Photo by Mitchell Mendis.*

entrance, New Orleans' Whispering Giant seems to be guarding the sanctuary. He is an impressionable greeter, indeed.

Another surprising and more recent addition to the park is its upkeep team: a herd of goats. In 2014, the nonprofit that maintains the park, Parks and Parkways, hired a goat-landscaping company to get rid of Brechtel's invasive weeds.[627] The group has reported saving thousands of dollars on labor as a result of the dozen goats feasting off the ground.[628] Meanwhile, the herd has become a big hit with visitors.

Festivals and Events

Brechtel Park hosts Warren Easton Charter School's annual Kite Day, a culminating project for geometry students. The Friends of Brechtel Park organization runs an annual Easter egg hunt, Arbor Day celebration and guided eco-hikes, among other rotating events.

LOWER COAST ALGIERS (NEW AURORA/ENGLISH TURN)

A Note on Identity

Most locals refer to this large sweep of land as "Lower Coast" or "Lower Coast Algiers." The city's "New Aurora" moniker is seldom used, and "English Turn" is reserved for the area's English Turn Development and Golf Course. It is also the historic name for this last big bend of the Mississippi River, where Bienville tricked the English into "turning away" by announcing to a ship that the French had already colonized the coast upriver in 1699.[629]

At the Heart of It

Lower Coast Algiers is a rural oasis made up of sanctuaries. Its public roads can be counted on two hands, and even those are sometimes made of gravel, cutting through swampy forests and pastures. In 2013, the Woodlands Conservancy nonprofit acquired 190 acres of wetlands here, with the aim of protecting them from development.[630] Wild boar run free on the Lower Coast, and the area is one of New Orleans' best for bird watching. Residents who live far downriver fondly call their area "horse country." Some live here full time, but because the area lacks gas and other services, many instead come for weekend visits with their campers.

It is not just horse lovers, however, who have made a refuge out of this former sugar plantation. The Audubon Institute has its Endangered Species Complex in Lower Coast Algiers, where programs are dedicated to boosting the populations of disappearing animals.[631] The campus includes Wilderness Park, which is seasonally open to the public. A natural and secluded green space, Wilderness Park brims with trees and plants that support a vast variety of local birds.[632]

In addition to making scientific gains possible, Lower Coast forests have inspired artistic creativity, too. Since 2001, A Studio in the Woods has provided space for more than fifty resident writers and visual and material artists to work uninterrupted. The retreat is on 7.6 acres filled with oak, elm, hickory, hackberry, cypress and sweetgum trees.[633] Recognizing the power of nature to ignite the imagination, founders Joe and Lucianne Carmichael developed the program to share their haven. Although residencies are not

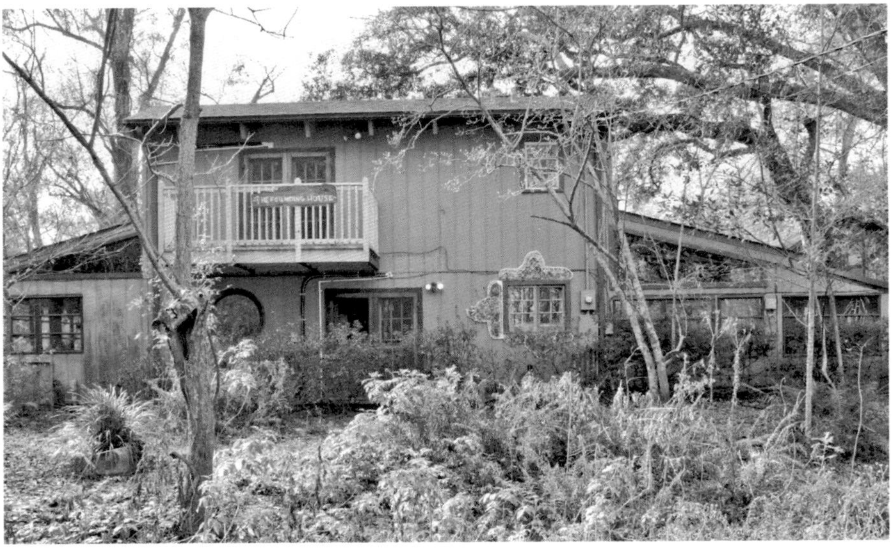

The Founding House at A Studio in the Woods provides office space and lodging to resident artists. *Photo by author.*

available to students, Tulane University operates A Studio in the Woods today. The Carmichaels sold the land to the Tulane/Xavier Center for Bioenvironmental Research to ensure the forest's preservation.[634]

Religious sanctuaries in Lower Coast Algiers include Chua Bo De Buddhist Temple and the Wat Wimuttayaram Buddhist Meditation Center. Gold and red inside and out, the impressionable Chua Bo De is one of the first structures people see after crossing the Intracoastal Waterway. It was built in 1983 in traditional Vietnamese style and is named for the Bodhi Tree, which Buddha sat under when he reached enlightenment.[635] Tucked away on Stanton Road, the Wat Wimuttayaram Buddhist Meditation Center aims to promote the teaching of the Buddha and peaceful living among people of different beliefs.[636] It is open to anyone with an interest in the religion and culture.

Finally, in the English Turn gated community, there is the sanctuary of comfortable country living. Just ten miles from New Orleans' downtown, where many English Turn residents work, this wealthy subdivision seems a world away. While enjoying their clubhouse, swim and tennis club and private golf course built by Jack Nicklaus's development corporation, English Turn residents can also appreciate pods of pelicans feeding in the area's canals and acres of open fields teeming with wildlife.

Festivals and Events

A Studio in the Woods hosts an annual FORESTival, a celebration of art and nature that showcases the work of resident artists.

Chua Bo De hosts special ceremonies for Phat Dan Sanh, Buddha's birthday, and Phat Thanh Dao, the day marking Buddha's enlightenment. Wat Wimuttayaram has a festival and food fair for the Thai New Year, Songkran, and the Loy Krathong Festival, Thailand's "festival of lights."

Notes

PREFACE

1. Richard Campanella, "A Glorious Mess: A Perceptual History of New Orleans Neighborhoods," *New Orleans Magazine* (June 2014).

INTRODUCTION

2. Richard Campanella, *Time and Place in New Orleans: Past Geographies in the Present Day* (Gretna, LA: Pelican Publishing Company, 2002), 38.
3. Ibid.
4. Richard Campanella, *Geographies of New Orleans: Urban Fabrics Before the Storm* (Lafayette: Center for Louisiana Studies, 2005), 5.
5. Ibid.
6. Campanella, "Glorious Mess."
7. Campanella, *Geographies of New Orleans*, 206.
8. Richard Campanella, "An Ethnic Geography of New Orleans," *Journal of American History* (December 2007).
9. Ibid.

CHAPTER 1

10. Campanella, *Geographies of New Orleans*, 17.
11. Henry Renshaw, "Jackson Square," *Louisiana Historical Quarterly* 2 (1919): 42.
12. Sally Asher, *Hope and New Orleans: A History of Crescent City Street Names* (Charleston, SC: The History Press), 12.

13. Campanella, *Geographies of New Orleans*, 298.
14. Campanella, "Ethnic Geography of New Orleans."
15. Arnold R. Hirsch and Joseph Logsdon, *Creole New Orleans: Race and Americanization* (Baton Rouge: Louisiana State University Press, 1992), 189.
16. Campanella, *Geographies of New Orleans*, 206.
17. Campanella, "Ethnic Geography of New Orleans."
18. Campanella, *Geographies of New Orleans*, 215.
19. Ibid.
20. Ibid., 328.
21. Ibid., 325.
22. Ibid.
23. New Orleans Convention & Visitors Bureau, "Frequently Asked Questions for Visitors to New Orleans," October 2014, www.neworleanscvb.com/visit/faq.
24. *Preservation in Print*, "Preservation Resource Center Board of Directors Action on Issues" (February 2003): 11.
25. Preservation Resource Center of New Orleans, *Living with History in New Orleans' Neighborhoods: Central Business District*, brochure.
26. Ibid.
27. Peggy Laborde and John Magill, *Canal Street: New Orleans' Great Wide Way* (Gretna, LA: Pelican Publishing Company Inc., 2006), 31.
28. Campanella, "Ethnic Geography of New Orleans."
29. Campanella, *Geographies of New Orleans*, 299.
30. Gordon Chadwick, "Government Forces and Fighting on Canal Street," New Orleans Historical, www.neworleanshistorical.org/items/show/149 (accessed December 7, 2014).
31. Gordon Chadwick., "The Battle of Liberty Place Monument," New Orleans Historical, www.neworleanshistorical.org/items/show/150 (accessed December 7, 2014).
32. From Common and Basin to Tulane and Loyola: 150 Years of Change in Our Neighborhood, "Duncan Plaza," New Orleans Public Library exhibit.
33. Rebecca Mowbray, "All that's Left of New Orleans' Historic Jazz Infrastructure: 3 Moldering Buildings on South Rampart Street," *Times-Picayune*, May 8, 2011.
34. Ibid.
35. Ben Schwartz, "What Louis Armstrong Really Thinks," *New Yorker*, February 25, 2014.
36. *Daily Picayune*, "New Orleans Negroes Lead Their Race in Enterprise," August 19, 1909.
37. Elizabeth Kovacevic, "Pythian Temple Building," Media NOLA: A Project of Tulane University, November 2012, http://medianola.org/discover/place/869/Pythian-Temple-Building.

38. Greater New Orleans Data Center Pre-Katrina website, "Central Business District Neighborhood Snapshot," 2002, www.datacenterresearch.org/pre-katrina/orleans/1/47/snapshot.html; Zulu Social Aid and Pleasure Club, "History of the Zulu Social Aid and Pleasure Club," www.kreweofzulu.com/history (accessed May 30, 2015).
39. Campanella, *Geographies of New Orleans*, 22.
40. Ibid.
41. *Preservation in Print*, "PRC Memorializes Lost Jazz Landmarks" (September 2001): 9.

CHAPTER 2

42. *Preservation in Print*, "A Classical Neighborhood Reborn in the 1970s and Still Growing" (April 2004): 22–23.
43. Campanella, *Geographies of New Orleans*, 244.
44. The Kingsley House first opened in today's Warehouse District but was moved to its current location on Constance Street in 1924. Kingsley House, www.kingsleyhouse.org/about-us (accessed May 30, 2015).
45. Billy Sothern, "Goodbye, St. Thomas," *The Nation* (August 27, 2007).
46. Campanella, "Ethnic Geography of New Orleans."
47. Richard Webster, "River Garden Residents March in Protest, Management Pushes Back," NOLA.com and the *Times-Picayune*, January 24, 2013.
48. Campanella, *Geographies of New Orleans*, 229–41.
49. Ibid., 234.
50. Ibid.
51. Ibid., 244.
52. Campanella, *Time and Place in New Orleans*, 86.
53. Campanella, *Geographies of New Orleans*, 17.
54. Irish Channel St. Patrick's Day Club, www.irishchannelno.org (accessed May 31, 2015); Parasol's Bar and Restaurant, www.parasolsbarandrestaurant.com (accessed May 31, 2015).
55. Allison Plyer and Denice Warren Ross, "Change in the Irish Channel: Thirty Years of Data About a Historic New Orleans Neighborhood," Greater New Orleans Community Data Center Pre-Katrina website, March 2004, www.datacenterresearch.org/pre-katrina/articles/IrishChannel.html.
56. Ibid.
57. Ibid.
58. Author analysis of "Irish Channel Statistical Area," analysis of data from U.S. Census 2000 Summary File 1 (SF1) and U.S. Census 2010 Summary File 1 (SF1), the Data Center, March 2014.

59. Jed Lipinski, "Nola Brewing Co. Owner Kirk Coco Offers Tips on Branding," NOLA.com and the *Times-Picayune*, March 25, 2014.
60. Garden District Association, https://gardendistrictassociation.com (accessed June 1, 2015).
61. Preservation Resource Center of New Orleans, *Living with History in New Orleans' Neighborhoods: Garden District*, brochure.
62. Ibid.
63. Charlotte Seidenberg, *The New Orleans Garden: Gardening in the Gulf South* (Jackson: University Press of Mississippi, 1993), 449.
64. Ibid.
65. S. Frederick Starr, *Southern Comfort: The Garden District of New Orleans* (Princeton, NJ: Princeton Architectural Press, 2005), 17.
66. Campanella, "Ethnic Geography of New Orleans."
67. Jim Fraiser, *The Garden District of New Orleans* (Jackson: University Press of Mississippi), 173.
68. Commander's Palace, "Our Story," www.commanderspalace.com/our-story (accessed June 1, 2015).
69. Dryades YMCA School of Commerce, www.dryadesymcaschoolofcommerce.com (accessed June 1, 2015).
70. Katy Reckdahl, "HANO to Remove Tons of Contaminated Dirt from Former B.W. Cooper Site," *Times-Picayune*, November 25, 2011.
71. Sothern, "Goodbye St. Thomas."
72. *Louisiana Weekly*, "New Orleans' Desegregation Was Rooted in the 1960 Dryades St. Boycott," August 4, 2014.
73. Shannon Frystak, "Oretha Castle Haley," *KnowLA Encyclopedia of Louisiana* (July 22, 2011), Louisiana Endowment for the Humanities.
74. *Times-Picayune*, "1941: The First Public Housing Complexes Are Built in New Orleans," November 14, 2011.
75. Billes Architecture LLC, "Central City Neighborhood, Planning District 2," *New Orleans Neighborhood Revitalization Plans* (Lambert Plans), 2006, 7.
76. Ashé Cultural Arts Center, "History and Values," www.ashecac.org/main/index.php/about-us/history.html (accessed June 1, 2015).
77. Café Reconcile, "History," http://cafereconcile.org/about/history (accessed June 1, 2015).
78. Billes Architecture LLC, "Central City Neighborhood, Planning District 2."
79. Tram Nguyen, "Pushed Out and Pushing Back in New Orleans," *Colorlines* (April 7, 2010).
80. This figure combines Central City and the B.W. Cooper census tracts. "Central City Statistical Area" and "B.W. Cooper Statistical Area," analysis of data from U.S. Census 2000 Summary File 1 (SF1) and U.S. Census 2010 Summary File 1 (SF1)," the Data Center, March 2014.
81. Sothern, "Goodbye, St. Thomas."

82. All plantation land here had been subdivided by 1850 except for the Delachaise plantation, which was not divided and incorporated until 1855, making it the "last agricultural operation in the Central Crescent." Campanella, *Time and Place in New Orleans*, 91.
83. La Petite Grocery Restaurant and Bar, "La Petite Grocery and History," http://www.lapetitegrocery.com/history (accessed June 1, 2015).
84. William McG. Keefe, "Big Plans for Lyons Dedication," *Times-Picayune*, December 13, 1948.
85. Marilyn Stewart, "Global Maritime Ministries in New Orleans Serves Seafarers from Around the World," NOLA.com, August 20, 2014.
86. Tipitina's, "History in the Music," http://tipitinas.com/history-music (accessed June 1, 2015.)
87. Data Center, "Extent of Katrina Flooding Map," November 2005, www.datacenterresearch.org/maps/reference-maps.
88. Blake Hanson, "Lyons Center to Reopen Monday," *WDSU News*, June 3, 2013.
89. Campanella, *Time and Place in New Orleans*, 91.
90. Rayne Memorial United Methodist Church, "Our Mission," http://raynenola.org/about/our-mission (accessed June 1, 2015); Joy Dickinson, *Haunted City: An Unauthorized Guide to the Magical, Magnificent New Orleans of Anne Rice* (New York: Citadel Press, 2004), 182.
91. Touro Infirmary, "Touro Timeline," www.touro.com/timeline (accessed June 1, 2015).
92. Karen Kingsley, "Touro Synagogue," *KnowLA Encyclopedia of Louisiana* (October 17, 2014).
93. Touro Synagogue, "Our History," https://tourosynagogue.com/about-us/ourhistory (accessed June 1, 2015).
94. Ibid.
95. Touro Infirmary, "Touro Timeline."
96. Ibid.
97. Ibid.
98. Rayne Memorial United Methodist Church, "Our Mission."
99. New Orleans Musicians' Clinic, "About NOMC," www.neworleansmusiciansclinic.org/about (accessed June 1, 2015).
100. "Milan Statistical Area," analysis of data from U.S. Census 2000 Summary File 1 (SF1) and U.S. Census 2010 Summary File 1 (SF1)," the Data Center, March 2014.
101. Greater New Orleans Data Center Pre-Katrina website, "Milan Neighborhood Snapshot," 2002, www.datacenterresearch.org/pre-katrina/orleans/2/66/snapshot.html.
102. Ibid.

103. Billes Architecture LLC, "Milan Neighborhood, Planning District 5," *New Orleans Neighborhood Revitalization Plans* (Lambert Plans), 2006, 13.
104. *USTA News*, "Nehemiah Atkinson, Tennis Pioneer, Passes Away at 84," May 25, 2008.

CHAPTER 3

105. Campanella, "Glorious Mess."
106. German Jews were part of the Reform movement. Orthodox Jews who preceded them in the city settled near today's Oretha Castle Haley Boulevard in Central City. Campanella, *Geographies of New Orleans*, 10.
107. Manuscripts Collection, Tulane University Special Collections, "Jewish Children's Home (New Orleans, La.)."
108. David Cuthbert, "Storied House—A Historic Home on St. Charles Avenue Became a Library 50 Years Ago," *Times-Picayune*, November 7, 1998.
109. Pascal's Manale, "Our History," http://pascalsmanale.com/history (accessed June 2, 2015); Prytania Theatre, "Prytania History," http://prytaniatheatreneworleans.com/prytania-theatre-history (accessed June 2, 2015).
110. JCC New Orleans, "Our Rich History," www.nojcc.org (accessed June 2, 2015).
111. New Orleans Tourism Marketing Corporation, "Streetcars in New Orleans," www.neworleansonline.com/tools/transportation/gettingaround/streetcars.html (accessed June 2, 2015).
112. Friends of the Cabildo, *The University Section*, vol. 8, *New Orleans Architecture* (Gretna, LA: Pelican Publishing Company, 2000), 11.
113. Campanella, *Geographies of New Orleans*, 8.
114. Dorothy Mahan, "A Site to See: The United States Public Health Service Hospital Grounds," *Preservation in Print* (March 1994).
115. Ibid.
116. Jonathan Fricker, "Saving White Elephants," *Preservation in Print* (March 2003).
117. New Orleans Public Belt, "History of the Public Belt Railroad," www.nopb.com/history (accessed June 3, 2015).
118. Hansen's Sno-Bliz, www.snobliz.com (accessed June 3, 2015).
119. F&M's opened in 1905, but its popularity picked up in the 1930s, when it added its dance hall; Domilise's Po-Boys and Bar, "About Domilise's Po-Boys & Bar," www.domilisespoboys.com (accessed June 3, 2015).
120. Mahan, "Site to See."
121. Rebecca Catalanello, "Children's Hospital Proposes $250 Million Expansion onto Historic Marine Hospital Campus," NOLA.com and the *Times-Picayune*, March 17, 2015.
122. Fricker, "Saving White Elephants."

123. "West Riverside Statistical Area," analysis of data from U.S. Census 2000 Summary File 3 (SF3) and 2008–2012 American Community Survey, the Data Center, March 2014.
124. Asher, *Hope and New Orleans*, 93.
125. Ibid., 94.
126. Mary Fitzpatrick, "National Main Street Program Adopts Freret Street" *Preservation in Print* (September 2001).
127. Greater New Orleans Community Data Center Pre-Katrina website, "Freret Neighborhood Snapshot," 2002, www.datacenterresearch.org/pre-katrina/orleans/3/64/snapshot.html.
128. Fitzpatrick, "National Main Street Program."
129. Ibid.
130. Billes Architecture LLC, "Freret Neighborhood, Planning District 3," *New Orleans Neighborhood Revitalization Plans* (Lambert Plans), 2006, 10.
131. Louisiana Office of Cultural Development, Division of the Arts, "Louisiana Cultural Districts Announcements," October 2008, www.crt.state.la.us.
132. *The New Freret*, "Business Listing," http://thenewfreret.com/business-listings (accessed June 2, 2015).
133. Greater New Orleans Data Center Pre-Katrina website, "Broadmoor Neighborhood Snapshot," 2002, www.datacenterresearch.org/pre-katrina/orleans/3/63/snapshot.html.
134. Ibid.
135. Ibid.
136. Ibid.
137. Amy Biederman, "Field Report: Broadmoor Development Corporation," "Americorps Tulane Vista Blog," August 18, 2013, https://tulanevista.wordpress.com/2014/03/18/field-report-broadmoor-development-corporation-4.
138. Ibid.
139. Angela Hill, "From the Front Porch: On the Broadmoor Area," WWL.com, June 30, 2014.
140. Campanella, *Time and Place*, 95.
141. Walter Hill, "Exploring the Life and History of the 'Buffalo Soldiers,'" *The Record*, March 1998.
142. Campanella, *Time and Place*, 95.
143. Ibid.
144. Ibid.
145. Billes Architecture LLC, "Audubon-University Neighborhood, Planning District 3," *New Orleans Neighborhood Revitalization Plans* (Lambert Plans), 2006, 10.
146. Friends of the Cabildo, *University Section.*

147. Ibid.
148. Fontainebleau Improvement Association, "The Arch," http://fia-nola.org/6678.html (accessed June 3, 2015).
149. Billes Architecture LLC, "Marlyville/Fontainebleau Neighborhood, Planning District 3," *New Orleans Neighborhood Revitalization Plans* (Lambert Plans), 2006, 10.
150. *Neighborhood Profiles Project*, "Black Pearl," City of New Orleans Office of Policy Planning and the City Planning Commission, 1980, 3.05.
151. Laurraine Goreau, *Just Mahalia Baby: The Mahalia Jackson Story* (Gretna, LA: Pelican Publishing Company, 1975), 16.
152. Ibid., 15.
153. Dave Walker, "Witness Recalls Role of New Orleans' Mahalia Jackson in Martin Luther King's 'I Have a Dream Speech,'" NOLA.com and the *Times-Picayune*, August 23, 2013.
154. Campanella, "Glorious Mess."
155. David Marcello, "Naming Black Pearl," *New Orleans Magazine* (August 2014).
156. "East Carrollton Statistical Area," analysis of data from U.S. Census 2000 Summary File 3 (SF3) and 2008–2012 American Community Survey, the Data Center, March 2014.
157. Before being developed as part of the Town of Carrollton, today's East Carrollton was part of Barthelemy Macarty's sugar plantation, which made up the entire western edge of the crescent. Campanella, *Time and Place*, 93.
158. Greater New Orleans Data Center Pre-Katrina website, "East Carrollton Neighborhood Snapshot," 2002, www.datacenterresearch.org/pre-katrina/orleans/3/11/snapshot.html.
159. Ibid.
160. New Orleans Tourism Marketing Corporation, "Maple Street," www.neworleansonline.com/tools/streets/maplestreet.html (accessed June 3, 2015).
161. Ibid.
162. Before being developed as part of the Town of Carrollton, today's Leonidas was part of Barthelemy Macarty's sugar plantation, which made up the entire western edge of the crescent. Campanella, *Time and Place*, 93.
163. Preservation Resource Center of New Orleans, *Living with History in New Orleans' Neighborhoods: Carrollton*, brochure.
164. Greater New Orleans Data Center Pre-Katrina website, "Leonidas Neighborhood Snapshot," 2002, www.datacenterresearch.org/pre-katrina/orleans/3/13/snapshot.html.

165. *National Historic Mechanical Engineering Landmarks*, "St. Charles Avenue Streetcar Line, 1835" (1984): 7, American Society of Mechanical Engineers, New York.
166. Robert McClendon, "Pigeon Town or Pension Town? In One New Orleans Neighborhood, That Is the Question," NOLA.com and the *Times-Picayune*, April 30, 2015.
167. Ibid.
168. Kevin McQueeney, "Race and Palmer Park," New Orleans Historical, www.neworleanshistorical.org/items/show/661 (accessed June 14, 2015).
169. Alena Anderson and Michelle Thompson, *"Where Y'at?": An Evaluation of Commercial Corridor Revitalization Programs in New Orleans*, Planning and Urban Studies Reports and Presentations (New Orleans, LA: University of New Orleans, 2012), 24.
170. Molly Kramer, "Fresh in the Chair: Joseph Henry Brings the Speed," *Nola Vie*, December 9, 2013, www.nolavie.com.
171. Greater New Orleans Data Center Pre-Katrina website, "Hollygrove Neighborhood Snapshot," 2002, www.datacenterresearch.org/pre-katrina/orleans/3/12/snapshot.html.
172. Ibid.
173. Jarvain Bingmon, personal interview with author.
174. Ibid.
175. City of New Orleans Programs, "Healthy Start New Orleans," www.nola.gov/health-department/programs/healthy-start (accessed June 3, 2015).

CHAPTER 4

176. Katy Reckdahl, "Discovery of Human Remains Delays Iberville Redevelopment," *The Lens* (December 13, 2012); Campanella, *Geographies of New Orleans*, 8.
177. Greater New Orleans Data Center Pre-Katrina website, "Iberville Development Neighborhood Snapshot," 2002, www.datacenterresearch.org/pre-katrina/orleans/4/41/snapshot.html.
178. Emily Epstein Landau, *Spectacular Wickedness: Sex, Race, and Memory in Storyville, New Orleans* (Baton Rouge: Louisiana State University Press, 2013), 23.
179. Ibid., 31.
180. Ibid., 16.
181. Ibid., 9.
182. *Times-Picayune*, "A Visit to Storyville, New Orleans' Most Famous Red Light District," October 7, 2011.
183. Greater New Orleans Data Center Pre-Katrina website, "Iberville Development Neighborhood Snapshot."

184. Ibid.
185. *HANO News*, "The Transformation of Iberville" (Fall 2011): 4, Housing Authority of New Orleans.
186. Reckdahl, "Discovery of Human Remains."
187. Ibid.
188. Yvonne Estrade, "The Accidental Place: Louis Armstrong Park Out of Place on the North Side," master's thesis, University of New Orleans, Paper 49, 2003, 6.
189. Ibid.
190. Ibid., 9.
191. Hirsch and Logsdon, *Creole New Orleans*, 189.
192. St. Augustine Catholic Church of New Orleans, "Summary of Church History," www.staugustinecatholicchurch-neworleans.org/hist-sum.htm (accessed June 4, 2015).
193. Ibid., "Famous Parishioners," www.staugustinecatholicchurch-neworleans.org/hist-famous.htm (accessed June 4, 2015).
194. Dooky Chase's Restaurant, "History of Dooky Chase's Restaurant," www.dookychaserestaurant.com/about (accessed June 3, 2015).
195. Greater New Orleans Data Center Pre-Katrina website, "Treme/Lafitte Neighborhood Snapshot," 2002, www.datacenterresearch.org/pre-katrina/orleans/4/42/snapshot.html.
196. Ibid.
197. Ibid.
198. Ibid.
199. Julie Raimondi, "Treme Brass Band," *KnowLA Encyclopedia of Louisiana* (July 26, 2011); Backstreet Cultural Museum, "History," www.backstreetmuseum.org (accessed June 4, 2015).
200. Greater New Orleans Data Center Pre-Katrina website, "Seventh Ward Neighborhood Snapshot," 2002, http://www.datacenterresearch.org/pre-katrina/orleans/4/14/snapshot.html.
201. Hirsch and Logsdon, *Creole New Orleans*, 189.
202. Ibid.; Greater New Orleans Data Center Pre-Katrina website, "Seventh Ward Neighborhood Snapshot."
203. Michael P. Smith, "Buffalo Bill and the Mardi Gras Indians," *Louisiana Cultural Vistas Magazine* (January 5, 2015).
204. Ibid.
205. Mark Cave and Thomas Walsh, "AP Tureaud Jr.'s Creole Perspective: Memories of the 7th Ward," *WWNO*, November 3, 2014.
206. Ibid.
207. Amistad Research Center online database, "Tureaud, A.P." (1899–1972), www.amistadresearchcenter.org (accessed June 5, 2015).

208. Ibid.
209. Ibid.
210. *The Advocate*, "N.O. Honors Mardi Gras Indian Legend Montana," January 9, 201).
211. Ibid.
212. Billes Architecture LLC, "Seventh Ward Neighborhood , Planning District 4," *New Orleans Neighborhood Revitalization Plans* (Lambert Plans), 2006, 8.
213. *New Orleans Local Network*, "Porch 7th Ward Cultural Organization," National Performance Network, http://npnweb.org (accessed June 5, 2015).
214. Nora Goddard, "The Destruction of Public Housing in New Orleans," *NOLA Tour Guy*, November 27, 2012, www.nolatourguy.com/public-housing.
215. Housing Authority of New Orleans, "Our Communities," www.hano.org/communities.aspx (accessed April 6, 2015); Richard A. Webster, "Columbia Parc in New Orleans Is Showcased as National Mixed-Income Housing Model," NOLA.com and the *Times-Picayune*, October 3, 2013.
216. Leroy Jones, "The Fairview Baptist Church Christian Marching Band," Spirit of New Orleans Productions, www.spiritofneworleans.com/Fairview.htm (accessed June 14, 2015).
217. Ibid.
218. Ibid.
219. *Times-Picayune*, "Helen Washington Lang, Public Housing Advocate, Dies at 80," August 20, 2010.
220. Ibid.
221. Goddard, "Destruction of Public Housing."
222. "St. Bernard Area Statistical Area," analysis of data from U.S. Census 2000 Summary File 1 (SF1) and U.S. Census 2010 Summary File 1 (SF1)," the Data Center, March 2014.
223. Billes Architecture LLC, "St. Bernard Neighborhood, Planning District 4," *New Orleans Neighborhood Revitalization Plans* (Lambert Plans), 2006, 7.
224. Tram Nguyen, "Pushed Out and Pushing Back."
225. Ibid.
226. Goddard, "Destruction of Public Housing."
227. *Facing South*, "Scandal-Plagued HUD Chief Quits, but Affordable Housing Crisis Continued in the Gulf" (April 4, 2008), Institute for Southern Studies.
228. Webster, "Columbia Parc in New Orleans."
229. Campanella, *Geographies of New Orleans*, 5.
230. Ibid.
231. Ibid.
232. Preservation Resource Center of New Orleans, *Living with History in New Orleans' Neighborhoods: Esplanade Ridge*, brochure.

233. Jean Étienne de Boré preceded Pitot as New Orleans' mayor before the city was incorporated.

234. Greater New Orleans Data Center Pre-Katrina website, "Fairgrounds Neighborhood Snapshot," 2002, www.datacenterresearch.org/pre-katrina/orleans/4/25/snapshot.html.

235. Ibid.; Preservation Resource Center of New Orleans, *Esplanade Ridge*, brochure.

236. Parkway Bakery & Tavern, "Our History," www.parkwaypoorboys.com/history.html (accessed June 5, 2015).

237. The New Orleans Jazz & Heritage Festival, "History," www.nojazzfest.com/info/history (accessed June 5, 2015).

238. *Mid-City Messenger*, "Bayou St. John Resident Look into Restricting Activity Near the Waterway," January 12, 2014.

239. Billes Architecture LLC, "Faubourg St. John Neighborhood, Planning District 4," *New Orleans Neighborhood Revitalization Plans* (Lambert Plans), 2006, 8.

240. Peggy Scott Laborde, "Mid-City: The Heart of New Orleans," *Preservation in Print* (June 1992).

241. The Irish suffered from the yellow fever epidemic disproportionately to other immigrants because of the unskilled digging work they did in New Orleans' canals. Leonard V. Huber, *New Orleans Architecture: The Cemeteries*, vol. 8 (Gretna, LA: Pelican Publishing, 1996), 33.

242. Jane Place Neighborhood Sustainability Initiative, "History & Neighborhood Snapshot," http://jpnsi.org/history--neighborhood-snapshot (accessed June 5, 2015).

243. Greater New Orleans Data Center Pre-Katrina website, "Mid-City Neighborhood Snapshot," 2002, www.datacenterresearch.org/pre-katrina/orleans/4/45/snapshot.html.

244. Campanella, *Geographies of New Orleans*, 21.

245. Jane Place Neighborhood Sustainability Initiative, "History & Neighborhood Snapshot."

246. Billes Architecture LLC, "Mid-City Neighborhood, Planning District 4," *New Orleans Neighborhood Revitalization Plans* (Lambert Plans), 2006, 8.

247. Richard Campanella, "Gentrification and Its Discontents: Notes from New Orleans," *newgeography*, March 1, 2013, www.newgeography.com.

248. Katherine Sayre, "As New Orleans Rents Rise, Nonprofit Creates 'Permanently Affordable' Apartments," NOLA.com and the *Times-Picayune*, April 22, 2015.

249. Richard Campanella, "Where the Hell Is Plum Orchard: How New Orleanians Perceive, Delineate, Name—and Argue About—Urban Space in Their City," posted on richcampanella.com and nolafender.com, based on Richard Campanella, *Bienville's Dilemma: A*

Historical Geography of New Orleans (Lafayette: University of Louisiana Press, 2008).

250. Charity moved five times before opening in its final building in 1939.
251. Greater New Orleans Data Center Pre-Katrina website, "Tulane/Gravier Neighborhood Snapshot," 2002, www.datacenterresearch.org/pre-katrina/orleans/4/46/snapshot.html.
252. Danielle Del Sol, "Mid-City Mid-Transformation," *Preservation in Print* (April 2014).
253. Ibid.
254. "Tulane/Gravier Statistical Area," analysis of data from U.S. Census 2000 Summary File 1 (SF1) and U.S. Census 2010 Summary File 1 (SF1)," the Data Center, March 2014.
255. Del Sol, "Mid-City Mid-Transformation."
256. Ibid.
257. Campanella, *Geographies of New Orleans*, 259.
258. Allen Toussaint, "The House with 88 Keys," *Wall Street Journal*, September 26, 2013.
259. Xavier University of Louisiana, "History of Xavier," www.xula.edu/about-xavier/history.php (accessed June 15, 2015).
260. Ibid.
261. Blue Plate Artists Lofts, "History of the Blue Plate Building," www.blueplatelofts.com/history (accessed June 5, 2015).
262. Xavier University of Louisiana, "History of Xavier."
263. Xavier University of Louisiana, "2014 Accomplishments," www.xula.edu/mediarelations/2014_xavieraccomplishments.pdf (accessed June 5, 2015).
264. Billes Architecture LLC, "Gert Town Neighborhood, Planning District 4," *New Orleans Neighborhood Revitalization Plans* (Lambert Plans), 2006, 9-13.
265. Xavier University of Louisiana, "Quick Facts," www.xula.edu/mediarelations/quickfacts.php (accessed June 5, 2015).
266. Jed Lipinski, "Norman Francis to Retire After 46 Years as University President," NOLA.com and the *Times-Picayune*, September 4, 2014.
267. Xavier University of Louisiana, "History of Xavier."
268. *NolaVie*, "Blue Plate Lofts Get Artistic Touch," NOLA.com, June 13, 2012.

CHAPTER 5

269. Author analysis of "St. Bernard Area Statistical Area," analysis of data from U.S. Census 2000 Summary File 1 (SF1) and U.S. Census 2010 Summary File 1 (SF1)," the Data Center, March 2014.

270. Greater New Orleans Data Center Pre-Katrina website, "Marigny Neighborhood Snapshot," 2002, www.datacenterresearch.org/pre-katrina/orleans/7/21/snapshot.html.
271. Campanella, "Ethnic Geography of New Orleans."
272. Ibid.; Hirsch and Logsdon, *Creole New Orleans*, 189.
273. The train depot was at Royal and Press Streets, within the Marigny's National Historic Boundaries but in the city's Bywater neighborhood. Keith Weldon Medley, "Plessy vs. Ferguson," *KnowLA Encyclopedia of Louisiana* (August 16, 2013).
274. Campanella, *Geographies of New Orleans*, 215.
275. Campanella, "Gentrification and Its Discontents."
276. Greater New Orleans Data Center Pre-Katrina website, "St. Roch Neighborhood Snapshot," 2002, www.datacenterresearch.org/pre-katrina/orleans/7/24/snapshot.html.
277. Ibid.
278. Ibid.
279. Ibid.
280. "St. Roch Statistical Area," analysis of data from U.S. Census 2000 Summary File 1 (SF1) and U.S. Census 2010 Summary File 1 (SF1)," the Data Center, March 2014.
281. Billes Architecture LLC, "St. Roch Neighborhood, Planning District 7," *New Orleans Neighborhood Revitalization Plans* (Lambert Plans), 2006, 11.
282. St. Roch CDC, "About Us," http://strochcdc.org/about-us (accessed June 5, 2015).
283. Dancing Grounds, "Our Mission & Impact," http://dancingrounds.org/mission-vision (accessed June 5, 2015).
284. Ibid.
285. Doug MacCash, "Bywater Art Lofts 2, an $11.3 Million Investment, Holding Grand Opening Tonight," NOLA.com and the *Times-Picayune*, October 12, 2012.
286. Mimi Read, "Where the Walls Do Talk," *New York Times*, June 6, 2012.
287. Eve Abrams, "Along Saint Claude," *WWNO* audio documentary, April 11, 2014.
288. Arthur White, "Bywater Past and Present," *Preservation in Print* (August 1984): 4.
289. Abrams, "Along Saint Claude."
290. Doug MacCash, "Crescent Park on New Orleans Riverfront Is a Severe Masterpiece," NOLA.com and the *Times-Picayune*, February 27, 2014.
291. Read, "Where the Walls Do Talk."
292. Doug MacCash, "Gentrification of Bywater and St. Claude Avenue Was Sped Up by Flood and 2008 Economic Slump," NOLA.com and the *Times-Picayune*, January 15, 2013.

293. Dan Swenson, "Flash Flood: Hurricane Katrina's Inundation of New Orleans, August 29, 2005," Interactive Graphics, NOLA.com and the *Times-Picayune*, www.nola.com/katrina/graphics/flashflood.swf; Dan Swenson, "Lagniappe: Flood Depths," Interactive Graphics, NOLA.com and the *Times-Picayune*, www.nola.com/katrina/graphics/depths.swf.

294. David Hammer, "Road Home's Grant Calculations Discriminate Against Black Homeowners, Federal Judge Rules," *Times-Picayune*, August 16, 2010.

295. Ruby Bridges Foundation, "History of the Florida Neighborhood," www.rubybridgesfoundation.org (accessed March 26, 2015).

296. Ibid.

297. Ibid.

298. PBS.org, "Ruby Bridges Desegregates a School," November 19, 2013, www.pbs.org/wnet/african-americans-many-rivers-to-cross/video/ruby-bridges-goes-to-school.

299. Ibid.

300. New Orleans Area Habitat for Humanity, "Musicians' Village," www.habitat-nola.org/about/musicians_village (accessed June 5, 2013).

301. Housing Authority of New Orleans, "Our Communities: Florida," accessed June 6, 2015.

302. Greater New Orleans Data Center Pre-Katrina website, "Desire Area Neighborhood Snapshot," 2002, www.datacenterresearch.org/pre-katrina/orleans/7/15/snapshot.html.

303. Ibid.

304. Orissa Arend, *Showdown in Desire: The Black Panthers Take a Stand in New Orleans* (Fayetteville: University of Arkansas Press, 2009), 4.

305. Goddard, "Destruction of Public Housing."

306. Arend, *Showdown in Desire*, 4–5.

307. Ibid.

308. Amistad Research Center online database, "Free Southern Theater (1963–1978)," www.amistadresearchcenter.org (accessed June 6, 2015).

309. Greater New Orleans Data Center Pre-Katrina website, "Desire Area Neighborhood Snapshot."

310. Ibid.

311. Arend, *Showdown in Desire*, 25.

312. Ibid., 26.

313. Ibid.

314. Stacy Dittrich, *Murder Behind the Badge: True Stories of Cops Who Kill* (Westminster, MD: Prometheus Books, 2009), 198.

315. Ibid.

316. Desire Street Ministries, "FAQ, Fact Sheet," May 2013, www.desirestreet.org/wp-content/uploads/2013/05/Media-Fact-Sheet-5-7-2013.pdf.

317. Rob Walker, *Letters from New Orleans* (New Orleans, LA: Garret County Press, 2005), 151.
318. Housing Authority of New Orleans, "Our Communities: The Estates," accessed June 6, 2015.

CHAPTER 6

319. Richard Campanella, "Urban Transformation in the Lower Ninth Ward," in *Architecture in Times of Need: Make It Right—Rebuilding New Orleans' Lower Ninth Ward* (New York: Prestel Publishing, 2009), 86, 93.
320. *A Framework for Sustainable Resilience in the Lower Ninth Ward*, H3 Studio Project team, January 2007, 1.8.
321. Campanella, "Urban Transformation," 92.
322. *Framework for Sustainable Resilience*, 1.12.
323. Only one other black student integrated a white school that day: Ruby Bridges, in the Upper Ninth Ward.
324. Restore the Bayou.org, "Background," http://restorethebayou.org/background (accessed June 6, 2015).
325. Ibid.
326. Campanella, "Urban Transformation," 94.
327. Juliette Landphair, "'The Forgotten People of New Orleans': Community, Vulnerability, and the Lower Ninth Ward," *Journal of American History* (December 2007): 94.
328. Campanella, "Urban Transformation," 95.
329. Swenson, "Flash Flood."
330. Swenson, "Lagniappe."
331. Hammer, "Road Home's Grant Calculations."
332. Vicki Mack and Allison Plyer, "Neighborhood Growth Rates: Growth in New Orleans Neighborhoods Continues in 2014," the Data Center, August 6, 2014.
333. Lowernine.org, "About," http://lowernine.org/about (accessed March 26, 2015).
334. Make It Right staff, "Our Response to the *New Republic*," Makeitright.org, March 18, 2013.
335. Mary Rickard, "With MRGO Closed, Groups Seek to Restore Bayou Bienvenue Ecosystem," *New Orleans Advocate*, November 27, 2013.
336. Rachel Breunlin, Ronald W. Lewis and Helen Regis, *The House of Dance and Feathers: A Museum by Ronald Lewis* (New Orleans, LA: Neighborhood Story Project, 2009), 8.
337. City of New Orleans Historic District Landmarks Commission, "Holy Cross Historic District," May 2011, www.nola.gov.

338. Campanella, "Urban Transformation," 87–88.
339. Greater New Orleans Data Center Pre-Katrina website, "Holy Cross Neighborhood Snapshot," 2002, www.datacenterresearch.org/pre-katrina/orleans/8/20/snapshot.html.
340. Preservation Resource Center of New Orleans, *Living with History in New Orleans' Neighborhoods: Holy Cross*, brochure.
341. Campanella, "Urban Transformation," 91.
342. The second Doullut house was built in 1913. Doug MacCash, "Unusual Flood-Resistant 'Steamboat House' Helped Keep Neighborhood Afloat," *Times-Picayune*, August 28, 2010.
343. Campanella, "Urban Transformation," 91.
344. Ibid., 88.
345. Ibid., 94.
346. "Holy Cross Statistical Area," analysis of data from U.S. Census 2000 Summary File 1 (SF1) and U.S. Census 2010 Summary File 1 (SF1), the Data Center, March 2014.
347. Swenson, "Lagniappe."
348. Ibid.
349. *Sustainable Restoration: Holy Cross Historic District & Lower 9th Ward*, Lower Ninth Ward Residents Recommendation Report, June 2006, 1.
350. Lower 9th Ward Center for Sustainable Engagement & Development, "Natural Environment," "Built Environment: Community Mapping" and "Volunteers," www.sustainthenine.org (accessed June 6, 2015).
351. Kickstarter Campaign, "The Center: A Sustainable Historic House," www.kickstarter.com/projects/312337143/the-center-a-sustainable-historic-house (accessed June 6, 2015).
352. Jed Lipinski, "Lil Wayne Skatepark Failure a Setback for Lower Ninth Ward Community Center," NOLA.com and the *Times-Picayune*, April 29, 2014.
353. Ibid.

CHAPTER 7

354. New Orleans City Park, "Live Oaks of City Park," http://neworleanscitypark.com/live-oaks-of-city-park (accessed May 26, 2015).
355. Works Progress Administration, *New Orleans City Park: Its First Fifty Years* (New Orleans, LA: Gulf Printing Company, 1941).
356. New Orleans City Park, "City Park History," http://neworleanscitypark.com/new-orleans-city-park-history (accessed May 26, 2015).
357. New Orleans Historical, "City Park Tour," http://neworleanshistorical.org/tours/show/9 (accessed May 26, 2015).

358. Ibid.
359. New Orleans City Park, "City Park History."
360. Ibid.
361. Ibid.
362. New Orleans City Park, *New Orleans City Park Master Plan: Vision for the 21st Century—City Park 2018*, 8. Adopted March 25, 2005, and amended in 2007, 2009 and 2011.
363. New Orleans City Park, "City Park History"; Swenson, "Lagniappe."
364. New Orleans City Park, *New Orleans City Park Master Plan*, 3.
365. Grow Dat Youth Farm, "Our Farm," http://growdatyouthfarm.org/our-farm-1 (accessed May 26, 2015).
366. Delgado Community College, "Fast Facts," www.dcc.edu/about/fast-facts (accessed May 26, 2015).
367. Delgado Community College, "History," www.dcc.edu/about/history.aspx (accessed May 26, 2015).
368. Ibid.
369. Save Our Cemeteries, "Holt Cemetery," www.saveourcemeteries.org/holt-cemetery (accessed June 6, 2015).
370. *Times-Picayune*, "Jazz Funeral for Legend to Correct Big Oversight," September 6, 1996.
371. Greater New Orleans Data Center Pre-Katrina website, "Navarre Neighborhood Snapshot," 2002, www.datacenterresearch.org/pre-katrina/orleans/5/40/snapshot.html.
372. Delgado Community College, "History."
373. Ibid.
374. Delgado Community College, "Fast Facts."
375. Delgado Community College, "Why Choose Delgado?" www.dcc.edu/about/fast-facts/why-delgado.aspx (accessed May 26, 2015).
376. Delgado Community College, "Fast Facts."
377. Country Club Gardens Association, "About CCGA," http://countryclubgardens.net(accessed May 27, 2015).
378. Campanella, *Geographies of New Orleans*, 57–58.
379. Ibid., 14.
380. Huber, *New Orleans Architecture: The Cemeteries*, 52.
381. Ibid.; Save Our Cemeteries, "Metairie Cemetery," accessed May 27, 2015.
382. Billes Architecture LLC, "Lakewood Neighborhood, Planning District 5," *New Orleans Neighborhood Revitalization Plans* (Lambert Plans), 2006, 3.
383. *Times-Picayune*, Real Estate, October 5, 1924.
384. Ibid.

385. Longue Vue House & Gardens, "Edith and Edgar Stern," https://longuevue.com/about/history/stern (accessed May 27, 2015).
386. Longue Vue House & Gardens, "History: A Masterpiece of Beauty and Elegance," https://longuevue.com/about/history (accessed May 27, 2015).
387. Greater New Orleans Data Center Pre-Katrina website, "West End Neighborhood Snapshot," 2002, www.datacenterresearch.org/pre-katrina/orleans/5/39/snapshot.html.
388. Ibid.
389. Ibid.; Southern Yacht Club, "A Brief History," www.southernyachtclub.org (accessed May 28, 2015).
390. Greater New Orleans Community Data Center Pre-Katrina website, "West End Neighborhood Snapshot."
391. New Orleans History: Lake Pontchartrain, "Resorts at West End," www.pontchartrain.net/491323 (accessed May 28, 2015).
392. Greater New Orleans Community Data Center Pre-Katrina website, "West End Neighborhood Snapshot."
393. Ibid.
394. Dan Ellis, "West End," Dan Ellis New Orleans website, http://neworleans.danellis.net/west_end.htm (accessed May 28, 2015).
395. Greater New Orleans Community Data Center Pre-Katrina website, "West End Neighborhood Snapshot."
396. Lake Pontchartrain Basin Foundation, "History of the Pontchartrain Basin," www.saveourlake.org/basin-history.php (accessed May 28, 2015).
397. Ibid.
398. The clubhouse that was destroyed was erected in 1949 as the yacht club's third clubhouse. Southern Yacht Club, "A Brief History," accessed May 28, 2015.
399. Ibid.
400. Greater New Orleans Community Data Center Pre-Katrina website, "Lakeview Neighborhood Snapshot," 2002, www.datacenterresearch.org/pre-katrina/orleans/5/37/snapshot.html.
401. Ibid.; Mount Carmel Academy, "Our History," www.mcacubs.com (accessed May 28, 2015).
402. Campanella, "Ethnic Geography of New Orleans."
403. Ibid.
404. Swenson, "Flash Flood."
405. Susan Langenhennig, "New Orleans' Lakefront Neighborhoods Rank in the Top 10 Most Searched Zip Codes Nationwide on Realtor.com," NOLA.com and the *Times-Picayune*, December 28, 2014.
406. Campanella, *Geographies of New Orleans*, 153.
407. Joseph H. De Grange, "Historical Data of Spanish Fort," *Louisiana Historical Quarterly* 2 (1919): 268.

408. Ibid., 269.
409. Ibid., 270.
410. National Park Service, "Jazz Neighborhoods," www.nps.gov/jazz/learn/historyculture/jazz-map.htm (accessed May 30, 2015).
411. Greater New Orleans Data Center Pre-Katrina website, "Lakeshore/Lake Vista Neighborhood Snapshot," 2002, www.datacenterresearch.org/pre-katrina/orleans/5/35/snapshot.html.
412. John D. Cramer, "Lake Vista: New Orleans' Own Garden City," "HPRESIST" blog, October 26, 2011, https://johndcramer.wordpress.com.
413. U.S. Department of Veterans Affairs, "VA New Orleans: The Legacy of Service Continues," www.neworleans.va.gov/Legacy_of_service.asp (accessed May 30, 2015).
414. Ibid.
415. Arthur Hardy, "A Few Things You Might Not Know About Mardi Gras Fountain on New Orleans' Lakefront," *New Orleans Advocate*, February 17, 2015.
416. Ibid.
417. "Navarre Statistical Area," analysis of data from U.S. Census 2000 Summary File 1 (SF1) and U.S. Census 2010 Summary File 1 (SF1), the Data Center, March 2014.
418. Lakeshore Property Owners' Association, "History of Lakeshore," www.lakeshorenola.com/History.html (accessed May 30, 2015).
419. Mack and Plyer, "Neighborhood Growth Rates."

CHAPTER 8

420. Campanella, *Geographies of New Orleans*, 153.
421. Ibid., 143, 153.
422. Ibid., 143.
423. Ibid.
424. Ibid., 144.
425. Ibid., 149.
426. Ibid., 145.
427. Ibid., 149.
428. Ibid.
429. Ibid., 145.
430. Greater New Orleans Data Center Pre-Katrina website, "Lake Terrace & Oaks Neighborhood Snapshot," 2002, www.datacenterresearch.org/pre-katrina/orleans/6/34/snapshot.html.
431. Campanella, *Geographies of New Orleans*, 148.
432. Greater New Orleans Data Center Pre-Katrina website, "St. Anthony Neighborhood Snapshot," 2002, www.datacenterresearch.

org/pre-katrina/orleans/6/32/snapshot.html; and "Milneburg Neighborhood Snapshot," 2002, www.datacenterresearch.org/pre-katrina/orleans/6/30/index.html.

433. Author analysis of "St. Anthony Statistical Area," analysis of data from U.S. Census 2000 Summary File 1 (SF1) and U.S. Census 2010 Summary File 1 (SF1), the Data Center, March 2014.

434. "Milneburg Statistical Area," analysis of data from U.S. Census 2000 Summary File 1 (SF1) and U.S. Census 2010 Summary File 1 (SF1), the Data Center, March 2014.

435. Adriane Quinlan, "9 Years After Hurricane Katrina, a Gentilly Church Re-Opens Its Doors," NOLA.com and the *Times-Picayune*, August 29, 2014.

436. Swenson, "Flash Flood" and "Lagniappe."

437. "Milneburg Statistical Area" and "St. Anthony Statistical Area," the Data Center; Mack and Plyer "Neighborhood Growth Rates."

438. Kweilyn Murphy, "Hurricane Katrina: Gentilly Church Reopens for Community with Various Events," *WDSU News*, August 29, 2014.

439. Richard Webster, "Work on Milne Boys Home in Gentilly Begins, Seven Years after Hurricane Katrina," *Times-Picayune*, October 11, 2012.

440. Ibid.

441. Scott Gold and Ann Simmons, "Geographic Quirk Saved 'the Island' in New Orleans," *Los Angeles Times*, March 12, 2006.

442. Campanella, *Geographies of New Orleans*, 57–58.

443. Ibid., 57.

444. Preservation Resource Center of New Orleans, *Living with History in New Orleans' Neighborhoods: Gentilly Terrace*, brochure.

445. Campanella, *Geographies of New Orleans*, 152.

446. Ibid.

447. Ibid.

448. Ibid.

449. Ibid., 305.

450. Ibid.

451. Cowen Institute for Public Education Initiatives Report, *New Orleans Public Schools History: A Brief Overview* (New Orleans, LA: Tulane University, 2007), 2.

452. Donna Fricker, "The Founding of Dillard University," *Preservation in Print* (June 2003).

453. Ibid.; State University Study Guide, *Booker T. Washington (1856–1915)—Early Years, The Black Commitment to Free Education, Industrial Education*, http://education.stateuniversity.com/pages/2542/Washington-Booker-T-1856-1915.html (accessed June 14, 2015).

454. Dillard University President's Staff Task Force, "A Brief History of Dillard University," www.dillard.edu (accessed June 14, 2015).
455. Campanella, *Geographies of New Orleans*, 305.
456. Ibid., 58.
457. Ibid.
458. Dillard University President's Staff Task Force, "Brief History of Dillard University."
459. Campanella, *Geographies of New Orleans*, 305.
460. Ibid.
461. Greater New Orleans Data Center Pre-Katrina website, "Dillard Neighborhood Snapshot," 2002, www.datacenterresearch.org/pre-katrina/orleans/6/27/snapshot.html.
462. Billes Architecture LLC, "Dillard Neighborhood, Planning District 6," *New Orleans Neighborhood Revitalization Plans* (Lambert Plans), 2006, 15.
463. Dillard University President's Staff Task Force, "Brief History of Dillard University."
464. Gold and Simmons, "Geographic Quirk."
465. Dillard University President's Staff Task Force, "Brief History of Dillard University."
466. Ibid.
467. Campanella, *Geographies of New Orleans*, 5.
468. Ibid.
469. Independent Levee Investigation Team, "History of New Orleans Flood Protection System," New Orleans Levee Systems: Hurricane Katrina, July 31, 2006, 4–14.
470. Greater New Orleans Data Center Pre-Katrina website, "Filmore Neighborhood Snapshot," 2002, www.datacenterresearch.org/pre-katrina/orleans/6/33/snapshot.html.
471. Ibid.; Holy Trinity Greek Orthodox Cathedral, "History," http://holytrinitycathedral.org/history.html (accessed June 7, 2015).
472. Holy Trinity Greek Orthodox Cathedral, "History."
473. Author analysis of "Filmore Statistical Area," analysis of data from U.S. Census 2000 Summary File 1 (SF1) and U.S. Census 2010 Summary File 1 (SF1), the Data Center, March 2014.
474. Ibid. These figures are from 2000.
475. Swenson, "Flash Flood" and "Lagniappe."
476. Author analysis of "Filmore Statistical Area," the Data Center.
477. Greater New Orleans Data Center Pre-Katrina website, "Gentilly Woods Neighborhood Snapshot," 2002, www.datacenterresearch.org/pre-katrina/orleans/6/29/snapshot.html.
478. Galvin Richard, *Katrina: Eyes Have Not Seen, Ears Have Not Heard* (n.p.: AuthorHouse, 2008), 8.

479. *New Orleans History: Lake Pontchartrain*, "Higgins Huts," January 2000.
480. Richard, *Katrina.*
481. New Orleans Baptist Theological Seminary, "Our Heritage," www.nobts.edu (accessed June 6, 2015).
482. Jonathan Fricker, "The Past as Inspiration," *Preservation in Print* (October 2012): 13.
483. Ibid.
484. "Gentilly Woods Statistical Area," analysis of data from U.S. Census 2000 Summary File 1 (SF1) and U.S. Census 2010 Summary File 1 (SF1), the Data Center, March 2014.
485. Swenson, "Flash Flood" and "Lagniappe."
486. Mack and Plyer, "Neighborhood Growth Rates."
487. Katherine Sayre, "Walmart Opens on Once-Blighted Gentilly Woods Property," NOLA.com and the *Times-Picayune*, August 13, 2014.
488. St. Gabriel the Archangel Roman Catholic Church, "History of St. Gabriel the Archangel Parish," www.stgabrielstl.org/ParishInformation/History.aspx (accessed June 14, 2015).
489. Campanella, *Geographies of New Orleans*, 309.
490. Ibid.
491. Ibid.
492. Pontchartrain Park Neighborhood Association, "Post-War Promise," www.pontchartrainpark.org/history (accessed June 7, 2015).
493. Crawford Homes development company constructed both Gentilly Woods and Pontchartrain Park. Greater New Orleans Data Center Pre-Katrina website, "Pontchartrain Park Neighborhood Snapshot," 2002, www.datacenterresearch.org/pre-katrina/orleans/6/31/snapshot.html; Pontchartrain Park Neighborhood Association, "Post-War Promise."
494. Greater New Orleans Community Data Center Pre-Katrina website, "Pontchartrain Park Neighborhood Snapshot."
495. Pontchartrain Park Neighborhood Association, "Joseph M. Bartholomew, Sr., Golf Architect," www.pontchartrainpark.org/history (accessed June 7, 2015).
496. Southern University of New Orleans, "History," http://suno.edu/about/history (accessed March 29, 2014).
497. Pontchartrain Park Neighborhood Association, "In a Sense, It Was Kind of Like a Mayberry," www.pontchartrainpark.org/history (accessed June 7, 2015).
498. Ibid.
499. Pontchartrain Park Neighborhood Association, "National Historic Preservation," www.pontchartrainpark.org/history (accessed June 6, 2015).

500. Tricia Escobedo and Katie Pyne, "New Orleans Suburb Rises from Katrina's Shadow," CNN.com, August 19, 2010.
501. Swenson, "Flash Flood" and "Lagniappe."
502. Mack and Plyer, "Neighborhood Growth Rates."
503. Hammer, "Road Home's Grant Calculations"; Michelle Krupa, "Pontchartrain Park Rebuilding Initiative Reaches Milestone with Opening of a Model Home," *Times-Picayune*, May 14, 2010.
504. David Hammer, "8,800 Road Home Properties to Return to Private Hands," *Times-Picayune*, September 28, 2009.
505. Mack and Plyer, "Neighborhood Growth Rates."
506. Southern University of New Orleans, "History."
507. Hammer, "8,800 Road Home Properties."
508. Campanella, *Geographies of New Orleans*, 153.
509. John Pope, "33 Vintage Pontchartrain Beach Amusement Park Photos for #Throwbackthursday," NOLA.com and the *Times-Picayune*, August 21, 2014.
510. Greater New Orleans Data Center Pre-Katrina website, "Lake Terrace & Oaks Neighborhood Snapshot," 2002, www.datacenterresearch.org/pre-katrina/orleans/6/34/snapshot.html.
511. University of New Orleans, "History," www.uno.edu/about/history.aspx (accessed March 31, 2015).
512. Ibid.
513. Ibid.
514. University of New Orleans, "At a Glance," www.uno.edu/about/at-a-glance.aspx (accessed March 31, 2015).
515. University of New Orleans, "Research and Technology Park," www.uno.edu/research/rtp.aspx (accessed June 7, 2015).
516. Swenson, "Lagniappe."
517. University of New Orleans, "History."
518. Jarvis DeBerry, "Saying Goodbye to the University of New Orleans," NOLA.com and the *Times-Picayune*, December 9, 2014.
519. Ibid.
520. University of New Orleans, "History."

CHAPTER 9

521. Richard Campanella, "Addressing New Orleans East's Core Problem," NOLA.com and the *Times-Picayune*, December 10, 2013.
522. Campanella, *Geographies of New Orleans*, 58.
523. Campanella, "Addressing New Orleans East's Core Problem."
524. Ibid.

525. Greater New Orleans Data Center Pre-Katrina website, "Little Woods Neighborhood Snapshot," 2002, www.datacenterresearch.org/pre-katrina/orleans/9/49/snapshot.html.
526. Ibid.
527. Ibid.
528. Ibid.
529. Campanella, "Addressing New Orleans East's Core Problem."
530. Ibid.
531. Ibid.
532. Campanella, *Geographies of New Orleans*, 309.
533. Ibid., 362.
534. Greater New Orleans Data Center Pre-Katrina website, "West Lake Forest Neighborhood Snapshot," 2002, www.datacenterresearch.org/pre-katrina/orleans/9/55/snapshot.html.
535. Ibid.
536. Swenson, "Flash Flood."
537. Ibid.
538. Swenson, "Lagniappe."
539. Mack and Plyer, "Neighborhood Growth Rates."
540. Casey Ferrand, "Celebrating Grand Opening of New Orleans East Hospital," *WDSU News*, August 20, 2014.
541. Benjamin Alexander-Bloch, "Audubon Louisiana Nature Center Restoration Finally Begins After Sitting in Tatters since Katrina," NOLA.com and the *Times-Picayune*, January 24, 2014.
542. Jennifer Larino, "Folgers Expansion Perks Up Louisiana," *New Orleans CityBusiness*, March 24, 2010.
543. NASA Michoud Assembly Facility, "History," http://mafspace.msfc.nasa.gov/history.html (accessed June 7, 2015).
544. Dan Swenson, "War Machines, Space Exploration and Michoud's Role in History: Timeline," NOLA.com and the *Times-Picayune*, January 6, 2015.
545. Greater New Orleans Data Center Pre-Katrina website, "Viavant/Venetian Isles Neighborhood Snapshot," 2002, www.datacenterresearch.org/pre-katrina/orleans/11/54/snapshot.html.
546. NASA Michoud Assembly Facility, "History."
547. Campanella, *Geographies of New Orleans*, 58.
548. Billes Architecture LLC, "Viavant/Venetian Isles/Lake Catherine Neighborhood, Planning District 11," *New Orleans Neighborhood Revitalization Plans* (Lambert Plans), 2006, 13.
549. Dan Swenson, "War Machines."
550. NASA Michoud Assembly Facility, "History."

551. NASA Michoud Assembly Facility, "Tenants: United States Coast Guard," http://mafspace.msfc.nasa.gov/tenants_uscg.html (accessed June 7, 2015).
552. Greater New Orleans Data Center Pre-Katrina website, "Viavant/ Venetian Isles Neighborhood Snapshot."
553. Jennifer Larino, "From Michoud to Mars: New Orleans Workers Building NASA's Next Generation Spacecraft," NOLA.com and the *Times-Picayune*, January 6, 2015.
554. Ibid.
555. Karen J. Leong, Christopher A. Airriess, Wei Li, Angela Chia-Chen Chen and Verna M. Keith, "Resilient History and the Rebuilding of a Community: The Vietnamese American Community in New Orleans East," *Journal of American History* (December 2007): 94.
556. Ibid.
557. Ibid.
558. Ibid.
559. Campanella, *Geographies of New Orleans*, 362.
560. Ibid., 365.
561. Ibid., 358.
562. Leong, Airriess, Li, Chen and Keith, "Resilient History."
563. Swenson, "Flash Flood" and "Lagniappe."
564. Leong, Airriess, Li, Chen and Keith, "Resilient History."
565. Ibid.
566. Ibid.
567. *VietNOLA Podcast*, "Eric Tang on Vietnamese and African American Solidarity Post-Katrina," January 20, 2015, It's New Orleans podcast network.
568. Ibid.
569. Ibid.
570. Ibid.
571. Ibid.
572. VAYLA New Orleans, "Mission, Vision, Values," http://vayla-no.org/about (accessed June 7, 2015).
573. Campanella, *Bienville's Dilemma*, 110.
574. Todd Smith, *Louisiana and the Gulf Frontier, 1500–1821* (Baton Rouge: Louisiana State University Press, 2014), 181.
575. Ibid.
576. New Orleans Historical, "Fort Petite Coquilles," www.neworleanshistorical.org/items/show/119 (accessed June 7, 2015).
577. New Orleans Historical, "Fort Macomb," www.neworleanshistorical.org/items/show/117, and "Fort Pike," www.neworleanshistorical.org/items/show/120 (accessed March 25, 2015).

578. Charles Castner, "A Brief History of the Louisville & Nashville Railroad," Louisville & Nashville Railroad Historical Society, www.lnrr.org/History.aspx (accessed June 8, 2015).
579. New Orleans Historical, "Town of Lake Catherine," www.neworleanshistorical.org/items/show/121 (accessed March 25, 2015).
580. Ibid.
581. NOLAcitymuseum, "Camps and Lodges," Town of Lake Catherine exhibit, www.nolacitymuseum.org (accessed March 25, 2015).
582. Campanella, *Geographies of New Orleans*, 24.
583. U.S. Fish and Wildlife Service: Southeast Louisiana National Wildlife Refuges, "Bayou Sauvage National Wildlife Refuge," www.fws.gov/refuge/Bayou_Sauvage (accessed June 8, 2015).
584. New Orleans Historical, "Fort Pike Volunteer Fire Department," www.neworleanshistorical.org/items/show/118 (accessed March 25, 2015).
585. Mack and Plyer, "Neighborhood Growth Rates."

CHAPTER 10

586. Ferry Foundation, "1817 Shipbuilding," www.theferryfoundation.org/page10a.html (accessed June 8, 2015).
587. Jane Tiller, "World War II Veteran Celebrates 90th Birthday at Home in Algiers," NOLA.com and the *Times-Picayune*, May 31, 2012.
588. Algiers Historical Society, "The History of Algiers," www.algiershistoricalsociety.org/algiers-history.html (accessed June 8, 2015).
589. Ibid.
590. Ibid.
591. Allen Powell II, "Algiers Landmark Could Be Destroyed in Fight Against Mississippi River Flooding," *Times-Picayune*, May 13, 2011.
592. Ibid.
593. Algiers Historical Society, "Over Da River Jazz Tour," http://algiershistoricalsociety.org/page35.html (accessed June 8, 2015).
594. Old Algiers Main Street, "A Condensed History of Old Algiers," www.oldalgiersmainstreet.org/history.html (accessed June 8, 2015).
595. *The African-American Mosaic: Colonization*, Library of Congress Resource Guide for the Study of Black History & Culture, www.loc.gov/exhibits/african/intro.html (accessed January 18, 2015).
596. Ray Brassieur, Lionel Lyles and Michael S. Martin, *"Freetown as It Was and as It Is": The Freetown History Project Final Report* (University of Louisiana–Lafayette, 2013), 22.
597. Old Algiers Main Street, "Condensed History of Old Algiers."
598. Campanella, "Ethnic Geography of New Orleans."

599. Algiers Historical Society, "3 Walking Tours of Algiers Point," http://algiershistoricalsociety.org/walking-tours.html (accessed June 8, 2015).
600. ExhibitBe New Orleans, "Home," www.exhibitbe.com (accessed June 8, 2015).
601. Jeremy Alford, "Public Housing's 'Legacy Buildings,'" *Gambit*, July 24, 2012.
602. Allen Powell II, "Last Fischer Buildings Fall," *Times-Picayune*, January 9, 2008.
603. Old Algiers Main Street, "Condensed History of Old Algiers."
604. Paul Purpura, "Navy Gives Up Algiers Land for Federal City Development Tuesday," NOLA.com and the *Times-Picayune*, May 21, 2013.
605. Old Algiers Main Street, "Condensed History of Old Algiers."
606. Ibid.
607. Paul Purpura, "Navy's 110 Year Presence in New Orleans Comes to Close," *Times-Picayune*, September 16, 2011.
608. New Orleans Federal City, "The Opportunity," http://nolafederalcity.com/federal-city (accessed June 8, 2015).
609. Ibid.
610. Paul Purpura, "At Federal City in Algiers, Navy Fence Line Comes Down Three Years After Base Closed," NOLA.com and the *Times-Picayune*, September 15, 2014.
611. Ibid.
612. New Orleans Federal City, "The Opportunity."
613. *Defense Communities 360*, "Decision to Remove Fencing at Federal City Trouble Military Families," October 7, 2014.
614. Paul Purpura, "The New Federal City Complex in Algiers Won't Sweep Away the Past," *Times-Picayune*, July 14, 2009.
615. Ibid.
616. Ibid.; Paul Purpura, "After a Faithful Restoration, the Marine Corps' 'Quarters A' in Algiers Is Ship-Shape," *Times-Picayune*, July 21, 2012.
617. West Bank Living, "A Snapshot of Aurora Gardens History," http://westbankliving.com/westbank-communities/snapshot-of-aurora-gardens-history (accessed June 8, 2015).
618. Works Progress Administration, *A Guide to New Orleans* (reprint, New Orleans, LA: Garret County Press, 2009, originally published in 1938), 421.
619. New Orleans Public Library Online Exhibits, "Algiers: The Right Bank, Part II," 2000, www.neworleanspubliclibrary.org/~nopl/exhibits/algiers/algtitle.htm (accessed January 17, 2015).
620. Rebecca U. Brechtel, "Algiers: Life and Times in Louisiana History through the 20th Century," *Preservation in Print* (October 1993).
621. Tiller, "World War II Veteran."

622. Paul Finkelman, ed., "Maroons," *Encyclopedia of African American History 1619–1895; From the Colonial Period to the Age of Frederick Douglass*, vol. 2. (New York: Oxford University Press, 2006), 326.
623. Hugh Humphrey Jr., "Algiers Development Cited," *Times-Picayune*, March 16, 1970.
624. *America's Wetland Birding Trail on Louisiana's Great Gulf Coast*, "Barataria Loop: Bayou Birds" (Louisiana: Great American Trails Network, n.d.), 5.
625. *Times-Picayune*, "Brechtel Park Sculpture of American Indian Undergoing Repairs," September 9, 2010.
626. Melinda Morris, "Brechtel Park Sculpture Needs a Little TLC," *Times-Picayune*, June 1, 2010.
627. Melinda Morris, "Goats Are the Weed-Eaters at Brechtel Park in Algiers," NOLA.com and the *Times-Picayune*, July 15, 2014.
628. Ibid.
629. Campanella, *Time and Place*, 21.
630. Andrea Shaw, "Woodlands Conservancy Acquires 190 Acres in Lower Coast Algiers," NOLA.com and the *Times-Picayune*, January 13, 2013.
631. Audubon Nature Institute, "Freeport-McMoRan Audubon Species Survival Center," www.auduboninstitute.org/conservation/saving-species/research-center (accessed June 8, 2015).
632. Audubon Nature Institute, "Bird Watching at Wilderness Park," www.auduboninstitute.org/wilderness-park/events/bird-watching-wilderness-park (accessed June 8, 2015).
633. A Studio in the Woods, "Our Woods," http://astudiointhewoods.org/asitw_woods.html (accessed June 8, 2015).
634. Ibid.
635. Neeraj Gautam, *Buddha: His Life and Teaching* (Darya Ganj, New Delhi: Mahaveer & Sons, 2009).
636. Wat Wimuttayaram, "About Us," www.watwimuttayaram.org (accessed June 8, 2015).

Index

Index

D

E

R

S

T

About the Author

Maggy Baccinelli moved to New Orleans in January 2014 from Washington, D.C., where she covered neighborhoods for the *Hill Rag* and *Capital Community News*. She has a BA in journalism from the University of Maryland and is pursuing her MFA in nonfiction creative writing from the University of New Orleans. Her favorite thing about living in the Crescent City has been befriending and "befamilying" her Mid-City neighbors.

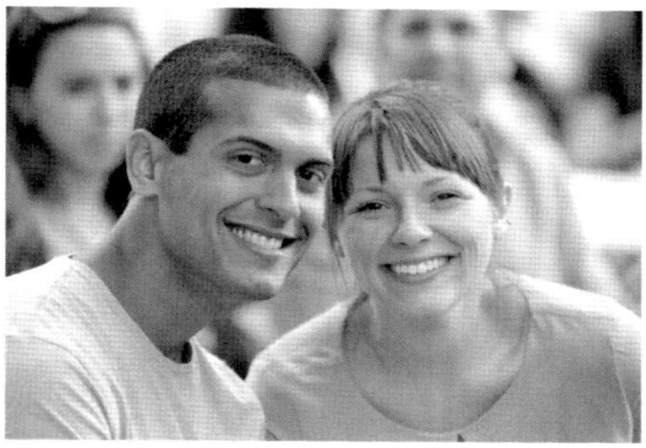

Photo by Sally Asher.

Visit us at
www.historypress.net

This title is also available as an e-book